QUICK ESCAPES® SERIES

QUICK ESCAPES®
FLORIDA

Third Edition

29 WEEKEND GETAWAYS
IN AND AROUND THE SUNSHINE STATE

BY

W. LYNN SELDON JR.

The Globe Pequot Press

GUILFORD, CONNECTICUT

Cover photo © Hoa Qui/Index Stock Imagery, Inc.
Cover design by Laura Augustine
Interior design by Nancy Freeborn
Interior photographs © W. Lynn Seldon Jr.
Maps by M.A. Dubé

ISSN: 1535-5705
ISBN: 0-7627-1047-0

Manufactured in the United States of America
Third Edition/First Printing

CONTENTS

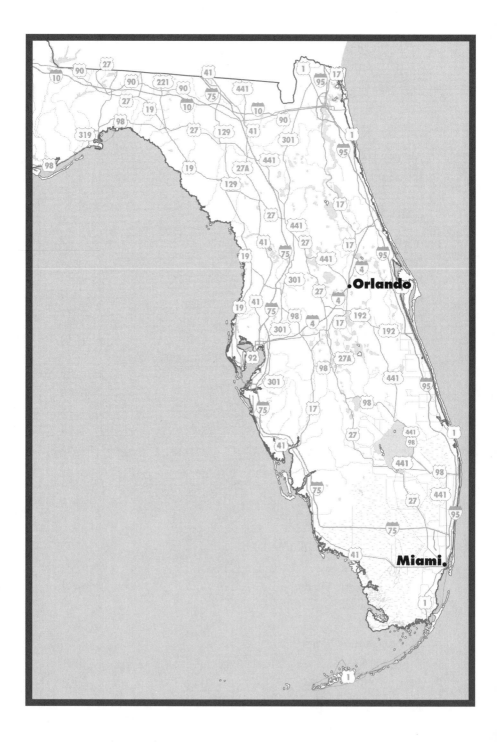

The information listed in this guidebook was confirmed at press time. We recommend, however, that you call establishments before traveling to obtain current information.

ACKNOWLEDGMENTS

With so many trips covered in this book, the hundreds of people who helped in researching it are far too numerous to mention individually. They all know who they are, and their love of the state and willingness to share it with me were greatly appreciated. The people of Florida make the places much more special.

Several firms and governmental agencies were particularly helpful in making this book a reality. In particular, I would like to thank Ed Stone & Associates; BSMG Worldwide; Geiger & Associates; Hill & Knowlton; JGR and Associates; Laura Davidson Public Relations; M. Silver Associates; Moore Consulting Group; Rosetta Stone Communications; St. John & Partners; Stuart Newman & Associates; Yesawich Pepperdine & Brown; The Zimmerman Agency; the Bimini Office of Tourism; Florida State Parks; Florida Division of Tourism; Sonesta Hotels & Resorts; and South Seas Resorts. Of course, many destination tourism offices were also helpful. I apologize in advance if I left anyone out in error.

My wife, Cele, was with me virtually every word and mile of the way. This book would not have been possible without her help. As always, my parents and the rest of my family should be thanked for supporting my unusual career choice. It must have been that very first family trip to Walt Disney World® that made me want to become a travel writer and photographer!

INTRODUCTION

From South Beach to the northwest Panhandle, Florida offers dozens of options for intriguing quick escapes. There's much more to the Sunshine State than bustling beaches, big cities, and thriving theme parks. It's amazing how quickly you can escape to a different Florida.

From five minutes to five hours away, these Florida destinations are easily reached by car. Whether you're a visitor with a rental car or a longtime resident, the Escapes make for ideal weekends or midweek adventures. Though written for traditional Friday-to-Sunday weekends, they can easily be expanded to three or more nights or adapted for midweek travel. Because of the proximity of many of these destinations, it's also easy to combine Escapes.

The detailed itineraries in this book are driving tours that feature extensive recommendations for sightseeing attractions, recreational activities, lodging, restaurants, shopping, and more. At the end of each Escape, **There's More** describes other attractions in the area. There are also sections labeled **Special Events** and **Other Recommended Restaurants and Lodgings. For More Information** gives you contacts to help with planning your escape.

Lodging and restaurant recommendations are included in three categories to indicate what general prices to expect. For lodging, inexpensive means less than $100 per night, double occupancy; moderate means $100–$200 per night; and expensive means more than $200 per night. For dining, inexpensive generally means you'll pay less than $10 per person, without alcohol; moderate means you should expect to pay $10–$20 per person; and expensive means you'll probably pay more than $20 per person. For anything that doesn't fit into those ranges, I provide the range.

The Florida Division of Tourism has a wide range of helpful publications, including a Florida Vacation Guide, Calendar of Events, Official Highway Map, Travel Tips Brochure, Florida Attractions Map, Value Activities Guide, and Florida Camping Directory. Contact them at (888) 7FLA–USA.

If you enjoy visiting Florida's fabulous state parks, you should seriously consider an annual pass, which offers a substantial savings after just a few visits. Contact Florida State Parks at (850) 488–9872 to learn more.

You may also want to visit Florida's extensive on-line travel guide, Destination Florida, which can be found on the World Wide Web at www.flausa.com.

But the best thing to do is hit the highways and byways. Few people realize how much Florida has to offer until they start exploring it. This book will help get you started.

Help Us Keep This Guide Up to Date

Every effort has been made by the author and editors to make this guide as accurate and useful as possible. However, many things can change after a guide is published—establishments close, phone numbers change, facilities come under new management, and so on.

We would love to hear from you concerning your experiences with this guide and how you feel it could be improved and be kept up to date. Though we may not be able to respond to all comments and suggestions, we'll take them to heart, and we'll also make certain to share them with the author. Please send your comments and suggestions to the following address:

The Globe Pequot Press
Reader Response/Editorial Department
P.O. Box 480
Guilford, CT 06437

Or you may e-mail us at:
editorial@globe-pequot.com

Thanks for your input, and happy travels!

MIAMI
ESCAPES

South Beach
AN ART DECO GETAWAY

2 NIGHTS

Art Deco architecture • Walking tours
Museums • Beach • Shopping • Dining

Even if you live or are vacationing nearby, South Beach is still a neon-hot destination for a quick escape. With the nation's largest Art Deco historic district, the trendiest of accommodations options, creative chefs in varied restaurants, designer shopping, the nonstop action of the ever-so-wide beach, the aqua Atlantic, and Ocean Drive's people-watching, SoBe is the place to be. It's like visiting a movie set (à la *Birdcage*), but this setting is ever so real.

South Beach is enjoying a tourism and economic boom that springs from the refurbishment of the area's Art Deco District. From the cafes and clubs along Ocean Drive, Washington Avenue, and Lincoln Road to the hot hotels and restaurants everywhere, South Beach is sizzling with the vibrant colors of Art Deco architecture and style.

The Art Deco Historic District, the first twentieth-century neighborhood on the National Register of Historic Places, has the highest concentration of Art Deco architecture in the world. It takes up about one square mile of South Beach, with most of it found between 5th Street and 23rd Street. Thanks to the work of the Miami Design Preservation League and many hardworking locals, many buildings have been saved from demolition and refurbished for all to enjoy as hotels, restaurants, shops, living space, and public buildings.

One of the best ways to tour the Art Deco Historic District is through a walking tour run by the Miami Design Preservation League (outlined later). For those who prefer other transportation, there are also organized tours by

bike, car, and bus. With a tour, you'll get a true sense of the history and flavor of the buildings. This perfect introduction allows you to return later to favorite buildings for a closer inspection.

Once you've explored the colorful buildings of South Beach, you can pursue as little or as much as you desire. The choices include swimming, sunning, and people-watching on the wide beach; strolling, biking, or in-line skating along Ocean Drive and Lummus Park; shopping until you drop; finding a favorite restaurant; and dancing the night away in one of many hot nightclubs. You'll never be bored in South Beach.

DAY 1

Afternoon

The best way to reach South Beach from Miami and the rest of South Florida is by driving east on I–395 off I–95. It's called the MacArthur Causeway and leads right past the towering cruise ships in the Port of Miami on your right, giving you an up-close view of the busiest cruise ship port in the world. Interstate 395 ends on 5th Street, right at the foot of South Beach. To reach Ocean Drive, just follow 5th Street to the end and turn left.

Try to arrive mid- to late afternoon, so you'll have some time to stroll along Ocean Drive before the nighttime crowds begin. It's also less crowded on the beach during the week. Whenever you head down to the beach, be sure to check out the brightly painted and architecturally unique array of lifeguard stands all along the strand.

DINNER: It's a good night to walk to a restaurant on Ocean Drive. Located at the Ocean Front Hotel (see below), **Les Deux Fontaines** (1230–38 Ocean Drive; 305–672–7878; moderate to expensive) brings a bit of Paris to Ocean Drive. The impeccable elevated terrace overlooking Ocean Drive is the setting for a meal that features generally low-fat health-conscious fresh and flavorful Provençal-style cuisine. Veterans swear by the Ceviche de Grouper or the Melon Champagne and Mint Soup to start, followed by the Snapper Provençal or Veal Valparaiso.

LODGING: There are many excellent Art Deco hotels in a wide range of styles and prices. If you want to stay in the heart and soul of South Beach and tend to enjoy the hustle and bustle of city life, Ocean Drive is your best bet. There are also many other excellent options on Collins Avenue, Washington Avenue, and further afield.

South Beach's Art Deco architecture and swaying palm trees are a national treasure.

One of my favorite spots here is the **Pelican Hotel** (826 Ocean Drive; 305–673–3373 or 800–7–PELICAN; moderate), the first property created by Diesel Jeans International. It's like a perfect South Beach rendition of the company's eccentric advertising campaigns. All twenty-five rooms have been furnished, decorated, and named with their own style. Examples include the Psychedelic room, complete with plastic furniture and posters from the 1970s; the African room, with its triumph of zebra stripes, furnished in old safari style; and a tribute to the American flag, the Stars and Stripes room. Other favorites include Best Whorehouse, Halfway to Hollywood, and Me Tarzan, You Vain. There are also three executive oceanfront suites, featuring the styles of the 1930s, 1950s, and 1960s, respectively.

If you're up to the club scene on your first night, check out the recommendations for Day 2.

DAY 2

Morning

BREAKFAST: For breakfast with the locals and in-the-know visitors, head just down the street to **News Cafe** (800 Ocean Drive; 305–531–0392; inexpensive to moderate). Grab a paper or magazine, sit inside or outside, and choose from a wide variety of breakfast items that are available twenty-four hours a day.

Be sure to be finished before 10:30 A.M., so you can head back up Ocean Drive to the **Art Deco Welcome Center** (1001 Ocean Drive; 305–672–2014; charge for walking tour). This is where the Saturday morning walking tour, sponsored by the Miami Design Preservation League, starts. While you wait, you'll enjoy browsing through the plethora of information, books, T-shirts, and much more at the Center.

The 1½-hour walking tour typically includes lots of history about the buildings, anecdotes about preservation efforts, and a few remarkable interior views. For most visitors, it ends much too quickly, and they usually head back out on their own. The tour is also available on Thursday nights at 6:30 P.M. There are also self-guided tours using a cassette tape and map for a small charge.

If you're not into a morning walk, other touring options include biking tours with **Art Deco Cycling Tour** (601 5th Street; 305–672–2014 or 305–674–0430); chartered car or coach tours with **Deco Tours Miami Beach** (420 Lincoln Road, Suite 412; 305–531–4465); and a wide variety of options with **Miami Nice Sightseeing Tours** (19250 Collins Avenue; 305–949–9180). Of course, spending the rest of the morning at the wide and active beach is also a fun option.

LUNCH: Joe's Stone Crab (11 Washington Avenue; 305–673–0365; moderate to expensive) leads the list of South Beach eateries, and for good reason. Quite simply, if you go to South Beach (or anywhere in South Florida, for that matter), you *must* go to Joe's. This legendary restaurant was famous before South Beach was a glimmer in Hollywood's intense lenses (one ad campaign states, "Before SoBe, Joe Be"). But nightly crowds mean a Saturday lunch is the perfect time to try it.

Family-owned and -operated for the past eighty years, the restaurant's veteran visitors and locals still love the sweet taste of fresh stone crabs, but they also enjoy some secrets (steaks, chops, and salads). Don't leave without trying the key lime pie. You can usually avoid two-hour waits by going there for lunch or an early or late dinner (5:00–6:30 P.M. or 10:00–11:00 P.M.). There's also a new Joe's Take Away & Coffee Bar as well as FedEx delivery to anywhere in the continental U.S. (800–780–CRAB).

Afternoon

Saturday afternoon is a good time for some culture or shopping, since some museums and shops are closed on Sundays. Though some would say that South Beach's culture is limited to people-watching on Ocean Drive, there's much more to this vibrant area, thanks to many creative minds and souls.

Possibilities for those in-the-know include the numerous art galleries on Lincoln Road; the **Bass Museum of Art** (2100 Park Avenue; 305–673–7530; admission charge), an Art Deco building housing fourteenth- to twentieth-century art; the **Wolfsonian** (1001 Washington Avenue; 305–531–1001; admission charge), a huge and eclectic collection of virtually anything from the late nineteenth to mid-twentieth centuries; and the **Sanford L. Ziff Jewish Museum of Florida** (301 Washington Avenue; 305–672–5044; admission charge), offering an interesting overview of Jewish history in Florida.

With so many fashion models and famous people (some of whom are fashion models living here) in town, it's natural that many of the shopping choices suit their tastes. Ocean Drive, Collins Avenue, Washington Avenue, Lincoln Road, and the accompanying cross streets provide the swankiest shopping locale.

The most popular shopping spots include **Gianni Versace, Armani Exchange, Kenneth Cole, Banana Republic, Succa, Nicole Miller, A.B.S.,** and **Island Trading,** all of which (and many more) are on or near Ocean Drive, Collins, or Washington. But there's also a huge roster of eclectic boutiques on Lincoln Road (e.g., **Books & Books** and **Pink Palm Company**), which is ideal for strolling and spending.

DINNER: If you ate on Ocean Drive your first night, now is the time to head up to Lincoln Road for an evening of window-shopping (many stores stay open late) and dining. Lincoln Road has rebounded to become one of South Beach's best dining and shopping spots, featuring a 10-block retail district stretching from ocean to bay (including a sharply renovated 7-block pedestrian mall). Many Lincoln Road aficionados shop until they drop into one of the many excellent restaurants.

Though residents and visitors may never have dreamed of trading their stone crabs for Mongolian lamb salad, they are definitely finding the time to try **Pacific Time** (915 Lincoln Road; 305–534–5979; moderate to expensive). Serving what chef/co-owner Jonathan Eismann calls "Asian-influenced American food with a 'French head'," Pacific Time puts out masterful food in a soaring space where South Beach surfers sit next to Hollywood elite. Eismann combines the American affinity for experimentation with the spices, flavors, and textures of the Far East, resulting in dishes like Cedar Roast Atlantic Salmon. While Atlantic salmon rubbed with olive oil and roasted in the oven on a cedar plank epitomizes Western ingredients and cooking style, the accompanying raw, salted salmon rolls lend an Eastern sensibility to the dish. An East/West mustard sauce, blending French Pommery and Japanese wasabi, finishes the concept.

Be sure to have a drink at the **Van Dyke Cafe** (846 Lincoln Road; 305–534–3600; moderate), which has become a Lincoln Road magnet. The Van Dyke's sister restaurant, **News Cafe** (see above), is a busy all-day magnet on Ocean Drive for creative cafe fare, and the Van Dyke Cafe is just as popular.

Evening

After dinner, evening entertainment options are diverse. There is a wide variety of performances at the stunning **Jackie Gleason Theater** (1700 Washington Avenue; 305–673–7300) or a host of scheduled events with Lincoln Road's acclaimed **Miami City Ballet** (905 Lincoln Road; 305–532–7713) or **New World Symphony** (541 Lincoln Road; 305–673–3331).

The other option is to take advantage of the active club scene that's prevalent throughout South Beach. Keep in mind, however, that much of the activity doesn't even get started until midnight. From steam parties to Latin-style dancing till the wee hours, clubs like **Level, Crobar, N, 320, W6, Pearl, Mango's** (salsa), **Lola Salvation** (gay), **Shadow Lounge, Amnesia, Bash,** the **Clevelander Bar, Score** (gay), **Salvation** (gay), **Groove Jet, Liquid,** and **821** (gay) are all hot spots to nighttime-trotters. To avoid disappointment or embarassment, be sure to call first to see what's happening at particular clubs on particular nights as well as to make sure the club hasn't closed or moved in this quickly changing entertainment environment. The weekend section of the *Miami Herald* (available on Fridays) and the weekly *New Times* are also great club information resources.

LODGING: Of course, you could just stay at the Pelican Hotel for a second night, but it's also easy to move to another nearby hotel for a different South Beach overnight experience (see suggestions below).

DAY 3

Morning

Sunday mornings on the beach are a particularly nice and quiet time for a stroll along the sandy shore. A 2-mile-long boardwalk starts at 23rd Street, if you're up for a longer walk.

BREAKFAST: Sunday morning breakfast is also popular at the News Cafe (see Day 2), but a special treat is available 2 blocks over on Washington Avenue. The Astor Hotel's restaurant, **Astor Place Bar & Grill** (956 Washington Avenue; 305–531–8081; moderate), is already one of Washington Avenue's most popular eateries and is a wonderful spot for Sunday brunch.

For brunch, lunch, and dinner, chef Johnny Vinczincz has created a menu that can be best described as "Cowboy Caribbean," fusing grilled, smoked, or spit-fired meats, poultry, fruits, and tasty BBQ sauces with tropical ingredients like boniato, jicama, scotch bonnet pepper, yuca, and stone crab. Be sure to try the Zarzuela, a succulent stew of fresh Florida lobster, clams, local fish, shrimp, scallops, yuca, and peppers, in a habañero-mango broth (yes, this is a brunch item). There's also popular live entertainment to accompany the food.

Afternoon

The rest of the day can be spent on the beach, visiting museums missed on Saturday (check to see if they're open on Sundays), shopping (South Beach stores are generally open Sunday afternoons), or walking along busy Ocean Drive and Lummus Park, which are popular Sunday afternoon hangouts.

Heading back to Miami proper is easy. Just go back down to 5th Street, turn right, and take I–395 or I–95 to downtown.

THERE'S MORE

Other sightseeing attractions: The **Holocaust Memorial** (1933 Meridian Avenue; 305–538–1663; no entrance fee) is a stirring memorial that includes a bronze sculpture depicting Holocaust victims crawling up a huge open hand to freedom, pictures from concentration camps, and the etched names of many victims. It's just across the street from the helpful information counter and shop of the Miami Beach Chamber of Commerce.

Sightseeing by air: Chalk's Ocean Airways (1000 MacArthur Causeway; 305–373–1120 or 800–4–CHALKS) offers scheduled flights to the Bahamas and great views of Miami Beach, as well as floatplane sightseeing tours. **Action Helicopter** (1901 Brickell Avenue, B602; 305–358–4723) offers a wide range of sightseeing trips.

In-line skating: One of the most popular activities in South Beach is in-line skating. If you didn't bring your own, rent what you need at **Super Skates** (1360 Washington Avenue; 305–674–1912) or **Fritz's Skate Shop** (726 Lincoln Road Mall; 305–532–1954).

Bicycling: Along with the Art Deco biking tours mentioned above, rental bikes from **Two Wheel Drive** (1260 Washington Avenue; 305–534–2177) or **Miami Beach Bicycle Center** (601 5th Street; 305–674–0150) also offer a convenient way to get around South Beach for a day or more.

Watersports: For watersports enthusiasts, there are vendors all along the beach who rent equipment for sailboarding and sailing as well as Jet Skis. For inland boating along Indian Creek and Biscayne Bay, head up to **Beach Boat Rentals** (2380 Collins Avenue; 305–534–4307). For boating (and gambling) further afield, you may check into a short lunch or dinner cruise with **Sea Kruz** (1280 5th Street; 305–538–8300). Golfers can enjoy a fun short course at the **Bayshore Par 3 Golf Course** (2975 Prairie Avenue; 305–674–0305).

Fitness: If you want to keep up with all of the other hardbodies of South Beach, fitness facilities include **Crunch Fitness** (1253 Washington Avenue; 305–674–8222); **Gridiron Club** (1676 Alton Road; 305–531–4743); and the new **Gold's Gym** (1400 Alton Road; 305–538–GOLD).

Scuba diving: The artificial reefs (intentionally sunk ships and other items) make for surprisingly interesting dive sites. The marine life drawn to these reefs, as well as the unique structures, have made Miami Beach into a wreck diving mecca. Some good contacts include **Bob's Boat** (Miami

Beach Marina; 305–535–8334 or 800–657–2BOB); **Team Divers** (Miami Beach Marina; 305–673–3483); **R J Diving Ventures** (5332 Pine Tree Drive; 305–864–3040); and **H2O Scuba** (160 Sunny Isles Boulevard; 305–956–3483).

SPECIAL EVENTS

January. Art Miami. Artists and buyers at the Miami Beach Convention Center; (305) 220–2690.

Art Deco Weekend along Ocean Drive. Four-day festival, music, other entertainment, special events, and food; (305) 672–2014.

February. Miami International Boat Show. More than 250,000 boat lovers at Miami Beach Convention Center; (305) 531–8140.

Original Miami Beach Antique Show. Wide variety of antiques and dealers at Miami Beach Convention Center; (305) 754–4931.

March. World's Largest Indoor Flea Market, Miami Beach Convention Center; (305) 651–9530. Also held in June and December.

The Feast on the Beach, South Pointe Park. Fantastic food from around the world; (305) 672–1270.

April. Yamaha Outboards Miami Billfish Tournament, Miami Beach Marina; (305) 561–2868.

May. Miami Home Show, Miami Beach Convention Center. Wide array of home-oriented products; (305) 673–7311.

Antique Jewelry & Watch Show, Miami Beach Convention Center. Sparkles and ticks; (305) 754–4931. Also held in October.

October. International Women's Show, Miami Beach Convention Center. Events, booths, and products for females; (800) 849–0248.

November. South Florida Auto Show, Miami Beach Convention Center; (305) 758–2643.

Baron's Antique Show, Miami Beach Convention Center; (305) 754–4931.

OTHER RECOMMENDED RESTAURANTS AND LODGINGS

The list of additional restaurant and accommodations possibilities in South Beach is long and distinguished. Just pick any other place to eat or stay that seems to suit your style.

Ocean Drive offers many fine dining spots, with locals and visitors strolling along the busy sidewalks and making their dining choice by the look of the interior or the looks of the posted menus. If you're staying at The Pelican Hotel, as recommended, and don't feel like heading out to eat, **The Pelican Cafe** (826 Ocean Drive; 305–673–3373; moderate) is another of many great Ocean Drive choices. Chef Peter Masiello prepares his world cuisine versions of entrees like New Zealand Baby Lamp Chops (roasted with rosemary and balsamic reduction and served with mashed potatoes and spinach).

Right on Ocean Drive, **A Fish Called Avalon** (700 Ocean Drive; 305–532–1727; moderate) serves some of the area's best fresh seafood; both **Caffe Milano** (850 Ocean Drive; 305–532–0707; expensive) and **I Paparazzi** (940 Ocean Drive; 305–531–3500; moderate) serve excellent northern Italian fare; and **Gloria Estefan's Lario's Cafe** (820 Ocean Drive; 305–532–9577; moderate) specializes in Cuban cuisine.

Over on Washington Avenue, along with Astor Place Bar & Grill mentioned above, **China Grill** (404 Washington Avenue; 305–532–2211; expensive) is the hottest choice. Chef Ephraim Kadish has invented a number of dishes that intermingle Italian, Japanese, French, Chinese, and American ingredients. You can also enjoy terrific Thai dishes at **Ruen Thai Restaurant** (947 Washington Avenue; 305–534–1504; moderate) and down-home American cooking at **11th Street Diner** (11th Street and Washington Avenue; 305–534–6373; inexpensive).

Up on Lincoln Road, there's nouveau Cuban cuisine at **Yuca** (501 Lincoln Road; 305–534–4292; expensive). Over on Collins Avenue, the Raleigh Hotel features the "new American" cuisine of Marc Lippman at the **Raleigh Restaurant** (1775 Collins Avenue; 305–534–6300; moderate to expensive). **Grillfish** (1444 Collins Avenue; 305–538–9908; moderate) features some of the best seafood around.

Even further afield, if you have time, try a meal (or a night, see below) at Indian Creek Hotel's **Luna Rosa Restaurant** (2727 Indian Creek Drive; 305–531–2727; moderate), with creative Italian–Brazilian dishes.

On the lodging front, the choices are even more extensive. The **Hotel Ocean** (1230–38 Ocean Drive; 305–672–2579; moderate to expensive) is another excellent Ocean Drive option. Located in a quieter stretch of this busy street, the Ocean Front offers just twenty-three oceanview or oceanfront rooms as well as four with city views, all of which are soundproof. The oceanfront superior deluxe room, with an oceanfront balcony, is an excellent choice. The penthouse suite is simply one of the finest options (and views) in South Florida.

Situated on the southern end of Ocean Drive, the **Century Hotel** (140 Ocean Drive; 305–674–8855; inexpensive to moderate) offers tropical touches like mosquito-netted beds, painted wood floors, and an ever-present gecko logo. The **Park Central Hotel** (640 Ocean Drive; 305–538–1611 or 800–PARK CENTRAL; moderate) is another excellent Ocean Drive address. This member of the Historic Hotels of America features oceanview windows, ceiling fans, period furniture, and many other reminders of what drew the continent's chic and famous to the hotel in the 1930s. Other solid Ocean Drive choices include the "suite" (and more costly) life at **Casa Grande Suite Hotel** (834 Ocean Drive; 305–672–7003 or 800–OUTPOST; expensive); the classic 106-room **Colony Hotel** (736 Ocean Drive; 305–673–0088 or 800–226–5669; moderate); and the very lively and busy **Clevelander Hotel** (1020 Ocean Drive; 305–531–3485; moderate).

Though many ill-informed visitors think of South Beach and Ocean Drive as synonymous, you definitely don't have to stay on the ocean to get the full flavor of this multi-street mecca. In fact, many knowledgeable visitors head inland for a bit more sedate stay. Located two blocks off Ocean Drive, **Hotel Astor** (956 Washington Avenue; 305–531–8081 or 800–270–4981; moderate) provides a perfect example of the possibilities. This intimate forty-two-room hotel has attained a casual elegance typically associated with only the finest European-style concierge hotels. The eight one-bedroom junior suites are a great value at this Washington Avenue hideaway.

On Collins Avenue, a block off Ocean Drive and in the heart of South Beach, the **Marlin Hotel** (1200 Collins Avenue; 305–673–8770 or 800–OUTPOST; moderate) is the brainchild of Chris Blackwell, founder of Island Records. The funky hotel has just twelve units, ranging from studios to two-bedroom suites. If you want to stay right on the ocean, **The National** (1677 Collins Avenue; 305–532–2311 or 800–327–8370; expensive), a wonderfully renovated Art Deco hotel, is by far my favorite choice. As the first luxury hotel to be built on Miami Beach in more than thirty years, the best and most recent Collins Avenue choice is the **Loews Miami Beach** (1601 Collins Avenue; 305–604–1601 or 800–23–LOEWS; moderate to expensive).

If you want to stay completely away from the South Beach bustle, but still enjoy the proximity and flavor of the Art Deco district, look no further than the **Indian Creek Hotel** (2727 Indian Creek Drive; 305–531–2727; inexpensive to moderate). Indian Creek melds the graciousness of a small European hostelry with the informal charm of a Key West guesthouse.

FOR MORE INFORMATION

Miami Beach Chamber of Commerce, 1920 Meridian Avenue, Miami Beach, FL 33139. (305) 672–1270.

Greater Miami Convention & Visitors Bureau, 701 Brickell Avenue, Suite 2700, Miami, FL 33131. (305) 539–3034 or (800) 933–8448.

Key Biscayne

YOU CAN SEE MIAMI

2 NIGHTS

Beach • Watersports

It's hard to believe that an island getaway is so close to downtown Miami, but Key Biscayne can surprise even the staunchest urbanite. A world-class resort, a great beach with clear waters, and lots of activities make the skyscrapers seem even further away.

The beauty of a Key Biscayne quick escape is that it's so different and so quick. Within less than ten minutes, you can reach another world, where the toughest decisions revolve around what to do and where to dine.

DAY 1

Afternoon

Take I–95 or US 1 south to the Rickenbacker Causeway, where you turn left, following the signs to Key Biscayne. Traffic is generally lighter before 4:00 P.M.

DINNER AND LODGING: For the complete resort experience on Key Biscayne, the **Sonesta Beach Resort Key Biscayne** (350 Ocean Drive; 305–361–2021 or 800–SONESTA; moderate to expensive) is the perfect choice. With almost 300 rooms, you're sure to find the oceanfront accommodations to your liking. In addition to the large standard rooms, the tropically themed Sonesta also offers fifteen suites and three complete vacation homes for rent. The huge array of amenities includes an oceanfront pool, a fitness center, tennis, racquetball, lots of watersports and land rentals, shopping, and much more.

For your first night, it's easiest to stay right at the Sonesta for dinner. Once you see the options, you may never leave the resort. The signature restaurant, **Purple Dolphin,** is one of the best choices at the resort, on the island, and in South Florida. Creative seafood, continental cuisine, and theme nights make this casually elegant Sonesta landmark a great introduction to the resort's dining options. Other possibilities on this first (or any) night include unique Chinese, Thai, and Japanese fare at **Two Dragons,** the informal **Jasmine Cafe,** or the beachfront **Seagrape Bar and Snackerie** for the ultimate in casual oceanfront dining.

Evening

Because it's a quiet beach destination, the nightlife on Key Biscayne is rather limited. Several of the restaurants, however, also have bars or lounges with entertainment.

DAY 2

Morning

BREAKFAST: Sonesta Beach Resort Key Biscayne.

Use the morning to explore the resort and pursue one of the many watersports opportunities. The staff can help with Wave Runners, windsailing, and much more. If you just want to relax, the beach setting, complete with lounge chairs and huge towels, is hard to beat.

LUNCH: If you want lunch with the locals on this tourist-heavy island, head straight to **La Caretta** (12 Crandon Boulevard; 305–365–1171; inexpensive) for casual company and Cuban food.

Afternoon

Head south on Crandon Boulevard, following it for several miles all the way into **Bill Baggs Cape Florida State Recreation Area** (1200 Crandon Boulevard; 305–361–5811; entrance fee). Named after the late Miami newspaper editor who championed this area as a state park, it is a popular destination for a day at the beach, a visit to the historic lighthouse, or an afternoon of watersports pursuits.

One of the highlights of this natural area is the **Cape Florida Lighthouse,** which was built in 1825 to serve as an important link in the network of lighthouses along the East Coast. It is the oldest building in South Florida. After extensive renovations, it's now open to visitors for guided tours.

The concessionaire located near the beach offers a variety of rentals, including bikes, hydrobikes, in-line skates, ocean kayaks, windsurfers, beach chairs, and umbrellas. There are also eighteen covered pavilions for picnicking and The Lighthouse Cafe, which offers casual oceanfront dining if you didn't have lunch back at La Caretta. The western side of the park offers a great spot for viewing a sunset, if you're there that late before heading back to the Sonesta.

DINNER: Another popular spot for sunset, as well as a meal in a bayside setting, **Sundays on the Bay** (5420 Crandon Boulevard; 305–361–6777; moderate) is popular any day or night of the week. With wonderful views of the downtown area, as well as Coconut Grove, Sundays features the freshest seafood available and a befitting tropical setting. Though I recommend the Sonesta's spectacular Sunday brunch buffet, the Sundays version is also quite popular and bountiful.

LODGING: Sonesta Beach Resort Key Biscayne.

DAY 3

Morning

BREAKFAST/BRUNCH: Sleep in and then head to the huge Sonesta Sunday brunch buffet.

Sunday morning and early afternoon provide a quiet time to drive around Key Biscayne. Besides Bill Baggs Cape Florida State Recreation Area, there really aren't many other sightseeing attractions on the island. However, it's enjoyable just to drive around, taking in the seaside and bayside life. Some possible stops include the **Key Biscayne Chamber of Commerce** (328 Crandon Boulevard, Suite 217; 305–361–5207); Crandon Park's **Marjory Stoneman Douglas Biscayne Nature Center** (4000 Key Biscayne Boulevard; 305–361–8097), which was established to educate the public about the environment and to preserve Crandon Park's natural resources; and one of many shopping centers.

Key Biscayne's renovated Cape Florida Lighthouse was built in 1845 and is part of the Bill Baggs Cape Florida State Recreation Area.

Afternoon

After checking out from the Sonesta, be sure to budget time for a stop at the **Miami Seaquarium** (4400 Rickenbacker Causeway; 305–361–5705; admission fee) on your way back to Miami. This large complex features a number of interesting exhibits as well as four major shows featuring dolphins, killer whales, and many other sea mammals. It's well worth the stop.

Rickenbacker Causeway heads straight back into Miami, I–95, and US 1.

THERE'S MORE

Outdoor activities: Crandon Park (4000 Crandon Boulevard; 305–361–5421; parking fee), located on the northern end of Key Biscayne, features 3 miles of white beach, more than 3½ miles of bike paths and nature trails, and a variety of water- and land-based pursuits. Offshore, **Biscayne National Park** (P.O. Box 1369; 305–230–7275; no entrance fee), 95 percent of which is underwater, features the largest stretch of mangroves on the eastern coast of Florida (18 miles), excellent scuba diving, and canoeing. Along with the National Park diving concessionaire down in Homestead, scuba divers should also contact the Key Biscayne-based **Diver's Paradise** (Crandon Marina; 305–361–3483). Windsurfers should contact **Sailboards Miami** (Hobie Beach; 305–361–SAIL).

Boating: A wide variety of boat rentals are available through **Sailboats of Key Biscayne** (4000 Crandon Boulevard; 305–361–0328); **Key Biscayne Boat Rentals** (3301 Rickenbacker Causeway; 305–361–7368); and **Club Nautico of Key Biscayne** (Crandon Marina; 305–361–9217).

Tennis: The **Tennis Center at Crandon Park** (7300 Crandon Boulevard; 305–365–2300) and the **Key Biscayne Tennis Association** (6702 Crandon Boulevard; 305–361–5263) both welcome hackers for a modest fee.

Golf: Visiting duffers are welcome at the **Crandon Park Golf Course** (6700 Crandon Boulevard; 305–361–9129), which is considered one of the top public courses in the nation.

SPECIAL EVENTS

January. Key Biscayne Art Festival, along Crandon Boulevard. Features around 200 artists from around the country; (305) 361–5356.

The Royal Caribbean Senior PGA Golf Classic, The Links at Key Biscayne; (305) 365–0365.

March. The Ericcson Tennis Championship for men and women professionals; (305) 442–3367.

October. Columbus Day Regatta Events. More than 500 boats compete in various categories; (305) 666–8353.

November. Annual Key Biscayne Lighthouse Run. A 10-kilometer race, one of the oldest in South Florida; (305) 365–8900.

December. Key Biscayne Yacht Club Christmas Flotilla. Dozens of boats decked out in festive holiday decorations; (305) 361–9171.

OTHER RECOMMENDED RESTAURANTS AND LODGINGS

If you're on a tighter budget, the **Silver Sands Oceanfront Motel** (301 Ocean Drive; 305–361–5441; moderate) sits right next to the Sonesta. This family-friendly resort features about fifty large and clean rooms, which all include tropical decor, microwaves, and refrigerators. The amenities include a large pool and watersports facilities. If the Sonesta is full or a bit too pricey, this is a solid Key Biscayne choice.

For longer stays, **Key Colony for Guests** (121 Crandon Boulevard; 305–361–2170; expensive) is an interesting choice. The private community of Botanica at Key Colony offers elegant two-, three-, and four-bedroom apartments for short- and long-term vacation and business needs. Set in the midst of tropical gardens, the apartments come fully equipped and offer all the amenities of a luxury resort, including an 800-foot stretch of private beach, tennis, three swimming pools, dining, and a fitness center.

The Island Haven (472 Fernwood Road; 305–361–8123; moderate to expensive) offers a variety of weekly vacation rentals in three-bedroom accommodations. This service is ideal for families or couples vacationing together. All of the homes feature the amenities of home, but you're within easy walking distance of the beach, grocery store, and the Village Green.

Locals on Key Biscayne also enjoy the casual atmosphere of **Bayside Seafood Restaurant** and **Hidden Cove Bar** (3501 Rickenbacker Causeway; 305–361–0808; inexpensive), which is known locally as "The Hut" and specializes in fresh fish on paper plates; **The Rusty Pelican** (3201 Rickenbacker Causeway; 305–361–3818; moderate), which is another popular sunset and brunch spot; and the northern Italian cuisine at **Stefano's** (24 Crandon Boulevard; 305–361–7007; moderate to expensive).

FOR MORE INFORMATION

Key Biscayne Chamber of Commerce, 328 Crandon Boulevard, Suite 217, Key Biscayne, FL 33149. (305) 361–5207.

Greater Miami Convention & Visitors Bureau, 701 Brickell Avenue, Suite 2700, Miami, FL 33131. (305) 539–3034 or (800) 933–8448.

Upper Florida Keys
THE KEYS TO KEY LARGO

2 NIGHTS

Upscale "Keysey" atmosphere and accommodations
Water-oriented activities

Just an hour from the Miami area, Key Largo is another world. Jumping-off point to the Florida Keys, Key Largo is the longest island of the Keys chain. It's also the site where Humphrey Bogart and Lauren Bacall battled both Edward G. Robinson and a hurricane in the movie of the same name.

Key Largo's true star attraction is John Pennekamp Coral Reef State Park—the first underwater preserve in the United States—and the adjacent Key Largo National Marine Sanctuary. Watersports—including boating, scuba diving, and snorkeling—are big business (and fun) around Key Largo. The water orientation and the people provide Key Largo with a unique atmosphere in which you can quickly immerse yourself. Even after a short stay, you may never want to return to mainland Florida.

DAY 1

Afternoon
Head south on the Florida Turnpike until it ends at US 1 in Homestead. Take US 1 south toward Key Largo. For a short diversion (or if traffic is really bad), you can take the slightly longer and more scenic route along Card Sound Road, which eventually intersects with US 1 in the Keys. Either way, you'll follow US 1 (the Overseas Highway) all the way to Key Largo and the Upper Keys. Take US 1 to Mile Marker (MM) 98 (Mile Markers are used for

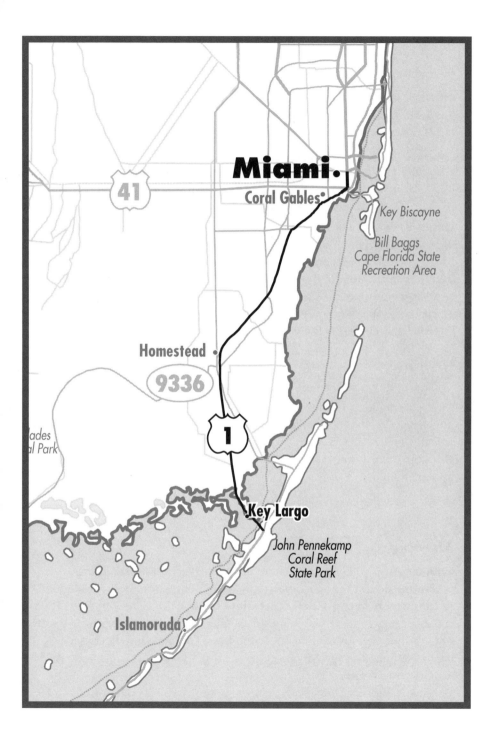

directions and locations in the Keys) and then look for Kona Kai Resort on the right just two-tenths of a mile further.

DINNER: Right across the street from the Kona Kai Resort, **Ballyhoo's Seafood Grille** (MM 97.8 oceanside; 305–852–0822; inexpensive to moderate) offers the freshest of seafood in a casual and friendly setting.

LODGING: If you want ideal "tropical upscale Keysey" accommodations in Key Largo, head straight for **Kona Kai Resort** (MM 97.8 bayside, 97802 Overseas Highway; 305–852–7200 or 800–365–STAY; moderate to expensive). Joe and Ronnie Harris have lovingly restored this 1940s bayfront resort into a true Florida Keys gem. They offer eleven totally modern suites in a wide variety of styles and configurations, which are spread throughout the property (many have kitchens). The grounds are a tropical oasis and include a pool and Jacuzzi, a tennis court, a tropical fruit garden, and an art gallery (you can even buy the local art in your room). Whether you need a good restaurant recommendation or a friendly dive shop, Joe and Ronnie can help with practically anything during your stay. The Kona Kai is the perfect Key Largo base.

Evening

As with all of the Florida Keys, sunsets and later are popular times to be somewhere overlooking Florida Bay. Two of the best complexes in Key Largo for sunsets and other evening entertainment are **Sundowners** (MM 103.9 bayside; 305–451–4502) and **Senor Frijoles** (MM 103.9 bayside; 305–451–1592). **Coconuts Restaurant & Club** (MM 100; 305–453–9794) often features live entertainment.

DAY 2

Morning

BREAKFAST: In your Kona Kai suite or across the street at Ballyhoo's.

For the perfect introduction to Key Largo's outdoor options, head straight to **John Pennekamp Coral Reef State Park** (MM 102.5; 305–451–1202; entrance fee). This state park was the first underwater park in the United States and is a showcase for ecotourism in the Keys. This park and the adjacent Key Largo National Marine Sanctuary are 21 miles long and contain about 165 square nautical miles.

The residents at Pennekamp include more than 500 species of fish and 55

Kona Kai Resort provides an upscale "Keysey" base in the upper Florida Keys.

varieties of coral, along with 27 species of gorgonians (marine life forms, such as anemones). The coral can also be home to crabs, sea urchins, snails, lobsters, shrimps, worms, chitons (mollusks), starfishes, sea cucumbers, sand dollars, barnacles, sponges, and much more.

The excellent visitor center provides a great overview of the park and is also the place to get more information about what there is to see and do. There are four basic ways to explore this area: various boating options; scuba diving; "snuba" (breathing air from a tube sent underwater); and snorkeling. You can also hike on several boardwalks through the mangroves. All of these options offer unique insights into natural life in the Florida Keys. You'll end up spending more than a half-day in this fascinating park.

LUNCH: There are many excellent local seafood restaurants in the Key Largo vicinity. Among them, **Crack'd Conch** (MM 105 oceanside; 305–451–0732;

inexpensive to moderate) is a perfect casual spot for excellent sandwiches and chowders. Many places along the Overseas Highway feature similar food and atmosphere, but the Crack'd Conch is particularly popular and friendly.

Afternoon

You'll probably want to spend more time exploring John Pennekamp Coral Reef State Park with outfitters inside or outside the park grounds (many other watersports operators dot the Overseas Highway), but there are many other sightseeing choices. One of the most popular is to take a boat tour aboard the original *African Queen* (MM 100 oceanside; 305–451–2121 or 800–843–5397), which was used in the filming for the movie of the same name. Tours aboard the steam-engine vessel are typically in the Port Largo Canal and last about an hour.

You may see dolphins during any boat tour, which will whet your appetite for a visit to the fascinating complex at **Dolphins Plus** (MM 99.5 bayside; 305–451–1993; various entrance and program fees). This interesting operation provides several recreational and educational programs with its dolphins, including "swim with the dolphins" offerings, classroom sessions, and basic tours.

DINNER: For another good local meal, be sure to eat at **Mrs. Mac's Kitchen** (MM 99.4, 99336 Overseas Highway; 305–451–3722; inexpensive to moderate). Again, sandwiches, chowders, and seafood reign here, where license plates from around the world are plastered on the walls.

LODGING: Kona Kai Resort.

DAY 3

Morning

BREAKFAST: In your Kona Kai suite or across the street at Ballyhoo's.

For an even closer tour of the Florida Keys environment, contact **Florida Bay Outfitters** (104050 Overseas Highway; 305–451–3018) about kayak and canoe rentals as well as tours. With your chosen boat (and, possibly, a guide) you can tour nearby Keys and also head north into Everglades National Park. It's a fascinating way to spend a quiet morning.

LUNCH: If you don't take a picnic lunch on your boat outing, try **Snapper's**

Waterfront Saloon & Raw Bar (MM 94.5 oceanside; 305–852–5956; moderate) for great raw and cooked seafood as well as nice views.

Afternoon

To continue your outdoors-oriented day, head to the **Florida Keys Wild Bird Center** (MM 93.6 bayside; 305–852–4486; no entrance fee, but donations are encouraged). This small nature center features an educational center, injured bird habitats, a boardwalk and nature trail, and lots of herons, hawks, ospreys, and pelicans in various states of recovery.

US 1 heads back to Homestead, where you can join the Florida Turnpike for the quick drive back to Miami.

THERE'S MORE

Scuba diving and snorkeling: A large number of excellent dive operators dot the Overseas Highway, including **Amy Slate's Amoray Dive Resort** (MM 104 bayside; 305–451–3595 or 800–4–AMORAY); **Captain Slate's Atlantis Dive Center** (two locations at MM 106.5 and 51 Garden Cove Drive; 305–451–1325 or 800–331–DIVE); **It's A Dive Watersports** (MM 103.8; 305–453–9881); **John Pennekamp Coral Reef State Park** (MM 102.5; 305–451–1621); **Sharky's Snorkel and Dive Center** (two locations at MM 106 and MM 100; 305–451–5533); **Silent World Dive & Snorkel Center** (MM 103.2 bayside; 305–451–3252 or 800–966–DIVE); and **Snuba Tours of Key Largo** (MM 97; 305–451–6391).

Boating: A wide variety of boats is available for rental throughout the boating-oriented Key Largo area. **John Pennekamp Coral Reef State Park** (MM 102.5; 305–451–1621) is a good place for rentals.

Fishing: Sailor's Choice Party Boat (MM 100; 305–451–1802) is the ideal choice for various fishing excursions. Further south, the Islamorada area is a fishing mecca, and **Bud 'N' Mary's Marina** (MM 79.8; 305–664–2461) is the place to head for party boats and charters.

SPECIAL EVENTS

April. Bay Jam, Music Festival on the Bay; (305) 451–9596.

November. Island Jubilee, four-day festival of food, shopping, music, and dancing; (305) 451–1414.

December. Key Largo Christmas Boat Parade, decorated boat parade along the shoreline of Blackwater Sound; (305) 451–1592.

OTHER RECOMMENDED RESTAURANTS AND LODGINGS

Accommodations options in the Key Largo area vary from large and bustling resorts to tiny and simple roadside motels. If Kona Kai Resort is full or you want something different, try **Amy Slate's Amoray Dive Resort** (MM 104 bayside; 305–451–3595 or 800–4–AMORAY; inexpensive to moderate); the "keysey" and friendly **Bay Harbor Lodge** (MM 97.7 bayside; 305–852–5695; inexpensive); the sprawling waterfront **Westin Beach Resort** (MM 97 bayside; 305–852–5553 or 800–539–5274; moderate to expensive); or the unusual underwater hotel room at **Jules' Undersea Lodge** (51 Shoreland Drive; 305–451–2353; expensive).

Other casual Key Largo area dining options include **Bogie's Cafe** (MM 100; 305–451–2121; moderate); **Coconuts Restaurant & Club** (MM 100; 305–453–9794; moderate to expensive); **Sundowners** (MM 104 bayside; 305–451–4502; moderate to expensive); and **Senor Frijoles** (MM 104 bayside; 305–451–1592; inexpensive to moderate).

FOR MORE INFORMATION

Florida Keys and Key West Visitors Bureau, P.O. Box 1147, Key West, FL 33041. (800) 352–5397 (FLA–KEYS).

The Key Largo Chamber of Commerce, 105950 Overseas Highway, Key Largo, FL 33037. (305) 451–1414.

Middle Florida Keys

YOUR OWN KEYS ESCAPE

2 NIGHTS

Resort activities • Bahia Honda State Park

Made up of narrow islands and small towns, the Middle Florida Keys aren't visited as often as the Upper Florida Keys around Key Largo or the Lower Florida Keys around Key West. But the area still offers the same laid-back Keys lifestyle and water-oriented activities.

Watersports and outdoors-oriented sightseeing are the main draws to the Middle Florida Keys, and resorts cater to visitors interested in these pursuits. From your own escape to one of the state's best state parks, you'll find the key to the Florida outdoors in the middle of the Florida Keys.

DAY 1

Afternoon

Head south on the Florida Turnpike until it ends at US 1 in Homestead. Take US 1 south toward Key Largo. For a short diversion (or if traffic is really bad), you can take the slightly longer and more scenic route along Card Sound Road, which eventually intersects with US 1 in the Keys. Either way, you'll follow US 1 (the Overseas Highway) all the way to the Middle Keys. Take US 1 to Mile Marker (MM) 61 (Mile Markers are used for directions and locations in the Keys) and turn left onto Duck Key, the location of Hawk's Cay Resort and Marina.

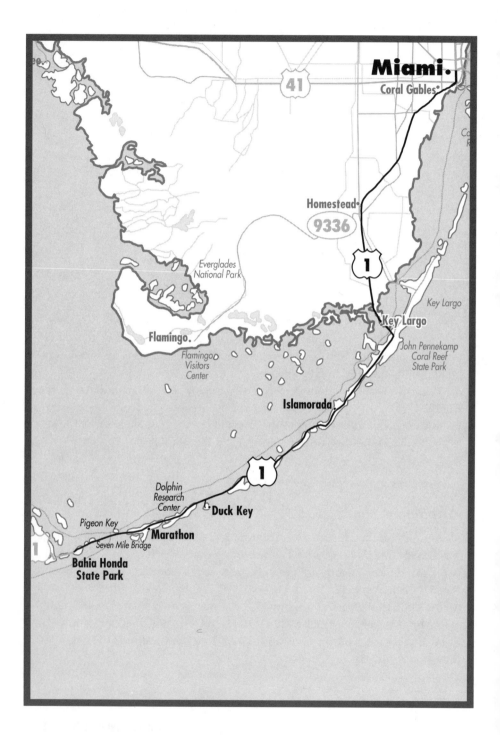

DINNER AND LODGING: Hawk's Cay Resort and Marina (MM 61, Duck Key; 305–743–7000 or 800–432–2242; moderate to expensive) is an ideal Middle Keys base. Located on a private 60-acre island in the five-island Duck Key formation, Hawk's Cay caters to guests of all ages and interests. The resort features 160 guest rooms and 16 suites, each with excellent views of the Gulf of Mexico, the Atlantic Ocean, or the island of Duck Key. All of the large rooms (including some villas) feature color TV, mini refrigerator, and an over-size private balcony (ask for one of the first-floor rooms, which offer a nice extended patio area). Amenities to enjoy during your stay include a full-service marina, freshwater swimming pool, whirlpool spas, a unique saltwater lagoon and private beach, a dolphin training center, tennis, a variety of restaurants and shops, and a fun bar. Many visitors never leave the resort.

On your first night at Hawk's Cay it's enjoyable to eat right at the resort. If you want to get right into the Keys lifestyle, head to the resort's **Water's Edge,** where grilled Angus steaks, fresh-off-the-boat seafood entrees, and an elaborate salad and soup buffet are served indoors or dockside at the Hawk's Cay Marina. Other options include **Cantina,** a tropical restaurant offering Mexican, Caribbean, and American fare, and **Porto Cayo,** a gourmet Italian restaurant with a hint of the islands.

Evening

Middle Keys life is generally pretty low-key at night. The resort's Water's Edge is also home to a nightclub that's popular with resort guests, visiting boaters, and locals.

DAY 2

Morning

BREAKFAST: Be sure to head to the resort's **Palm Terrace,** which serves a lavishly famous breakfast buffet seven days a week.

Your first morning provides a great time to explore the resort's offerings, which are typical of properties in the Middle Keys. An *Activities Guide* is published weekly, but head straight to Pool Hut for an update on the possibilities. The options include glass-bottom boat trips to the spectacular reefs, sailing excursions, sunset cruises, parasailing and Wave Runner rentals, shallow and deep-sea fishing, scuba diving and snorkeling on the United States' only living barrier coral reef, tennis, nearby golf, ecology tours, dolphin interaction, fitness programs, and a full-fledged "Island Adventure Club" for children aged 5–12.

After pursuing your chosen morning activity, head off Duck Key and turn left (south) on US 1 toward Marathon. If you have time and interest, stop in the **Dolphin Research Center** (MM 59; 305–289–1121; admission fee), which conducts dolphin research and provides entertainment and education. The guided tour includes explanations of dolphin behavior and interaction with dolphins. There is also a "swim with the dolphins" program (reservations required).

The Marathon area was the base camp for workers on Flagler's Florida East Coast Railway, completed in 1912 (you'll see the remains of the bridge all along the Overseas Highway). The crews were said to have made a "marathon" effort to complete the railway to Key West.

LUNCH: Right before you get to the legendary Seven Mile Bridge (MM 46.5), look for **Seven Mile Grill** (1240 Overseas Highway, MM 47; 305–743–4481; moderate). This Middle Keys mecca has been around since the 1950s, including the huge red, white, and blue sign that you can't miss. You sit at a long counter, which opens out to the Overseas Highway through a number of open garage doors. They specialize in friendly service, fried seafood, and great key lime pie.

Afternoon

Seven Mile Bridge starts a half-mile after the restaurant. This engineering wonder is the longest segmented bridge in the world, with 288 sections linking the keys. Though you can't stop on the bridge, you do get some great views. If you'd like to visit part of the **Old Seven Mile Bridge** and the former railroad camp on **Pigeon Key** (MM 45; 305–289–0025; admission fee), turn right off the Overseas Highway right before the new bridge. Cars aren't allowed on the old bridge, so you can take the trolley or walk the 2 miles out to Pigeon Key. Once there, visitors see one of the old houses occupied by crew members and can also take in the shark research facility that is now based on the island.

Continue south on the Overseas Highway to MM 37.5, where you'll turn left into **Bahia Honda State Park** (36850 Overseas Highway, MM 37.5; 305–872–2353; admission fee). With a name that is Spanish for "deep bay," this 490-acre park features one of the state's best beaches, mangroves, hiking, waterfront camping, and watersports activities like snorkeling, kayaking, and fishing. It's a great place to spend the afternoon.

Seven Mile Bridge is the longest segmented bridge in the world.

Head back north on the Overseas Highway to Hawk's Cay Resort and Marina.

DINNER: You can try one of the other restaurants right at Hawk's Cay or take the short drive down to the **Grassy Key Dairy Bar** (MM 58.5, Grassy Key; 305–743–3816; inexpensive), a typical local fish house. This very casual restaurant features fresh fish and sandwiches at budget prices. It's perfect for families.

LODGING: Hawk's Cay Resort and Marina.

DAY 3

Morning

BREAKFAST: Palm Terrace breakfast buffet at Hawk's Cay Resort and Marina.

Use the morning to pursue additional activities at the resort. Of special interest, the **"Dolphin Encounter"** at Hawk's Cay provides an in-depth view of these fascinating mammals as guests learn firsthand about dolphins through up-close and personal sessions with mammal husbandry experts. Participants are allowed to walk out onto the docks and into shallow depths with the trainer and dolphins, participating in a forty-five-minute informative presentation on dolphin behavior and current research. The experience is held three times daily.

Begin making your way back up the Keys to Miami, taking the time to explore some sightseeing possibilities along the way. Just north of Hawk's Cay, pull into **Long Key State Recreation Area** (Long Key, MM 67.5; 305–664–4815; admission fee). This 912-acre park borders both the ocean and the bay, with an interesting boardwalk trail, a long beach, canoeing, and camping as highlights.

Islamorada is one of the world's best deep-sea fishing hubs, so you'll see lots of busy marinas, including famed **Bud 'N' Mary's Marina** (MM 79.8; 305–664–2461 or 800–742–7945). Be sure to look on the right for the Hurricane Memorial just before MM 83, which marks the mass burial spot of some 400 people killed in the massive hurricane of 1935. Just north of Islamorada proper, the **Theater of the Sea** (Windley Key, MM 84.5; 305–664–2431; admission fee) is one of those old-style Florida amusement parks. It opened in 1945, making it the second oldest marine park in the United States (St. Augustine's Marineland is the oldest). Established in an old railroad quarry, the four-acre facility features dolphin and sea lion shows as well as other marine-life programs and displays.

One new option is the **Alison Fahrer Environmental Education Center** at Windley Key Quarry Fossil Reef State Geological Site (MM 85; 305–664–2540; no entrance fee). This former coral quarry, saved from condominium development, shows through displays and exploration of the actual reef how coral develops.

LUNCH: The fishing capital of Islamorada is a great place for a lunch of fresh fish. Located across the Overseas Highway from Bud 'N' Mary's Marina, **Papa Joe's** (MM 79.9; 305–664–8109; inexpensive to moderate) is another Keys dining landmark. The fresh fish of the day as an entree or sandwich is the order of choice for veterans. The tiki bar downstairs and raw bar upstairs are both sunset hangouts.

Afternoon

Continue on up the Keys and, if you have time, refer to Miami Escape Three (Upper Keys) for additional ideas.

US 1 continues to Homestead, where you can join the Florida Turnpike for the quick drive back to Miami.

THERE'S MORE

Other outdoor activities: Along with the array of outdoor possibilities right at Hawk's Cay Resort and Marina, many other outfitters provide more options in the Middle Keys. For general boating, contact **Captain Pip's** (MM 47.5; 305–743–4403) or **Robbie's Rent-a-Boat** (MM 77.5; 305–664–9814). Along with Bud 'N' Mary's Marina in Islamorada (mentioned above), **The Bounty Hunter** (15th Street; 305–743–2446) is another good fishing contact.

SPECIAL EVENTS

February. Annual Pigeon Key Festival; (305) 289–0025.

Annual Pigeon Key Art Festival; (305) 743–7664.

Rotary Island Festival. Local seafood delights; (305) 743–5417.

March. Islamorada Art & Music Festival; (305) 852–0511.

Marathon Seafood Festival. Gourmet delicacies from the waters of the Florida Keys; (305) 743–5417.

April. Annual Seven Mile Bridge Run; (305) 743–8513.

Earth Day at Cheeca Lodge. Entertainment, food, and sand-shaping contest on the beach; (305) 664–4651.

Taste of Islamorada. Area's best chefs prepare island delicacies for all to enjoy; (305) 664–4503.

July. Annual Underwater Music Festival, Looe Key National Marine Sanctuary. Underwater radio broadcast; (305) 872–2411.

OTHER RECOMMENDED RESTAURANTS AND LODGINGS

If Hawk's Cay Resort and Marina is full or a bit too pricey for your budget, contact **Banana Bay Resort & Marina** (4590 Overseas Highway, MM 49.5; 305–743–3500 or 800–BANANA–1; moderate) for a similar experience, though with less overall amenities. For a "keysey" cottage experience, **Marathon's Conch Key Cottages** (MM 62.3; 305–289–1377 or 800–330–1577; moderate) offers ten unique apartments and one- or two-bedroom waterfront cottages, which are a peaceful bargain.

Other fun restaurants in the area include **Manny & Isa's** (MM 81.6 oceanside; 305–664–5019; inexpensive); **Sid & Roxie's Green Turtle Inn** (MM 81.5 oceanside; 305–664–9031; inexpensive to moderate); **Lorelei** (MM 82 bayside; 305–664–4656; moderate); and **Lazy Days Oceanfront Bar and Seafood Grill** (MM 79.9 oceanside; 305–664–5256; inexpensive to moderate).

FOR MORE INFORMATION

Florida Keys and Key West Visitors Bureau, P.O. Box 1147, Key West, FL 33041. (800) 352–5397 (FLA–KEYS).

The Greater Marathon Chamber of Commerce, 12222 Overseas Highway (MM 53.5), Marathon, FL 33050. (305) 743–5417 or (800) 842–9580.

Key West

THE END OF THE ROAD

2 NIGHTS

Sightseeing • Key West street life

Key West is the end of the road in the United States. The nation's southern-most city has an atmosphere all its own, drawing a wide variety of characters for sunshine, assorted sightseeing, and some inevitable tackiness. But in addition to the constant party that has come to symbolize Key West, you'll also find fine dining, excellent sightseeing, and lots of watersports and other outdoor activities.

DAY 1

Afternoon

Head south on the Florida Turnpike until it ends at US 1 in Homestead. Take US 1 south toward Key West. For a short diversion (or if traffic is really bad), you can take the slightly longer and more scenic route along Card Sound Road, which eventually intersects with US 1 in the Keys. Either way, you'll follow US 1 all the way to Key West.

DINNER: Depending on when you hit the Keys, you may want to stop for dinner along the way. Two good "keysey" possibilities are **Mrs. Mac's Kitchen** (MM 99.4; 305–451–3722; inexpensive to moderate) in Key Largo and **Papa Joe's** (MM 79.9; 305–664–8109; inexpensive to moderate) in Islamorada. Both offer fresh seafood and a very laid-back atmosphere. If you make it all the way to Key West, get right into the swing of things at **Jimmy Buffett's Margaritaville Cafe** (500 Duval Street; 305–292–1435; moderate). The

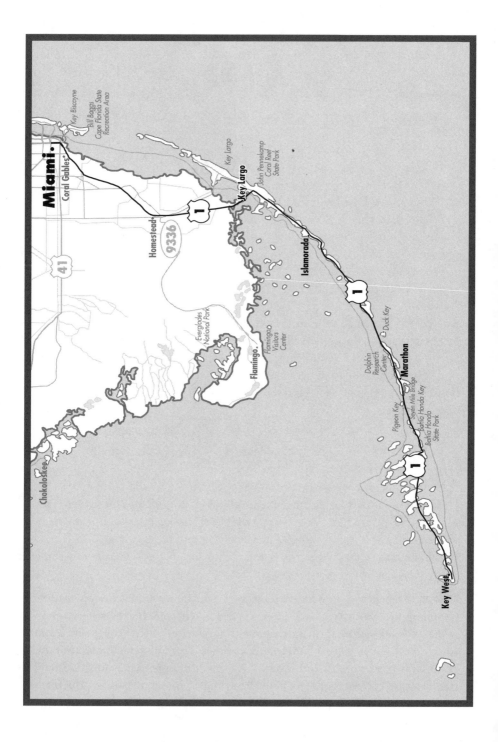

sandwiches and entrees are not really renowned, but you're actually here to be on Duval Street, watch the people, and drift into the Key West mentality.

LODGING: There are big-name hotels and quaint little B&Bs or inns in Key West, but if you want the best of both worlds, call the **Marquesa Hotel** (600 Fleming Street; 305–292–1919 or 800–869–4631; moderate to expensive). This twenty-seven-room inn has all of the amenities and services of a luxury hotel, coupled with the feel of a B&B. Originally built in 1884 as a single-family Greek Revival–style home, the completely renovated house and several adjoining structures have welcomed guests to Key West since 1988. Rooms and the hotel's popular Cafe Marquesa (creative "food of the Americas") are now located in four buildings surrounding two pools and an elaborate garden and three-tier waterfall. Each of the rooms and suites features a different decor of West Indies–style furnishings. The location just off Duval Street and the intimate yet full-service accommodations make the Marquesa an ideal Key West base.

Evening

Duval Street and other parts of Key West come alive after sunset. You can't come to Key West and not toast Hemingway at least once at **Sloppy Joe's** (201 Duval Street; 305–294–5717), but you'll definitely want to head further afield to the original Hemingway bar at **Captain Tony's Saloon** (428 Greene Street; 305–294–1838); **Hog's Breath Saloon** (400 Front Street; 305–296–4222); **Durty Harry's** (208 Duval Street; 305–296–4890); **Schooner Wharf Bar** (202 William Street; 305–292–9520); and **Jimmy Buffett's Margaritaville Cafe** (500 Duval Street; 305–292–1435).

DAY 2

Morning

BREAKFAST: If you want to have your coffee with lots of locals and fishermen, head to **Breakfast Anytime** (934 Truman Avenue; no phone; inexpensive) or **Camille's** (703 Duval Street; 305–296–4811; inexpensive).

Key West is definitely a walking town, so put on your walking shoes and start exploring. First, head up Duval Street or quieter Whitehead Street to the **Hemingway House** (907 Whitehead Street; 305–294–1575; admission fee). This large and airy house was Hemingway's base for fishing and writing from 1929 to 1939. He wrote *A Farewell to Arms, Death in the Afternoon,* and *For*

Sloppy Joe's Bar is among many Key West tourist attractions.

Whom the Bell Tolls while living here. He also built Key West's first swimming pool in the side yard and raised a huge brood of six-toed cats (you'll see many of their descendants during the entertaining half-hour tour).

Just a bit farther up the street, stop by the **Key West Lighthouse** (938 Whitehead Street; 305–294–0012; admission fee) for an interesting tour and a great view of Key West. The 1848 lighthouse and grounds include a museum in the former lighthouse keeper's house and an eighty-eight-step climb to the top.

LUNCH: Head back down Whitehead Street to **Kelly's Caribbean Bar & Grill** (301 Whitehead Street; 305–293–8484; moderate), which is located in the original office of Pan Am. Kelly McGinnis and her husband own this place, which features casual indoor and outdoor dining, with an island flair to its food and decor. The brewed-on-site beer is great after a hot morning of sightseeing.

Afternoon

Walk a block farther on Whitehead Street to the **Audubon House** (205 Whitehead Street; 305–294–2116; admission fee). Though naturalist John James Audubon never lived in this renovated house, he did visit the area, and many of the resulting lithographs are now displayed throughout the three-story home. The tropical gardens alone are worth the entrance price.

Located at the foot of Whitehead Street, the **Key West Aquarium** (1 Whitehead Street; 305–296–2051) will probably take up the rest of your afternoon. This old-style attraction opened in 1932 and features lots of large aquariums and touch tanks for the kids and kids at heart.

Depending on the time of year, you'll definitely want to enjoy the **sunset celebration at Mallory Square** before or after dinner. The sunsets at this spot can truly be stunning, but it's the street life that draws crowds. Musicians, jugglers, mimes, and many others provide the entertainment. It must be seen at least once to be believed.

DINNER: Make a reservation early for at least one meal at **Louie's Backyard** (700 Waddell Avenue; 305–294–1061; expensive). This classic Key West restaurant is perhaps one of the state's best. The outdoor deck provides a perfect setting for nearly perfect Caribbean cuisine. Current chef Doug Shook creatively combines fresh ingredients to come up with unusual takes on Cuban and "Floribbean" appetizers, entrees, and desserts.

LODGING: Marquesa Hotel.

Evening

If you're not into late nights of drinking along Duval Street, take heart. Plays and other cultural fare can be found at the **Red Barn Theater** (319 Duval Street; 305–296–9911) and the **Waterfront Playhouse** (Mallory Docks; 305–294–5015).

DAY 3

Morning

BREAKFAST: For another breakfast (or any meal) with locals in-the-know, head to **Blue Heaven** (729 Thomas Street; 305–296–8666; moderate). This former bordello and cockfight arena now hosts residents and a few visitors for all

three meals. Hemingway used to officiate boxing matches here. Healthful breakfasts include giant pancakes stuffed with varied fruits.

After a big breakfast, the long walk over to the **Key West Cemetery** feels good. Located off Olivia Street between Windsor Lane and Frances Street, this unique "attraction" includes whimsical tombstones with inscriptions like "I Told You I Was Sick."

LUNCH: Back on Duval Street, **Mangoes Restaurant** (700 Duval Street; 305–292–4606; moderate) is perhaps the quintessential Key West lunch spot. The huge brick patio has large trees providing shade from the sun, and the substantial menu features fresh soups, sandwiches, entrees, and tasty wood-stove pizza.

Afternoon

Use the afternoon for an outdoors-oriented pursuit, of which Key West has many. One fun way to explore more of Key West is with a bike, the local form of transportation for most residents. It's easy to ride around the entire island, including many of Old Town's peaceful side streets. Another option is to head over to Smather's or Key West Municipal Beaches off South Roosevelt Boulevard, which are the only two real public beaches on Key West. If two-wheeling or lying on the beach aren't your style, the Keys' famed scuba diving and fishing are also easy to pursue.

Heading back north, US 1 goes to Homestead, where you can join the Florida Turnpike for the quick drive back to Miami.

THERE'S MORE

Other sightseeing attractions: East Martello Museum and Gallery (3501 South Roosevelt Boulevard; 305–296–3913; admission fee) is one of the least-visited and -appreciated museums on Key West. Located in an old fort, the museum features a wide array of Key West history, including local art, a horse-drawn hearse, a raft from the Mariel boatlift, and old ship models. **Mel Fisher's Treasure Museum** (200 Greene Street; 305–294–2633; admission fee) showcases the finds of treasure hunter Mel Fisher, including gold and silver coins, gold bars, and lots of jewels. **Conch Train** (1805 Staples Avenue, No. 101; 305–294–5161; admission fee) and **Old Town Trolley** (1910 North Roosevelt Boulevard; 305–296–6688; admission fee) both run interesting loop tours of Key West, if you want to get an overview before exploring on your own.

Biking: Contact **The Bike Shop** (1110 Truman Avenue; 305–294–1073) or **Tropical Bicycles & Scooter Rentals** (1300 Duval Street; 305–294–8136).

Fishing: Contact the **Municipal Marina** (1801 North Roosevelt Boulevard; 305–292–8167) for deep-sea fishing outings.

Scuba Diving: Southpoint Divers (714 Duval Street; 305–292–9778) and **Key West Pro Dive Shop** (3128 North Roosevelt Boulevard; 305–296–3823 or 800–426–0707) are two of the biggest and best operations in the state.

SPECIAL EVENTS

January. Old Island Days House & Garden Tour. Part of Old Island Days, a four-month run, beginning in December, of events including an art festival, conch shell blowing contests, and house and garden tours; (305) 294–9501.

Red Barn Theater. Full schedule of performances fills the theater season; (305) 293–3035.

Annual Key West Literary Seminar. Themed workshops, walking tours, and panel discussions with distinguished writers; (305) 293–9291.

Key West Race Week. Top sailing vessels competing in a five-day race; (781) 639–9545.

February. Old Island Days Arts Festival; (305) 294–9501.

Heritage Festival. Civil War reenactments; (305) 292–6713.

April. Conch Republic Independence Celebration. Parades, parties, and fun to commemorate the "founding" of the Conch Republic; (305) 296–0213.

June. Offshore Powerboat Race. Superboat and other class races; (305) 296–8963.

July. Hemingway Days Festival. Annual celebration of the legendary author's work, lifestyle, and looks, highlighted by a look-alike contest; (305) 296–2388.

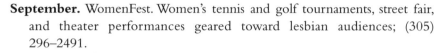
September. WomenFest. Women's tennis and golf tournaments, street fair, and theater performances geared toward lesbian audiences; (305) 296–2491.

Annual Florida Keys Poker Run. Motorcycles cruise from Miami to Key West in an effort to raise funds for local children's charities; (305) 294–3032.

October. Goombay Festival. Two-day street fair in Key West's historic Bahama Village; (305) 293–8305.

Fantasy Fest. Notorious 10-day celebration, outlandish costumes, sights, and sounds; (305) 296–1817.

Waterfront Playhouse. Theater and opera performances; (305) 294–0431.

November. Super Boat International Key West World Championship. World-class offshore powerboat races; (305) 296–8963.

December. Old Island Days begins; (305) 294–9501.

Tennessee Williams Fine Arts season. Four months of chamber music, theater performances, and special guests; (305) 296–1520.

OTHER RECOMMENDED RESTAURANTS AND LODGINGS

If you're looking for more of a large resort-style setting, try **The Pier House** (1 Duval Street; 305–296–4600 or 800–327–8340; expensive), with more than 140 rooms, virtually every amenity, and a great location at the foot of Duval Street. Similarly, the **Wyndham Casa Marina Resort and Beach House** (1500 Reynolds Street; 305–296–3535 or 800–626–0777; expensive) offers a resort experience, but away from the hustle and bustle of downtown Key West. For more of a B&B-style stay, contact **La Pensione** (809 Truman Avenue; 305–292–9923; moderate); **Southernmost Point Guest House** (1327 Duval Street; 305–294–0715; moderate); or **Wicker Guesthouse** (913 Duval Street; 305–296–4275 or 800–880–4275; moderate).

Meals are a big deal in Key West, and some other enjoyable possibilities include creative continental cuisine at intimate Marquesa Hotel's **Cafe Marquesa** (600 Fleming Street; 305–292–1244; expensive); upscale food and atmosphere at long-lived **Cafe des Artistes** (1007 Simonton Street; 305–294–7100; expensive); Mexican-influenced seafood at **Turtle Kraals**

(213 Margaret Street; 305–294–2640; moderate); and great budget meals all day at **Pepe's** (806 Caroline Street; 305–294–7192; inexpensive to moderate).

FOR MORE INFORMATION

Florida Keys and Key West Visitors Bureau, P.O. Box 1147, Key West, FL 33041. (800) 352–5397 (FLA-KEYS).

Key West Chamber of Commerce, 402 Wall Street, Key West, FL 33040. (305) 294–2587 or (800) 527–8539.

Southern Everglades

FLAMINGO FUN IN THE EVERGLADES

2 NIGHTS

Nature • Hiking • Canoeing and boating
Various outdoor tours

There is, quite simply, no place on earth like the Everglades. The extraordinary Everglades National Park occupies more than 1.5 million acres at the southern tip of the Florida peninsula. Diverse habitats in the park range from marine, estuarine, and mangrove communities to pinelands, hardwood hammocks, and extensive freshwater sloughs and prairies.

Historically, shallow water moved slowly south through the sawgrass toward the mangrove estuaries, inspiring early conservationists to describe the Everglades as a "River of Grass." Studies have revealed, however, that the Everglades are in great danger of being irreversibly destroyed. Restoration projects are attempting to reverse damage brought about by drainage for development and agriculture.

Even with the damage, the Everglades National Park is one of America's most fascinating outdoor destinations. A visit to the southern Everglades can include anything from a quick stop at one of many nature areas to a full day of organized activities in the Flamingo area. No matter what's chosen, the Everglades never cease to amaze visitors.

Alligators can be seen throughout the Everglades.

DAY 1

Afternoon

It's easy to reach your southern Everglades base from the Miami area. The quickest route is to head out to the Florida Turnpike and go south to where it intersects with US 1 in Florida City. State Road 9336 and prominent brown National Park signs will lead you directly to the Ernest F. Coe Visitor Center at the entrance of the park.

You can stop at the Coe Visitor Center for a wide variety of information. From there, a pretty 38-mile drive to the Flamingo Visitor Center runs past typical Everglades landscapes and also provides several excellent places to stop for an introduction to the unique environment. Depending on the amount of daylight left, some popular stops include the Royal Palm Visitor Center (be sure to walk on the Gumbo Limbo Trail and the Anhinga Trail), Long Pine

Key, Pinelands Trail, Pa-hay-okee Overlook, Mahogany Hammock, Nine Mile Pond, and West Lake. Keep in mind that it's easy to explore Nine Mile Pond, West Lake, and other natural areas once you've established yourself in the Flamingo area.

DINNER AND LODGING: There is no better base for Everglades exploration than the **Flamingo Lodge Marina & Outpost Resort** (#1 Flamingo Lodge Highway; 941–695–3101 or 800–600–3813 for reservations; inexpensive to moderate). The Flamingo Lodge provides the perfect place to stay (besides camping, it's the only lodging in the park). The resort is located at the conveniently close southern end of the park and offers accommodations, sightseeing tours, and many other activities. It is also near many of the park's other outstanding features that can be explored on your own.

The lodge features basic accommodations, with nice views of Florida Bay. But you'll want to spend as much time outdoors as possible. When you are outdoors, be prepared for mosquitoes with strong repellent and lots of clothing. They are definitely at their worst from June to November.

For dinner (and all meals), the lodge's **Flamingo Restaurant** provides a stunning view of Florida Bay (great sunsets are the norm) as well as surprisingly tasty and hearty food. You can enjoy anything from a simple hamburger to a full four-course meal, including a nice salad bar. Depending on crowds, the restaurant is seasonal (typically October through April).

Evening

There are typically evening programs led by rangers at the Flamingo campground amphitheater, with subjects ranging from manatees to mosquito fish. They usually last one hour. The Buttonwood Lounge (also seasonal) is a perfect place to trade stories about the day's adventures.

DAY 2

Morning

BREAKFAST: Flamingo Restaurant.

There's an incredible amount to see nearby and a wide range of sightseeing tours to help you see everything. One of the best morning tours to provide an overall view of the area is the *Dolphin* four-hour Wilderness Cruise. Shorter two-hour possibilities include the Pelican Backcountry Cruise and the Bald Eagle Florida Bay Cruise. Whichever introductory tour you choose

on this first morning, you'll have other times to explore other tours that interest you. All of them offer an opportunity to see the unique plants and animals of the Everglades and Florida Bay.

The flora and fauna encounters are astounding, with the sightings often including unique plants, raccoons, turtles, snakes, bobcats, herons, hawks, terns, bald eagles, egrets, pelicans, cormorants, ibis, ospreys, roseate spoonbills, alligators, crocodiles, manatees, dolphins, sea turtles, and sharks.

LUNCH: Flamingo Restaurant.

Afternoon

After lunch, exploration on your own is easy. Hiking is quite popular in the Everglades, with nearby options including pretty Eco Pond, the Coastal Prairie Trail to Clubhouse Beach, Christian Point Trail, Rowdy Bend Trail, and Snake Bight Trail. Canoe, skiff, and bike rentals are also available. As with the sightseeing tours, everything can be arranged right at the marina.

When you do head indoors, the Flamingo Lodge is accommodating. The resort features a well-stocked gift shop and marina store as well as a post office and laundry facilities.

In the early evening, sunset cruises on Florida Bay (seasonal) are also available at the marina. The Windfall Florida Bay Cruise lasts two hours and is very popular (get your tickets early).

DINNER AND LODGING: Flamingo Lodge Marina & Outpost Resort.

Evening

Ranger programs (seasonal) are often offered at the Flamingo campground amphitheater. Park visitors and employees often gather at the Buttonwood Lounge.

DAY 3

Morning

BREAKFAST: Flamingo Restaurant.

Use the morning for another sightseeing tour or to explore on your own by canoe, bike, or on foot.

LUNCH: Flamingo Restaurant.

Afternoon

Use the afternoon for another sightseeing tour or to explore on your own by canoe, bike, or on foot.

Head back to the Main Visitor Entrance and on to Homestead. Then, follow signs for the Florida Turnpike or US 1 back to the Miami area.

THERE'S MORE

In addition to the sightseeing tours described here, other options include deep wilderness cruises, beachcombing trips, birding cruises, sea kayaking tours, charter fishing, and houseboat rentals. For the longer trips, picnic box lunches are available seasonally from the Flamingo Restaurant (as well as limited supplies in the Marina store).

SPECIAL EVENTS

There aren't really any annual special events in the Flamingo area, but each week (seasonal) there's a schedule of ranger-led activities, including early-bird hikes, canoe trips (reservations required), presentations, hiking (including "wet walks"), and biking.

OTHER RECOMMENDED RESTAURANTS AND LODGINGS

Camping, which is located on Florida Bay and Long Pine Key, is available by calling (800) 365–CAMP.

FOR MORE INFORMATION

Everglades National Park, 4001 State Road 9336, Homestead, FL 33034. (305) 242–7700.

Western Everglades
TEN THOUSAND ISLANDS AND MORE

2 NIGHTS

Outdoor activities

At more than 1.5 million acres, the Everglades are a lot to see. Though many visitors head to the convenient southern portion of the national park, in the Flamingo area (see Miami Escape Six), the western Everglades are just as interesting and full of outdoor activity possibilities.

Like the Flamingo area, the western Everglades offer many exploration possibilities, including a wide range of boat tours from various outfitters, canoeing, hiking, and biking. Unlike Flamingo, there are no national park accommodations. Thus you have a choice of several excellent and varied lodging possibilities. Everglades City also offers many restaurants, in comparison to only one in Flamingo.

DAY 1

Afternoon

Take either I–75 (possibly faster) or US 41 (more scenic) to the Marco Island area. If you take US 41 (the Tamiami Trail), there are many enjoyable diversions along the way. Some of the possibilities include Everglades National Park trolley tours and biking at **Shark Valley** (US 41, about 25 miles west of Miami; 305–221–8455; entrance fee); **Miccosukee Indian Village and Airboat Tours** (US 41, about 25 miles west of Miami; 305–223–8380; entrance fee); hiking, canoeing, and animal viewing at **Big Cypress National Preserve** (US 41 near Ochopee; 813–695–2000; no entrance fee); and **Collier**

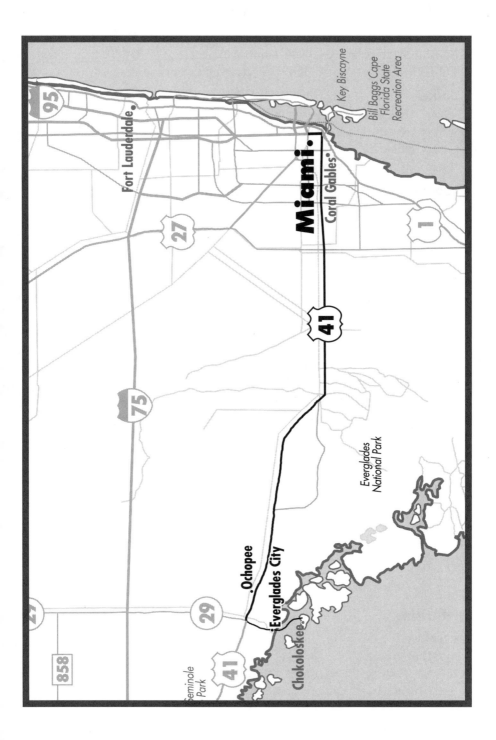

Seminole State Park (20200 Tamiami Trail; 941–394–3397; entrance fee). Off I–75 and US 41, State Road 29 leads right to Everglades City.

DINNER: There are many excellent seafood-oriented restaurants to enjoy while in the area. Along with lots of fresh fish and oysters, stone crab (in season) is particularly prevalent in the area. Nautically themed **Seafood Depot** (102 Collier Avenue; 941–695–0075; moderate), with fresh seafood and waterfront dining, is a local and visitor favorite.

LODGING: The **Rod & Gun Lodge** (200 Broadway; 941–695–2101; inexpensive) is one of those classic Florida establishments that everyone should experience at least once. With an old Florida fishing and hunting lodge ambience, the Rod & Gun Lodge was built as a private residence in 1930 on the site of the original structure built by the first settler of Everglades City. Barron Collier bought and ran it as a private club beginning in 1922, hosting many international dignitaries and several U.S. presidents. In 1972, the Bowen family from Michigan bought the club and is still operating it today. The sprawling white clapboard building offers simple rooms and wonderful public areas, including a very pleasant screened porch with ceiling fans.

The Rod & Gun Lodge has hosted presidents Hoover, Roosevelt, Truman, Eisenhower, and Nixon as well as John Wayne, Ernest Hemingway, Burl Ives, Gypsy Rose Lee, Burt Reynolds, Mick Jagger, Sean Connery, and many others. Its waterfront location and marina offer great boating opportunities as well as fishing with private local fishing guides. There's also a swimming pool, bike rental, and tennis.

Evening

Unless you head over to Marco Island, there's very little nightlife in this neck of the woods. Everglades City area visitors prefer to rise early for outdoors explorations.

DAY 2

Morning

BREAKFAST: Rod & Gun Lodge.

Head straight to the Everglades National Park **Gulf Coast Visitor Center** (State Route 29; 941–695–3311; no entrance fee) to review your Everglades exploration options with rangers and the national park boat tour

operator (seasonal). In addition to the Visitor Center's interpretive center, varied ranger programs (check the schedule), and canoe rentals, **Everglades National Park Boat Tours** (Gulf Coast Visitor Center, State Route 29; 941–695–2591 or 800–445–7724; entrance fees) offers several interesting routes through the western Everglades' saltwater gateway. Four variously sized boats run frequent seasonal one-hour-and-forty-five-minute or two-hour-and-thirty-minute tours through the mangrove wilderness islands. The boat captains also serve as fascinating guides, offering background information, and common spottings include dolphins, alligators, pelicans, ospreys, eagles, manatees, and much more. You'll surely want to schedule one or more trips with this well-run boat tour company.

LUNCH: The Oyster House (901 Copeland Avenue; 941–695–2073; moderate), across from the national park Visitor Center, serves fresh seafood in a friendly local atmosphere. The oysters, grouper, and fried platters are especially popular.

Afternoon

Use your afternoon to take one or more seasonal tours with one of the other operators. **Capt. Doug House's Florida Boat Tours** (200 State Route 29; 941–695–4000 or 800–282–9194; entrance fee) is definitely one of the best. With six airboats available and tours departing at least every thirty minutes, the professional guides provide a great overview of the Everglades environment, with frequent alligator, bird, and raccoon sightings.

If you want a longer and more intensive tour of the Everglades, **Majestic Everglades Excursions** (P.O. Box 241; 941–695–2777; entrance fee) is the top choice for a full afternoon of exploration. Husband-and-wife team Frank and Georgia Garrett are your fascinating hosts on the close to four-hour tour aboard a quiet covered deck boat that's limited to just six passengers. They provide a fascinating narrative that includes lots of flora and fauna as well as history of the early settlers. Fruits and cheeses are served on the afternoon tour, while a light lunch is served on the morning trip. If you're serious about exploring the Everglades, this is a great trip.

DINNER: For something a bit different, head to **Oar House Restaurant** (305 Collier Avenue; 941–695–3535; moderate), which specializes in local cuisine and atmosphere. The choices include frog legs, alligator, and turtle.

LODGING: Rod & Gun Lodge.

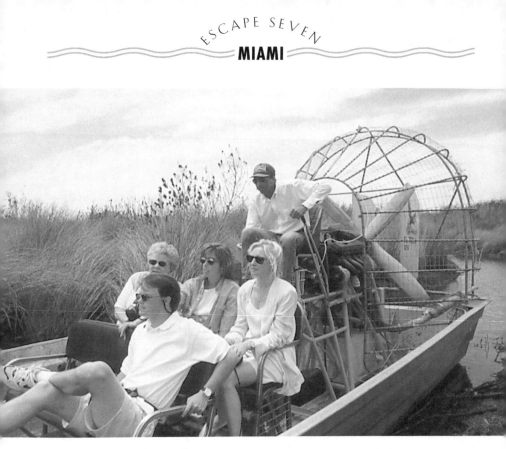

Airboat tours provide one of the best ways to visit the western Everglades.

DAY 3

Morning

BREAKFAST: Rod & Gun Lodge.

The early morning hours offer a perfect and peaceful opportunity to explore the area more intimately by canoe. The national park Visitor Center offers seasonal canoe rentals, but a far more interesting canoeing experience can be arranged by contacting David Harraden at **North American Canoe Tours** (107 Camellia Street; 941–695–4666). David has been running one-day, four-day, and one-week canoe (and kayak) trips in the area since 1978. If you try one of his daily tours, you're sure to book a longer trip during another visit. David and his family also run Ivey House Bed & Breakfast (see below), where they rent bikes as well (there's a nice 4-mile bike path to Chokoloskee Island).

LUNCH: If you're not enjoying a picnic lunch during your canoe trip, modern **Susie's Station** (1003 SW Copeland Avenue; 941–695–3666; inexpensive to moderate) features fresh soup, salads, and sandwiches.

Afternoon

No trip to the western Everglades would be complete without a visit to **Historic Smallwood Store** (Mamie Street; 941–695–2989; entrance fee), located south of Everglades City proper at the end of Chokoloskee Island. Human occupation of the area began more than 2,000 years ago, while white settlement didn't begin until near the end of the nineteenth century. This settlement brought the need for goods and mail, which led to the establishment of Smallwood Store by Ted Smallwood in 1906 as a trading post for buying and trading hides, furs, and farm produce. The bustling store was the site of the famed shooting of Ed Watson, who reputedly killed outlaw Belle Starr.

It was placed on the National Register of Historic Places in 1974 and operated as a store and post office until 1982. Ted's granddaughter kept the middle of the store as Ted would have known it and now runs it as a fascinating local museum, complete with 90 percent of the original store goods and many excellent displays concerning the area's history.

Take either US 41 or I–75 back to the Miami area.

THERE'S MORE

Other boat tours: Tours (seasonal) can be arranged through **Eden of the Everglades** (903 Dupont School Road; 941–695–2800); **Jungle Erv's Airboat World** (804 Collier Avenue; 941–695–2805); and **Wooten's Airboat Tours** (US 41, Ochopee; 941–695–2781), a popular and large operation that includes swamp buggy tours, an alligator farm, and animal exhibit.

Fishing: Fishing charters and guides are popular in the Ten Thousand Islands, with recommended captains including **Captain Tony Brock** (1 Turkey Trail Road, Ochopee; 941–695–4150); **Captain Bob Chipman** (Clary Drive; 941–695–2258); **Captain Max Miller** (210 North Starter Avenue; 941–695–2420); and **Captain Charles Tavernier** (166 US 29, Chokolosee; 941–695–4100).

SPECIAL EVENTS

February. Everglades Seafood Festival, Everglades City. Local seafood, music, and fun; (941) 695–3941.

April. Seminole Indian Days at Smallwood Store, Chokoloskee Island. Celebrates local Native American culture; (941) 695–2989.

OTHER RECOMMENDED RESTAURANTS AND LODGINGS

If the Rod & Gun Lodge isn't your style, **Ivey House Bed & Breakfast** (107 Camellia Street; 941–695–3299; inexpensive) is another excellent option. This one-time recreational center, boardinghouse, and dormitory is now a pleasant family-run B&B, with ten simple and clean rooms off a center hallway, a large living room and kitchen, and two porches. Bathrooms are shared, but there's also an excellent two-bedroom cottage for rent. A large cold breakfast is included with your room, and you can also enjoy a pleasant family-style dinner there each evening. The Harraden family are your friendly hosts, and David also operates the previously mentioned North American Canoe Tours.

Other accommodations in the Everglades City area include **Baron River Resort, Motel, & Villas** (803 Collier Avenue; 941–695–3591 or 800–535–4961; inexpensive to moderate); **Captain's Table Motel & Villas** (102 Collier Avenue; 941–695–4211; inexpensive to moderate); **River Wilderness Waterfront Villas** (210 Collier Avenue; 941–695–4499; inexpensive to moderate); and **Sportsman's Club Motel** (310 Collier Avenue; 941–695–4224; inexpensive).

Other dining options include **Glade's Haven Deli & Store** (801 Copeland Avenue; 941–695–2746; inexpensive) and **Under the Tower Cafe** (US 29; 941–695–3666; inexpensive).

FOR MORE INFORMATION

Everglades City Area Chamber of Commerce, US 41 and State Route 29, P.O. Box 130, Everglades City, FL 33929. (941) 695–3941.

Marco Island & the Everglades Convention & Visitors Bureau, 1102 North Collier Boulevard, Marco Island, FL 33937. (941) 394–7549 or (800) 788–MARCO.

Marco Island

A SOUTHWEST
FLORIDA ISLAND GETAWAY

2 NIGHTS

Beach • Resort activities • Ten Thousand Islands

Marco Island is the largest inhabited isle of the Ten Thousand Islands, with 3½ miles of sweeping beachfront and foam-flecked turquoise waters. Thanks to the development of several fine oceanfront resorts, Marco provides a perfect island escape as well as an ideal base for exploring the Ten Thousand Islands and the nearby Everglades. From sunning or shelling on the beaches to a variety of watersports and outdoor adventures, Marco Island is an ideal South Florida experience.

DAY 1

Afternoon

Take either I–75 (faster) or US 41 (more scenic) to the Marco Island area. If you take US 41 (the Tamiami Trail), there are many enjoyable diversions along the way. Some of the possibilities include Everglades National Park trolley tours and biking at **Shark Valley** (US 41, about 25 miles west of Miami; 305–221–8455; entrance fee); **Miccosukee Indian Village and Airboat Tours** (US 41, about 25 miles west of Miami; 305–223–8380; entrance fee); hiking, canoeing, and animal viewing at **Big Cypress National Preserve**

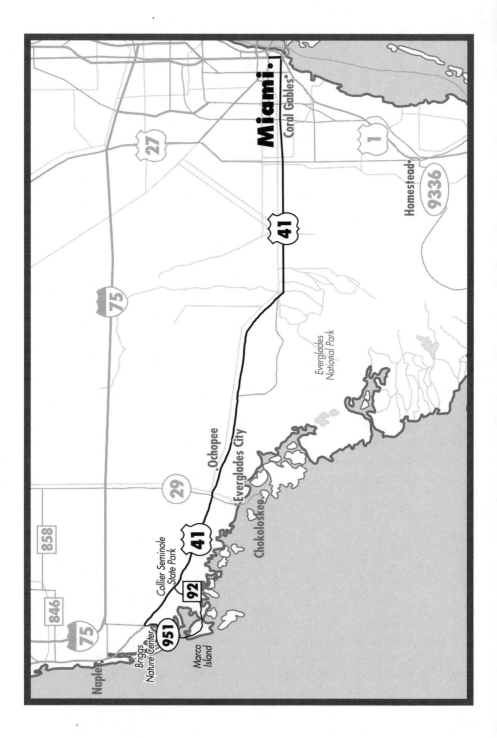

(US 41 near Ochopee; 813–695–2000; no entrance fee); and **Collier Seminole State Park** (20200 Tamiami Trail; 941–394–3397; entrance fee). Off I–75, State Road 951 leads right to Marco Island. Off US 41, State Road 92 leads onto the island.

DINNER AND LODGING: The **Marco Island Marriott Resort & Golf Club** (400 South Collier Boulevard; 941–394–2511 or 800–438–4373; moderate to expensive) is the perfect base for a Marco Island getaway. Located right on the wide and white sand beach, the resort features all of the amenities and activities needed to experience everything the island and surrounding area have to offer. These include a variety of spacious accommodations, shopping, three pools, spa, beach tiki huts, sailing, kayaking, Wave Runners, sailboarding, waterskiing, parasailing, fishing, biking, miniature golf, shelling and other out island excursions on a variety of watercraft, sixteen tennis courts, and golf on the Joe Lee championship course. The resort's popular Kids Klub program draws rave reviews from the many families who enjoy this kid-oriented Marriott. The resort was the first in North America to receive the distinguished National Parenting Center Seal of Approval.

For your first island meal, the resort has several excellent dining options. **Quinn's on the Beach,** named for the legendary pirate Captain Quinn, is a laid-back beach shack offering seafood right on the beach. For a true culinary experience, **Ristorante Tuscany** features an upscale northern Italian dining experience in the glow of candlelight and faint piano melodies. **Voyager Restaurant** offers grilled and charbroiled meats, fresh seafood, and an enormous salad bar. The resort also has several other casual eating choices, including a pizzeria and grocery.

Evening

The resort's **Quinn's on the Beach** is a very popular place with guests and locals, providing an ideal setting for the often spectacular sunsets as well as frequent live music right on the sand.

DAY 2

Morning

BREAKFAST: The resort's **Cafe del Sol** features a huge breakfast buffet, while **Quinn's on the Beach** offers cafeteria-style service, with dining right on the beach.

Wave Runner excursions to deserted islands are very popular for Marco Island visitors.

Use your first morning to explore Marco Island before deciding what particular activities you'd like to pursue. One way to get an overview of the island is to hop on one of the frequent trolleys that stop by the resort. **Marco Island Trolley Tours** (400 South Collier Boulevard; 941–394–1600; daily fares), based at the Marriott, runs a loop service around the island, with colorful commentary along the way. Otherwise, use your car for a quick driving tour of the island on and off Collier Boulevard, which can include several public beach areas; the undeveloped **Cushing Archaeological Site** (Bald Eagle Drive; no phone; no entrance fee), where significant excavations have unearthed 3,500-year-old Native American artifacts; and the **Olde Marco Inn** (100 Palm Street; 941–394–3131; no entrance fee), the first accommodations on the island and now a popular restaurant (see below).

Just off the island, on State Road 951, **Briggs Nature Center** (Shell Island Road; 941–775–8569; entrance fee) provides an interesting introduction to the natural side of the area. The facilities include a nature center, a half-mile boardwalk, boat tours, shelling trips, and nearby canoe rentals. In addition, **Collier Seminole State Park** (20200 Tamiami Trail; 941–394–3397; entrance fee), just off US 41 on State Road 92 leading off Marco Island, features additional canoeing (13-mile trail), boating, and hiking near the official boundary of the Big Cypress Swamp.

LUNCH: If you want to lunch with the local sailors and fishermen, stop by the **Snook Inn** (1215 Bald Eagle Drive; 941–394–3313; moderate) in the Old Marco section of the island. Located on the bustling Marco River, the restaurant's best bets are the seafood entrees and sandwiches. The outdoor Chickee Bar is a great place to eat, drink, or watch a sunset.

Afternoon

Head back to your resort to pursue any chosen outdoor activity. Along with boating or Wave Runner excursions to the quiet Ten Thousand Islands right from the beach, other options include **Marriott Sailing and Shelling** (400 South Collier Boulevard; 941–642–2740), located right at the Marriott and featuring small boats, sailing, shelling, and sightseeing; **Marco Island Sea Excursions** (1079 Bald Eagle Drive, #2A; 941–642–6400), offering sailing, fishing, shelling, and practically anything else on the water; and **Key West Excursions** (1081 Bald Eagle Drive; 941–389–2090 or 800–650–KEYS), featuring same-day and overnight excursions to Key West aboard one of the state's fastest cruise vessels.

DINNER: For a literal taste of history, you should have at least one meal at the **Olde Marco Inn** (100 Palm Street; 941–394–3131; moderate). Built in 1883 by Captain William Collier as the island's first hotel, the Victorian inn now features large dining rooms, elegant furnishings, and creative continental cuisine. It's definitely a Marco Island landmark.

LODGING: The Marco Island Marriott Resort & Golf Club.

Evening

You might want to visit one or more of several local hangouts for varied live music: **La Casita Mexican Restaurant** (San Marco Road and Barfield Drive; 941–642–7600); the **Snook Inn** (1215 Bald Eagle Drive; 941–394–3313); **Alan's Hideaway Piano Bar** (23 Front Street;

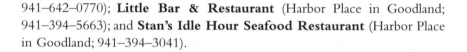
941–642–0770); **Little Bar & Restaurant** (Harbor Place in Goodland; 941–394–5663); and **Stan's Idle Hour Seafood Restaurant** (Harbor Place in Goodland; 941–394–3041).

DAY 3

Morning

BREAKFAST: **Susie's Diner** (1013 North Collier Boulevard; 941–642–6633; inexpensive) is a great place for breakfast with the locals.

Use the morning for additional outdoor activities. Be sure to take at least one excursion to the Ten Thousand Islands, one of Florida's most unique wilderness areas.

LUNCH: Take a drive out to Goodland, a small fishing village on the southeast end of Marco Island. Lunch at either **Little Bar & Restaurant** (Harbor Place in Goodland; 941–394–5663) or **Stan's Idle Hour Seafood Restaurant** (Harbor Place in Goodland; 941–394–3041) will be the highlight of this excursion. If you're on the island the week after the Super Bowl, ask about Stan's Goodland Mullet Festival, a huge seafood festival and party.

Afternoon

After checkout, you may want to consider a quick excursion into nearby **Everglades City and the Everglades National Park** (see Miami Escape Seven). This makes for an easy and convenient introduction to the area on the way back to Miami. It's just off US 41, on State Route 29.

Take US 41 or I–75 back to the Miami area (stops are outlined at the beginning of this Escape).

THERE'S MORE

Other boat tours: *Everglade Flyer* and *Marco Eagle* (Factory Bay Marina; 941–642–6717) also make Ten Thousand Islands trips.

SPECIAL EVENTS

January. Mullet Festival, Stan's Idle Hour, Goodland. Huge celebration of the local fish with food, fun, and music; (941) 394–3041.

February. Maritime Seafood Festival, Old Marco. More food, entertainment, and fun; (941) 394–7549.

June. Marco Island Amateur Sports Festival; (941) 394–7549.

OTHER RECOMMENDED RESTAURANTS AND LODGINGS

The two other large resorts on Marco Island are the **Radisson Suite Beach Resort** (600 South Collier Boulevard; 941–394–4100 or 800–992–0651; moderate to expensive) and the **Marco Island Hilton Beach Resort** (560 South Collier Boulevard; 941–394–5000 or 800–221–2424; moderate to expensive). If you want something smaller and less expensive, try the **Boat House Motel** (1180 Edington Place; 941–642–2400; inexpensive to moderate).

Because it's a resort island, Marco has many other excellent restaurants. Some of the best include **Konrad's Seafood & Grille Room** (599 South Collier Boulevard; 941–642–3332; moderate to expensive); **Kretch's** (527 Bald Eagle Drive; 941–394–3433; moderate to expensive); **Cafe de Marco** (244 Palm Street; 941–394–6262; moderate to expensive); and **La Casita Mexican Restaurant** (San Marco Road and Barfield Drive; 941–642–7600; moderate).

FOR MORE INFORMATION

Marco Island & the Everglades Convention & Visitors Bureau, 1102 North Collier Boulevard, Marco Island, FL 33937. (941) 394–7549 or (800) 788–MARCO.

Naples

A SOUTHWEST SOJOURN

2 NIGHTS

A family inn • Pier sunsets

Nestled between the Florida Everglades and the Gulf of Mexico, it's obvious why Naples is often called "simply charming." For one thing, it's worlds away from the glitter and crowds that typify some of South Florida. The town's pristine beaches and gracious hospitality are a far cry from the major urban centers less than two hours to the west.

This escape is for those who appreciate simple pleasures: a family-run inn with a legacy of serving guests for more than fifty years; the natural beauty of walking down a quiet white sand beach, while dolphins and diving pelicans make waves offshore; window-shopping along a tree-lined avenue; bicycling along a shaded path through a friendly neighborhood; or touring a throwback Florida beach town on a leisurely ride aboard a 1907 replica trolley.

DAY 1

Afternoon

It's a quick drive across southern Florida on I–75, which should take around two hours or less. Try to arrive before sunset, heading right downtown to the Third Street South area (it's well-marked). Walk along 12th Avenue South toward the Gulf of Mexico. Here you'll find the famed Naples Pier and one of the best settings for a Gulf of Mexico sunset you'll ever come across.

DINNER AND LODGING: The **Naples Beach Hotel & Golf Club** (851 Gulf Shore Boulevard North; 941–261–2222 or 800–237–7600; moderate to

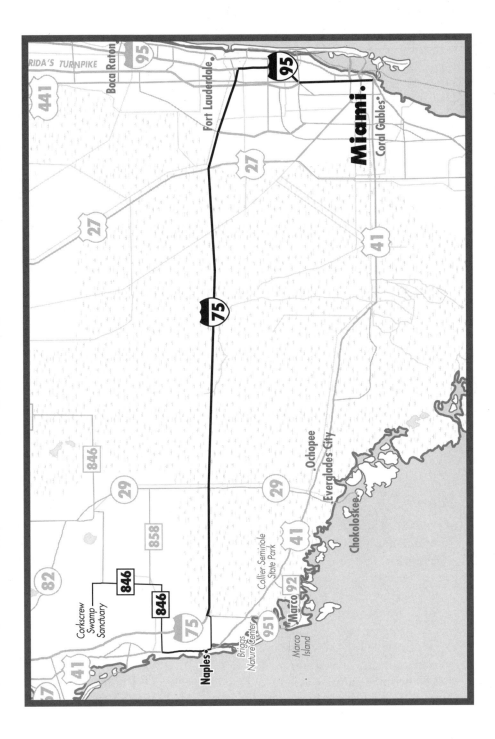

expensive) is one of the most appropriate places to stay in Naples, in that it fully evokes the "simply charming" feel of the area. Founded in 1946 by Henry Watkins Sr., the Naples Beach Hotel & Golf Club has become a legendary retreat for repeat guests and smart first-time Naples visitors.

Henry Watkins Jr. took over management of the hotel in 1979, and his son, Michael Watkins, is now its general manager. Three generations of management have also led to many third-generation guests, and an incredible repeat guest rate of 30 to 40 percent. It's a great place to start your own Florida quick escape tradition.

The eclectic resort now offers 316 rooms in 6 residential buildings spread over 125 acres and 1,000 feet of powdery sand beach. A popular eighteen-hole championship golf course is just a sand wedge across Gulf Shore Boulevard. The completely renovated accommodations include 41 suites, 22 efficiencies, and 253 brightly decorated guest rooms. Decorative touches in the rooms include prints of photographs by Clyde Butcher, who is known as the "Ansel Adams of the Everglades." In keeping with the owners' strong family tradition, this is a great base for families, with many specific programs and activities for kids, including a "Beach Klub for Kids."

The resort is a perfect place for your first Naples meal. **HB's on the Gulf** is the casual choice, with creative Florida cuisine served indoors or outdoors under cover. **The Everglades Dining Room** is the more elegant selection, with traditional continental cuisine served for dinner in-season (December to May). Both provide a great introduction to Naples dining.

DAY 2

Morning

BREAKFAST: The hotel's **Everglades Dining Room** serves an extensive breakfast buffet year-round.

The morning should be spent exploring what the hotel has to offer its guests. You may not want to leave the property, which exudes Old Florida family charm.

You'll naturally head right for the white sand beach, where you can rent your own lounge chairs (complete with your name) during your stay. Offshore activities include sailboarding, sailing, sea kayaking, pedal boating, and arrangements for deep sea and backwater fishing.

Another nice morning activity is a round of golf on the beautifully manicured and landscaped championship course. First built in the 1920s, but later

abandoned, the course underwent a major redesign by Ron Garl in 1980. You can follow in the footsteps of Gene Sarazen, Patty Berg, and modern-day Florida Seniors Open champions on this sporty layout. Serious golfers should definitely consider one of the hotel's excellent golf packages.

The Beach Klub for Kids entertains children daily with complimentary activities including swimming, crafts, beach walks, movies, finger painting, and games for kids ages five to twelve. A "kids' night out," which includes dinner, a movie, and games, is available on Friday and Saturday evenings for a nominal charge. Teens can meet other teens at complimentary tennis, volleyball, and golf clinics held every Saturday at the resort.

LUNCH: As a prelude to exploring "downtown" Naples, try one of the area's many excellent eateries for lunch. **Bistro 821** (821 5th Avenue South; 941–261–5821; moderate) is one of the best, and it's conveniently located in the heart of the shopping and dining area called "Third Street South."

Afternoon

Located in Old Naples (once the social center of southwest Florida in the 1920s), **Third Street South** (Broad Avenue to 14th Avenue South, between Second Street and Fourth Street South; 941–649–6707) is a major Naples attraction. There are more than 100 distinctive shops, art galleries, outdoor cafes, and award-winning restaurants. A copy of the *Historic Walking Tour of Old Naples* is available from sidewalk concierge booths.

Some top shopping recommendations include **The Beach House of Naples** (1300 Third Street South; 941–261–1366); **Johnston of Florida** (1190 Third Street South; 941–262–6637); **Tommy Bahama** (1220 Third Street; 941–643–6889); **The Mole Hole** (1201 Third Street South; 941–262–5115); or one of more than fifteen fine art galleries.

Depending on how long you can shop until you drop, you may have time to explore one or more other Naples area attractions in the late afternoon. By far the most popular and unusual is **Caribbean Gardens** (1590 Goodlette Road; 941–262–5409; entrance fee).

Caribbean Gardens was first opened in 1919 by Dr. Henry Nehrling and later developed by Julius Fleischmann. In 1969 the trustees of Fleischmann's estate contracted with the late Colonel Lawrence ("Jungle Larry") Tetzlaff and his wife, Nancy Jane ("Safari Jane"), to move their family and their collection of unusual and endangered animals within the garden. An expedition leader who brought back film footage and rare creatures to educate people, Tetzlaff

Third Street South is a popular Naples shopping and dining area.

and his family have taught millions of people about the plants and animals that live on the earth and the balance needed to sustain them. Nancy Jane and other family members are still active at Caribbean Gardens.

A visit to Caribbean Gardens includes a Primate Expedition Cruise; the Meet the Keeper Series; the Scales and Tails Show; big cats programs; an alligator lecture and feeding; Safari Canyon, a multimedia animal show; and lots of walking trails so you can explore the tropical gardens and animal exhibits on your own.

Try to be back at the Naples Beach Hotel & Golf Club before sunset to get a good seat at the Sunset Beach Bar, which is often voted one of the best places for a Gulf Coast sunset.

DINNER: For a night of casual Florida atmosphere and seafood, **The Dock at Crayton Cove** (City Dock, 845 12th Avenue South; 941–263–9940; moderate) is the place to go. Brothers Vin and Phil DePasquale run this large and open restaurant, which features fresh local seafood and some of the best chowders you'll find in the state.

LODGING: The Naples Beach Hotel & Golf Club.

DAY 3

Morning

BREAKFAST: The Naples Beach Hotel & Golf Club.

Outdoors enthusiasts will surely enjoy a morning excursion to the **Conservancy Naples Nature Center** (14th Avenue North; 941–262–0304; entrance fee). Operated by the Conservancy of Southwest Florida, this indoor/outdoor natural science museum features marine aquariums, a wildlife rehabilitation center, a nature store, self-guided trail walks, boat tours, and canoe and kayak rentals.

A bit farther afield, even more enthusiastic outdoors fans should head about 20 miles north of Naples to the **National Audubon Society's Corkscrew Swamp Sanctuary** (Immokalee Road; 941–348–9151; entrance fee). This 11,000-acre wilderness sanctuary is home to an array of wading birds, alligators, deer, bear, and giant bald cypress trees that are hundreds of years old.

LUNCH: Back in Naples, head to the mammoth Sunday brunch buffet at **Michelob's Rib Capital of Florida** (371 Airport-Pulling Road; 941–643–7427; moderate). Baby back ribs and much more are the specialties at this huge establishment. You'll probably be able to skip dinner.

Afternoon

For kids and kids at heart, there's nothing better than a cuddly teddy bear at the **Teddy Bear Museum** (2511 Pine Ridge Road; 941–598–2711; entrance fee). This unusual museum has more than 3,000 stuffed bears from throughout the world. The unique displays of bears are well worth the trip.

It's an easy trip back to the Miami area, taking I–75 back east.

THERE'S MORE

Watersports: Headboat fishing on the *Lady Brett* (1200 Fifth Avenue South, Tin City; 941–263–4949) is easy to pursue. Scuba divers interested in heading below the surface of the Gulf of Mexico should contact **SCUBAdventures** (971 Creech Road; 941–434–7477) or **Under Seas Dive Academy** (998 6th Avenue South; 941–262–0707) for details.

Boat tours: Tours of the Gordon River, Naples Bay, the Gulf of Mexico, and outlying islands are available through *Double Sunshine* (Tin City; 941–263–4949); *Naples Princess* (550 Port o' Call Way; 941–649–2275); **Nautilus Boat Tours** (Vanderbilt Beach; 941–597–4408); and *Sweet Liberty* (Boat Haven Marina; 941–793–3525).

SPECIAL EVENTS

January. Naples Doll Club Show and Sale, Florida Sports Park, Naples. Antique, reproduction, and artist dolls and accessories; (941) 566–9137.

February. Annual Shell Show, The Conservancy, Naples. Juried competition in scientific, artistic, and other divisions; (941) 775–7406.

Naples National Art Festival, Cambier Park. More than 200 artists from around the world display and sell their work; (941) 262–6517.

March. QMI Winter Classic, Florida Sports Park, Golden Gate. Part of a tri-annual nationally broadcast swamp buggy event; (941) 774–2701.

Naples Seafood Festival, Naples Airport; (941) 591–4212.

Mardi Gras Gala. Street music, open houses, and art exhibits, with grand masks or full costume the dress code of the event; (941) 434–3383.

April. Immokalee Harvest Festival, downtown Immokalee. Agricultural exhibits, lots of food vendors, a parade through town, live entertainment, and a rodeo; (941) 657–3237.

May. SummerJazz, Watkins Lawn, Naples Beach Hotel & Golf. Series of sunset concerts under the stars one Saturday every month from May to September; (941) 262–2222.

Mile o' Mud Swamp Buggy Races, Florida Sports Park, Golden Gate. Includes live musical entertainment and fun for the whole family; (941) 774–2701.

July. International Music Festival, Miccosukee Indian village. Bands, folk artisans, mariachi music, and much more, 70 miles southeast of Naples on US 41; (305) 223–8380, ext. 364.

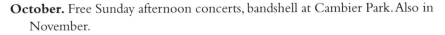
October. Free Sunday afternoon concerts, bandshell at Cambier Park. Also in November.

Naples Downtown Oktoberfest and Sidewalk Sale, Old Naples. European street carnival with oompah bands, fine arts and crafts, live entertainment, and more; (941) 435–3742.

Annual Bear Fair, Teddy Bear Museum. Arts and crafts by teddy bear and doll artisans, pony rides, games for children, live entertainment, and a flea market; (941) 598–2711.

November. Free outdoor concerts, Old Naples Pub, 255 13th Avenue South. Jazz up your Sunday afternoons, through April; (941) 649–8200.

Festival of Trees, Philharmonic Center for the Arts. More than 100 Christmas trees and decorated items; (941) 597–1111.

Annual Third Street and The Avenues' Festival of Lights, Neapolitan building, 1300 Third Street South. Breathtaking tree-lighting ceremony, music, and parade; (941) 649–6707.

December. Christmas in the Gardens. An evening of entertainment and refreshments at Caribbean Gardens; (941) 262–5409.

Naples Downtown New Year's Festival. Fine arts and crafts booths, International Food Courts, and music; (800) 605–7878.

OTHER RECOMMENDED RESTAURANTS AND LODGINGS

If the Naples Beach Hotel & Golf Club is full, the **Edgewater Beach Hotel** (1901 Gulf Shore Boulevard North; 941–262–6511 or 800–821–0196; expensive) and lagoon-like **Park Shore Resort** (600 Neapolitan Way; 941–263–2222 or 800–548–2077; moderate) also cater to families. If B&Bs are more your style, the historic **Inn by the Sea** (287 11th Avenue South; 941–649–4124; moderate) offers five rooms and an Old Florida ambience just 2 blocks from the beach in Old Naples. For a truly serious splurge, the **Ritz-Carlton Naples** (280 Vanderbilt Beach Road; 941–598–3300; expensive), the **Hotel Escalante** (290 Fifth Avenue South; 941–659–3466 or 877–GULFINN; expensive), and **The Registry Resort** (475 Seagate Drive; 941–597–3232 or 800–247–9810; expensive) all evoke an Old Naples beach resort elegance (and price).

For a really special meal, call **Sign of the Vine** (980 Solana Road; 941–

261–6745; expensive) to see if you can make a reservation. Nancy Christiansen plays host in a big old house with candlelit tables and creative home cooking from around the world. Another excellent option in Old Naples is **St. George and the Dragon** (936 5th Avenue South; 941–262–6546; moderate).

FOR MORE INFORMATION

Visit Naples, Inc. at 1400 Gulfshore Boulevard, Naples, FL 34102. (941) 430–0600.

The Lee Island Coast

SEASHELLS AND THE SEASHORE

2 NIGHTS

Sanibel Island nature • Outdoor activities

Tourism officials call the Lee Island Coast area "Florida's Tropical Island Getaway," and it's easy to see why. Many parts of this coastal region remind visitors of the days of a different Florida, when most of the state featured unspoiled white sand beaches, exotic wildlife, and lush subtropical foliage. It's still like that in much of this fascinating area.

The Lee Island Coast is made up of distinct areas, each with its own unique character. Best known is Sanibel Island (which is a perfect base), connected to the mainland by an alluring 3-mile-long causeway. To Sanibel's north, Captiva Island is reached by another, much shorter, bridge.

Sanibel is known worldwide for its shelling and the associated position referred to as the "Sanibel Stoop." Some fanatics attach flashlights to their heads in an effort to be first in the daily search for more than 200 varieties of shells. Sanibel Island also features the J. N. "Ding" Darling National Wildlife Refuge, which is home to many exotic species of birds and plants. The main attraction on Captiva is that there are very few attractions, except for time to explore the great outdoors. Off the coast of these main islands, hundreds of other small islands attract boaters and nature lovers, making it easy to see how the area got its name. Exploration possibilities include North Captiva, Cayo Costa Island Preserve, Cabbage Key, Pine Island, and Boca Grande.

Back on the mainland, another island draws visitors to the island-laced coast. Estero Island is the home of Fort Myers Beach. This area is popular for families, boating, and fishing as well as picnics or longer visits to Lovers Key.

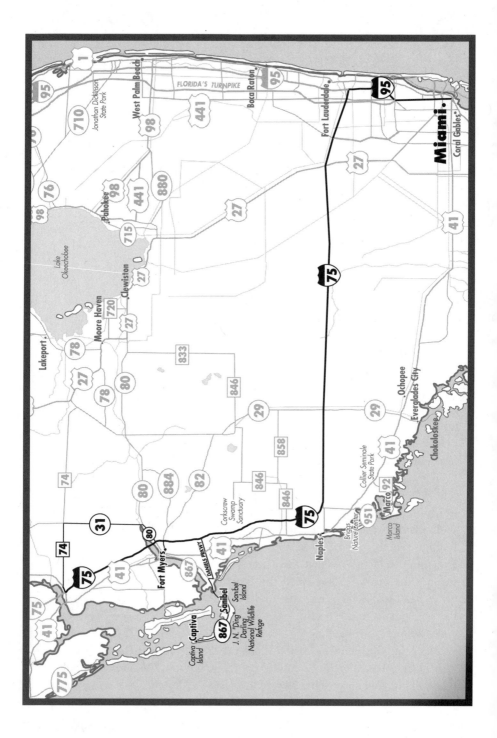

Continuing south, Bonita Beach occupies the southern boundary of the Lee Island Coast with some of the finest beaches in the area.

Anyone suffering from island fever can find instant relief by paying a call to town. Fort Myers, called "City of Palms," is a growing hub of history and activity. Inventor Thomas Edison and his friend, automobile magnate Henry Ford, decided to make their winter homes in Fort Myers. Today, visitors can tour their estates and Edison's laboratory and museum. Other in-town attractions include the Fort Myers Historical Museum, cruises out of the downtown yacht basin, and even the southernmost bonded winery in the continental United States.

Of course, you may not want to leave Sanibel Island, so you may have to leave further Lee Island Coast exploration to another visit.

DAY 1

Afternoon

Take I–75 north out of Miami and follow it all the way to exit 21 (Daniels Parkway) just south of Fort Myers proper. Head west on Daniels Parkway, crossing US 41, where the name of the road changes to Cypress Lake Drive. Turn left at McGregor Boulevard, which leads all the way to Sanibel Island. Depending on your timing, you can have dinner at the local spot recommended on the way or wait until you get on the island. You may also want to stop by one of several convenience or grocery stores along the way to pick up some breakfast or lunch items for your room's refrigerator.

DINNER: If you arrive in the area around dinnertime, be sure to stop for a meal right on the way to Sanibel Island at **Hickory Bar-B-Que** (15400 McGregor Boulevard; 941–481–2626; inexpensive to moderate). This popular locals' spot features barbecue sandwiches and platters that pack the large restaurant six days and nights a week (but only because they're closed on Sundays). If you decide to head right to Sanibel Island, the Sanibel Inn's **Portofino** (737 East Gulf Drive; 941–472–3181 or 800–237–1491; expensive) features acclaimed northern Italian cuisine in a stunning setting.

LODGING: The centrally located and low-key **Sanibel Inn** (937 East Gulf Drive; 941–472–3181 or 800–572–5998; expensive) is a perfect Lee Island Coast base. This beachfront property is located straight through the second stop sign on Sanibel Island (there are no traffic lights here). Several oceanfront buildings are located throughout the lushly landscaped grounds, offering ninety-six recently refurbished deluxe hotel rooms and one- or two-bedroom units. All of the bright accommodations feature a microwave, small refrigerator, coffee-maker, VCR, and balconies. Amenities at this quiet resort include its beachfront location, pool, bike and watersports rentals, and tennis. The Sanibel Inn is part of the varied South Seas Resorts, which owns and operates several highly recommended properties on Sanibel and Captiva Islands.

Evening

Sanibel and Captiva Islands are pretty quiet at night. Sunsets and supper choices are the big evening events.

DAY 2

Morning

BREAKFAST: Sanibel Inn.

The low sun of the early morning makes it more comfortable and better for pictures, so plan to head early to the **J. N. "Ding" Darling National Wildlife Refuge** (Sanibel-Captiva Road; 941–472–1100; entrance fee). The Visitor Center doesn't open until 9:00 A.M., but the 5-mile Wildlife Drive (which opens about an hour after sunrise) provides a perfect introduction to this fascinating refuge. Occupying more than 65 percent of Sanibel Island, "Ding" Darling features an array of birds, raccoons, alligators, and much more—all of which you're sure to see during your introductory drive.

After the early morning drive, you'll want to see more of the wild offerings at the refuge. Stop by the Visitor Center for information and programs. One of the best ways to learn and see more is with a two-hour tram tour, which is led by a naturalist with **Tarpon Bay Recreation** (Tarpon Bay Road; 941–472–8900; entrance and tour fees). In addition, the refuge's hiking trail, which starts before the entrance, is also well worth it.

LUNCH: You can't visit Sanibel Island without a casual seafood lunch, and one of two **Lazy Flamingo** locations will do the trick (6520–C Pine; 941–472–5353 and 1036 Periwinkle Way; 941–472–6939).

Afternoon

Along with "Ding" Darling, the **Bailey-Matthews Shell Museum** (Sanibel-Captiva Road; 941–395–2233; entrance fee) is one of the other major "nat-

J. N. "Ding" Darling National Wildlife Refuge on Sanibel Island is a birdwatching paradise.

ural" sightseeing highlights on Sanibel Island. Opened in 1995, this fascinating museum is devoted solely to shells from around the world. The colorful displays include thousands of shells, with the world's largest prominently featured. Fun for the entire family, this museum can get anyone motivated to walk the shell-strewn beaches of the Lee Island Coast.

Nearby, you should also stop at the **Sanibel/Captiva Conservation Foundation** (Sanibel-Captiva Road; 941–472–2329; entrance fee). This 1,500-acre property features hiking trails, guided tours, environmental programs, and a native plant center and nursery that displays and sells local varietals.

Depending on the time of year, you'll definitely want to arrange a sunset cruise before or after dinner.

DINNER: You cannot come to the Lee Island Coast without having dinner at **The Bubble Room** (15001 Captiva Road; 941–472–5558; moderate to expensive). This unusual restaurant is gaudy on the outside and inside, with brightly painted colors and memorabilia from the 1930s through today.

Distracted by the running toy trains and the waiters and waitresses in scouting uniforms, you may not notice that the menu is one of the most creative in the area. The huge platter is a favorite, with steak, quail, sausage, and pork in large portions.

LODGING: Sanibel Inn.

Evening

The cultural scene abounds on Sanibel Island, with frequent plays and other performances (usually December to April) at the **Old Schoolhouse Theatre** (1905 Periwinkle Way; 941–472–6862) and **J. Howard Wood Theatre** (2200 Periwinkle Way; 941–472–0006).

DAY 3

Morning

BREAKFAST: Sanibel Inn or, if you like omelettes, you'll want to try the **Lighthouse Cafe** (362 Periwinkle Way; 941–472–0303; inexpensive). Lynda and Ken's omelettes, homemade breads, and other breakfast items are popular with the local crowd (lunch isn't bad either).

Once you check out of your hotel, it's time to explore Fort Myers proper. Head back out to I–75 north to visit several north Fort Myers attractions first, since the Edison and Ford estates don't open until the afternoon on Sundays (if it's not a Sunday, you can reverse the morning and afternoon schedules easily).

Take I–75 north to exit 25 (SR 80), turning east. Just across from the large power plant, **Manatee Park** (SR 80; 941–432–2004; parking fee) will be on your right in 1½ miles. Manatees are naturally attracted to this area from November to March. The facility features viewing decks, a canoe launch, an "eco-torium" with exhibits and gifts, and guided programs during manatee season. There's also a butterfly garden.

Continue on SR 80 to SR 31, turning left (north). Follow this road for about 8 miles, turning right at the sign for **Babcock Wilderness Adventures** (8000 SR 31; 941–338–6367 or 800–500–5583; tour fee). This unexpected Florida attraction is definitely worth the drive. The interesting sights during the swamp buggy tours of this huge working cattle ranch include bison, alligators, cattle, horses, swampland, mangroves, and an enclosure with several panthers. It's a fascinating way to see more Lee County wildlife. Reservations are required.

Head back to I–75, where you'll go south to the Martin Luther King Boulevard exit and then head east into the city of Fort Myers. Your lunch spot on Edison Avenue is just a few blocks south on Cranford Avenue.

LUNCH: Located next to the bustling Fort Myers Farmers Market, the **Farmers Market Restaurant** (2736 Edison Avenue; 941–334–1687; inexpensive to moderate) is a popular after-church destination for many locals. This busy restaurant is open for three meals a day, seven days a week, and features serious Southern cooking. From ham hocks to the freshest country-style vegetables imaginable, this is a meal to remember.

Afternoon

Right in the middle of Fort Myers, the **Edison–Ford Winter Estates** (2350 McGregor Boulevard; 941–334–3614; entrance fee) is a highlight of the area. Thomas Edison built a winter home here in 1886 and came every year until he died in 1931. It appears just as it did during his lifetime, including light bulbs he invented and used in his laboratory (which visitors can also tour). Next door, friends Henry and Clara Ford built their winter house in 1916, and tour groups see it as the Fords used it in the 1920s. The lush grounds and a museum (including a Model T Ford given to Edison by Ford) are also featured on the tour.

If you have time, use the rest of the day to explore other Fort Myers attractions. Take I–75 back directly to the Miami area.

THERE'S MORE

Other sightseeing attractions: The Fort Myers area also features the **Fort Myers Historical Museum** (2300 Peck Street; 941–332–5955; entrance fee); the **Imaginarium** (2000 Cranford Avenue; 941–337–3332; entrance fee); living history tours of the early twentieth-century **Burroughs Home** (2505 1st Street; 941–332–6125; entrance fee); and the wetlands of **Six Mile Cypress Slough Preserve** (Six Mile Cypress Parkway; 941–338–3300; entrance fee).

Down in Estero, the **Koreshan State Historic Site** (US 41; 941–992–0311; entrance fee) was the home of the Koreshan Unity Movement during the nineteenth century, a religious group that believed people lived inside the earth (visitors can tour houses and the grounds).

SPECIAL EVENTS

January. The Welcome Back Manatees Celebration, Fort Myers. Learning activities and entertainment to celebrate the winter return of the manatees; (941) 432–2004.

February. The Edison Festival of Light celebrates the birthday of Thomas Edison with three weeks of events, including a spectacular parade of lights through downtown Fort Myers, a gala ball, a fashion show, and more; (941) 334–2999.

Sanibel Island Arts & Crafts Fair; (941) 472–6368.

Cape Coral Winter Festival. Parades, block parties, food, and more; (941) 549–2460.

March. Sanibel Shell Fair; (941) 472–2155.

Buckingham Historical Days, Fort Myers. Parade and reenactment of the Battle of Fort Myers; (941) 694–7116.

May. Sanibel Island's Taste of the Islands features a street festival and great food; (941) 472–3614.

The Bonita Springs Watermelon Festival. Watermelon eating and seed-spitting contests, crowning of Miss Bonita Springs Watermelon Queen; (941) 334–7007.

November. The Annual Fort Myers Beach Sandsculpting Contest. Creative sculptures, music, and refreshments; (941) 454–7500 or (800) 782–9283.

Fort Myers Boat Show, Harborside Convention Complex and City Yacht Basin; (954) 570–7785.

December. The Christmas Boat-A-Long, Bimini Basin in Cape Coral; (941) 574–0801.

OTHER RECOMMENDED RESTAURANTS AND LODGINGS

Sanibel Island

If the Sanibel Inn is full or you want something with another style or budget, there are many other excellent and varied options on Sanibel Island. By far, your best bet is to call **South Seas Resorts** (5400 Captiva Road, Captiva

Island; 800–572–5998 inexpensive to expensive). Along with the Sanibel Inn, they offer four other different styles of accommodations options on Sanibel Island. **Sundial Beach Resort** is a full-service family-oriented resort right on the beach. The more budget-minded **Best Western Sanibel Island Beach Resort** features forty-five units and offers a choice of hotel, studio, and one- and two-bedroom units, many of which include a kitchen, living room, and screened-in balcony overlooking the Gulf of Mexico. **Sanibel's Seaside Inn** is an intimate inn on the Gulf, with thirty-two poolside studios, one-bedroom units, and individual beach cottages. **Song of the Sea** is a romantic and European-style seaside inn, with eight one-bedroom suites and twenty-two studios.

In addition, **Casa Ybel Resort** (2255 West Gulf Drive; 941–472–3145 or 800–276–4753; expensive) is a popular choice with many veteran Sanibel visitors. Just before you cross the bridge to Sanibel Island, **Sanibel Harbour Resort & Spa** (17260 Harbour Pointe Road; 941–466–4000 or 800–767–7777; expensive) is a very popular mainland choice for active vacationers.

For other meals on Sanibel, the possibilities include fresh seafood at **McT's Shrimp House & Tavern** (1523 Periwinkle Way; 941–472–3161; moderate); creative American cuisine at **The Mad Hatter** (6467 Sanibel Captiva Road; 941–472–0033; expensive); and family-oriented fare at **Hungry Heron** (2330 Palm Ridge Road; 941–395–2300; moderate).

Captiva Island

If you want to stay on Captiva, choose **South Seas Plantation** (5400 Plantation Road; 941–481–6424 or 800–554–5454; expensive), a 330-acre full-service resort that has more than 2½ miles of beach and 600 accommodations, including deluxe hotel rooms; one-, two-, and three-bedroom units; beach cottages; and private homes. Amenities include twenty-one tennis courts, eighteen swimming pools, a nine-hole golf course, watersports, shopping, dining, and many other offerings at this large and popular resort.

Fort Myers Beach area

The **Best Western Pink Shell Beach Resort** (275 Estero Boulevard; 941–463–6161 or 800–572–5998; moderate) is an ideal choice in this traditional beach area, as are the efficiencies at **The Outrigger Beach Resort** (6200 Estero Boulevard; 941–463–3131 or 800–749–3131; moderate).

FOR MORE INFORMATION

Lee Island Coast Visitor and Convention Bureau, 2180 West First Street, Suite 100, Fort Myers, FL 33901. (888) 231–6933.

Fort Lauderdale
AMERICA'S VENICE

2 NIGHTS

Waterways • Las Olas Boulevard • Shopping

Fort Lauderdale is like a much more modern Venice, thanks to the large number of waterways that interlace the city and make convenient exploration by water quite possible. Add to the mix the cosmopolitan dining and shopping of Las Olas Boulevard, a refurbished beachfront, and more shopping further afield, and you have a perfect South Florida getaway that's a little bit of Venice and a lot of the Sunshine State.

DAY 1

Afternoon

Head north on I–95 to State Route 84 east, which takes you right into Fort Lauderdale proper.

DINNER AND LODGING: Situated on an ever-present waterway and near the ocean, the **Hyatt Regency Pier 66** (2301 17th Street Causeway; 954–525–6666 or 800–233–1234; moderate to expensive) provides the perfect Fort Lauderdale base. This 388-room full-service resort is also located close to famed Las Olas Boulevard and includes a large marina, spa, two pools, and a tropical garden setting. Every room has a balcony. If you really want to find out why Fort Lauderdale is like a modern Venice, this and a few other properties covered below are ideal. Situated at the resort, **California Cafe** (Pier 66; 954–728–3500; moderate to expensive) is a creative and convenient

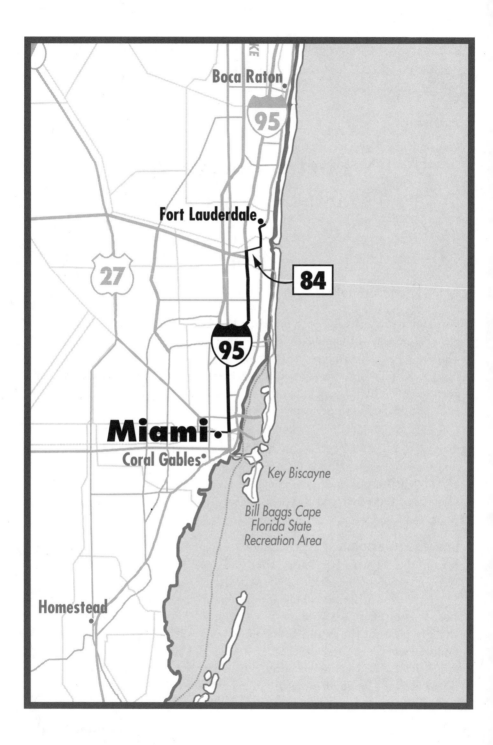

first-night choice right on the water. The extensive and ever-changing menu features a wide range of creative appetizers, salads, pastas, and many grilled and rotisserie items from the wood-fired stove.

Evening

Pier 66 has a large rotating rooftop lounge that provides a wonderful view of central Fort Lauderdale day and night.

DAY 2

Morning

BREAKFAST: During your walk along the beach, stop for breakfast at **Shula's Steakhouse** (in the Yankee Trader at 321 Beach Boulevard; 954–355–4000), which is popular with businesspeople and other locals for breakfast, lunch, and dinner overlooking the ocean.

Head over to Atlantic Boulevard (A1A) and the beach for a walk along the renovated **Fort Lauderdale Beach Promenade,** which runs along the beach for more than 3 miles between the 17th Street Causeway and Sunrise Boulevard. You can enjoy the European-like atmosphere along the promenade, walk along the wide beach, or check out shopping and more at **Beach Place.**

There are several excellent ways to get an overview of the area. Depending on your preference, you can take a boat tour, ride a water taxi and stop at several points, or take a trolley tour. The *Jungle Queen* (Bahia Mar Yacht Center; 954–462–5596; various tour fees) offers three-hour sightseeing tours on an old-style steamer that include the stunning waterfront houses, downtown, Old Fort Lauderdale, and the port. **Water Taxi of Fort Lauderdale** (651 Seabreeze Boulevard; 954–565–5507; per ride fees and daily passes) offers quick scheduled service to a wide variety of Fort Lauderdale hotels (including Pier 66), restaurants, and landmarks. Their daily pass provides a great way to get around the area.

Head up to Las Olas Boulevard for lunch and an afternoon of strolling and shopping.

LUNCH: Las Olas Boulevard has evolved into a South Florida dining mecca, with many cuisines and decor styles from which to choose. For a splurge (though less pricey at lunch), **Mark's Las Olas** (1032 East Las Olas Boulevard; 954–463–1000; moderate to expensive) is the preeminent Las Olas (and Fort Lauderdale) choice. Chef/owner Mark Militello has created a varied menu

Water Taxi of Fort Lauderdale provides the best way to see "America's Venice."

around his huge wood-fired grill. Try to sit overlooking the exhibition kitchen or by the floor-to-ceiling windows over Las Olas Boulevard. If the lunch menu seems a bit high, head to **Cheeburger! Cheeburger!** (708 East Las Olas Boulevard; 954–524–8824; inexpensive) for great cheeseburgers and diner atmosphere or **The Floridian Restaurant** (1410 East Las Olas Boulevard; 954–463–4041; inexpensive to moderate) for more diner food and flavor.

Afternoon

Spend the early afternoon in style by strolling, window-shopping, and finding a perfect Fort Lauderdale purchase along Las Olas Boulevard. There are many fine clothing stores as well as antiques shops and eclectic galleries and gift shops.

Try to head to **Butterfly World** (3600 West Sample Road, Coconut Creek; 954–977–4400; entrance fee) by midafternoon. This unusual all-ages attraction features more than 150 species of butterflies in an open environment as well as interesting educational displays, exhibits, and a new hummingbird display. Butterfly World is one of the largest breeders of these color-ful winged creatures. The large gift shop alone is worth the trip west.

DINNER: For a true taste of an old Sunshine State seafood restaurant, you shouldn't miss having at least one meal at **Old Florida Seafood House** (1414 NE 26th Street, Wilton Manors; 954–566–1044; moderate). The seafood is fresh, the service is friendly, and the atmosphere is simple. What more could you want from a seafood place?

LODGING: Hyatt Regency Pier 66.

Evening

O'Hara's Pub (722 East Las Olas Boulevard; 954–524–1764; moderate) is one of the region's best live jazz spots seven days a week, while the **Broward Center for the Performing Arts** (201 SW 5th Avenue; 954–462–0222; performance fees) offers a wide variety of plays, music, and other entertainment year-round. For something unusual, **Mai-Kai** (3599 North Federal Highway; 954–536–3272; moderate) supposedly offers the nation's longest-running Polynesian show.

DAY 3

Morning

BREAKFAST/BRUNCH: The Sunday brunch at the Hyatt Regency at Pier 66 **Mariner's Grill** is popular and outstanding, with a wide range of breakfast and lunch items.

The morning offers another opportunity to explore water-oriented Fort Lauderdale. **Bill's Sunrise Sports** (2051 East Sunrise Boulevard; 954–462–8962) can help you explore by water, with Wave Runners, power-boats, and party boats available for rent daily. It's the perfect way to see America's Venice by water, the way it's meant to be seen.

Afternoon

A Sunday (or any) afternoon is an ideal time for museum-hopping. For adults, the **Museum of Art** (1 Las Olas Boulevard; 954–763–6464; entrance fee) fea-tures a permanent collection of Copenhagen, Brussels, and Amsterdam (CoBrA) masters as well as world-renowned touring exhibitions. For families, the **Museum of Discovery & Science** (401 SW 2nd Street; entrance fee) is another one of those successful hands-on science museums that every city seems to have now. The IMAX theater is quite popular.

The afternoon is also a great time to pursue some additional shopping around Fort Lauderdale, which has become one of the state's biggest shopping destinations. Along with Las Olas Boulevard, the varied options include the world's largest flea market at **Fort Lauderdale Swap Shop** (3291 West Sunrise Boulevard; 954–791–SWAP), which also includes a movie theater, entertainment, and a remarkably large circus; the world's largest designer outlet mall, **Sawgrass Mills** (12801 West Sunrise Boulevard; 954–846–2300); and antiquing at more than 200 small shops on **Antique Row,** located along US 1 in Dania, just south of the airport (many shops are closed on Sunday).

Go over to I–95, which leads back south to the Miami area.

THERE'S MORE

Other sightseeing attractions: Bonnet House (900 North Birch Road; 954–563–5393; entrance fee) is a 1921 plantation house that was originally owned by artist Frederic Clay Bartlett and his wife, Evelyn, who also became a well-known painter. **Stranahan House** (335 SE 6th Avenue; 954–524–4736; entrance fee) is a 1901 structure that served as an Indian trading post, post office, general store, town hall, and a ferryman's house (Frank Stranahan, the "father of Fort Lauderdale"). It now houses an interesting historical collection. For an unusual attraction, head to **Dania Jai-Alai** (301 East Dania Beach Boulevard, Dania; 954–920–1511; entrance fee), where a fast-paced game with balls and wicker baskets provides a reason to gamble and gawk.

SPECIAL EVENTS

January. Las Olas Art Fair; (954) 472–3755.

April. Fort Lauderdale Seafood Festival, Smoker Park; (954) 764–7642.

May. Oceanfront scuba diving festival; (954) 776–1000.

Air & Sea Show: (954) 527–5600, ext. 88.

October. Fort Lauderdale International Boat Show, Convention Center; (954) 764–7642.

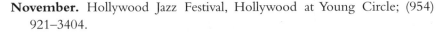
November. Hollywood Jazz Festival, Hollywood at Young Circle; (954) 921–3404.

October. Fort Lauderdale International Film Festival; (954) 960–9898.

December. Winterfest Boat Parade, Intracoastal Waterway. Holiday lighting on boats; (954) 767–0686.

OTHER RECOMMENDED RESTAURANTS AND LODGINGS

Other water-oriented Fort Lauderdale accommodations options include **Riverside Hotel** (620 East Las Olas Boulevard; 954–467–0671 or 800–325–3280; inexpensive to moderate), a 1936 inn off Las Olas and on the New River; **La Casa del Mar** (3003 Granada Street; 954–467–2037; inexpensive to moderate); and **A Little Inn by the Sea** (4546 El Mar Drive; 954–772–2450; inexpensive to moderate) up in quieter Lauderdale-by-the-Sea.

Dining-crazed Fort Lauderdale has many other creative choices, including **Mango's** (904 East Las Olas Boulevard; 954–523–5001; moderate) and **Las Olas Cafe** (922 East Las Olas Boulevard; 954–524–4300; moderate), right on Las Olas. Other interesting options include **Ernie's Bar-B-Q** (1843 South Federal Highway; 954–523–8636; inexpensive) and **Joe's 17th St. Diner** (1616 Eisenhower Boulevard; 954–527–5637; inexpensive).

FOR MORE INFORMATION

Greater Fort Lauderdale Convention & Visitors Bureau, 1850 Eller Drive, Suite 303, Fort Lauderdale, FL 33316. (954) 765–4466 or (800) 22–SUNNY.

Boca Raton

A CITY IN THE PINK (AND MINK)

2 NIGHTS

Boca Raton Resort & Club • Shopping • History • Museums

To visitors and residents, Boca Raton is anything but miserly when it comes to history, tradition, and modern elegance. But this special south Florida city is definitely "Miznerly" when it comes to its past and vibrant present.

Dreamers, risk-takers, moguls, and millionaires all contributed (and contribute) to Florida's Boca Raton, but none influenced the city more than Addison Mizner. With architecture often done in vibrant pink, the Mizner touch is everywhere, and it's certainly not miserly. This is a city that's at home in pink and real or designer faux mink.

DAY 1

Afternoon

Head north on I–95 and take the Hillsboro Boulevard exit east toward Boca Raton. Turn left (north) on US 1 and then right (east) on Camino Real, following the signs for Boca Raton Resort & Club.

DINNER AND LODGING: Boca Raton Resort & Club (501 East Camino Real; 561–447–3000 or 800–327–0101; moderate to expensive) is *the* resort and perfect Mizner-base-of-choice for your escape in Boca Raton. Set within a backdrop of casual Boca elegance, the resort's amenities include two eighteen-hole championship golf courses, thirty tennis courts, several pools, state-of-the-art fitness centers, a half-mile stretch of private beach, a wide range of dining, a full-service marina, a variety of watersports, and much more.

It retains its share of guests who remember a long-gone era but also boasts many newcomers, business travelers, couples, and families who come to enjoy the resort's unparalleled setting, luxurious accommodations and amenities, and the rich traditions of Mizner's famed resort and city. Day 2 provides a perfect schedule for further exploration of the resort.

For dinner, you have two excellent choices, depending on your mood and budget. Nick Nickolas, a well-known restaurateur who owns and operates award-winning restaurants in Chicago, Honolulu, and Miami, operates **Top of the Tower** (expensive) and **Nick's Fishmarket** (moderate).

Top of the Tower is situated at the top of the resort's sleek twenty-seven-story tower, with views of the Atlantic Ocean, Florida Intracoastal Waterway, and the historic resort grounds. The decor is reminiscent of a southern Italian villa, and the menu includes a creative selection of fresh pastas and entrees of seafood, chicken, veal, and lamb as well as handmade breads served tableside. As expected, Nick's Fishmarket features a wide variety of fresh seafood with simple or creative preparation.

Evening

For a unique evening at the resort, visit **Malone's Magic Bar.** Resident magician Bill Malone and his team of talented prestidigitators specialize in tableside magic and entertainment, making for a fun way to enjoy the bar's intimate atmosphere and beverage selection.

DAY 2

Morning

BREAKFAST: The Patio at the resort features an old-world elegant atmosphere with a huge breakfast buffet daily.

Spend a leisurely morning roaming around this historic resort. Boca Raton (Spanish for "mouth of the rat") was little more than a place on the map until Henry M. Flagler extended his railroad from West Palm Beach through Boca to Miami in 1895. In fact, it is only called Boca Raton because an 1823 mapmaker mistakenly moved a Miami inlet named Boca Ratones too far north on his drawing. The English version of the misplaced name stuck.

Except for occasional Spanish explorers, pirates, and Native Americans, no one stuck around in Boca Raton until the railroad brought the first settlers. A few hardy farmers who had been frozen out in north Florida pulled up stakes and moved to Boca Raton to raise citrus fruits and vegetables for the winter market. But Addison Mizner's arrival in south Florida in 1918 changed the region and, specifically, Boca Raton, forever. Self-taught architect, eccentric, and magnet for high society of the day, Mizner moved to Palm Beach from New York for health reasons at the recommendation of his friend Paris Singer, heir to the sewing-machine fortune.

As Mizner recuperated, he and Singer began planning a convalescent facility for wounded officers returning from the First World War. With Singer's money and Mizner's architectural skills, they built the swank Everglades Club in Palm Beach. This led to commissions from the area's elite for Mizner-designed mansions. Frank Lloyd Wright once said that many architects had imagination, but only Mizner had the courage to let it out of the cage.

Mizner also ventured to Boca Raton and decided his future lay there. By then, the frenzied Florida land boom was in full swing, with mangrove swamps and scrubland giving rise to whole towns. Real estate developers, land speculators, and quite a few swindlers flocked to Florida, hoping to become millionaires overnight by selling pieces of paradise to snowbound northerners.

To take advantage of this, Addison Mizner and his brother, Wilson (sometime playwright and full-time man-about-town), formed the Mizner Development Corporation. The company acquired 17,500 acres of Boca Raton property and proceeded to create what they called, "the greatest resort in the world," a happy combination of Venice and heaven, Florence and Toledo, with a little Greco-Roman glory and grandeur thrown in for good measure.

The Cloister Inn, which would eventually become the famed Boca Raton Resort & Club, opened its doors in 1926 at a cost of $1.25 million, the most expensive 100-room hotel ever built at the time. Mizner designed an elegant "pink palace" structure in an imaginative pseudo-Spanish style with courtyards and furnished it with his private collection of rare antiques from old churches and universities in Spain and Central America. The Cloister's luxury and ambience quickly attracted royalty, Wall Street wealth, movie stars, and the ranking hierarchy of the international social set, including General T. Coleman du Pont, Harold Vanderbilt, George Whitney, Florenz Ziegfeld, Al Jolson, and Elizabeth Arden. **The Cloister,** which still stands, is characterized by hidden gardens, barrel tile roofs, archways, ornate columns, finials, intricate mosaics, fountains, and beamed ceilings of pecky cypress.

The Cloister's original guests seemed attracted, rather than put off, by Addison Mizner's unconventional behavior. His previous trips to China gave him a fondness for silk pajamas, which he decided were perfectly proper for street wear. He also delighted in parading around with his pets and was reportedly seen on more than one occasion promenading with two chows, a small monkey on one shoulder, a macaw on the other, and leading two more larger monkeys.

However, the glory of The Cloister Inn lasted just one season. The land boom was faltering, and there were signs that the upcoming Depression was already taking its toll. Mizner's investors became apprehensive and demanded the reorganization of his company. Eventually, management was taken over by the Chicago-based Central Equities Corporation, run by Rufus Dawes and his brother, U.S. Vice President Charles Dawes.

The Dawes brothers were unable to rescue the company from bankruptcy, which was hastened by a deadly hurricane in the fall of 1926 that killed nearly 400 people and destroyed many of the boom-time buildings. Even though Mizner's plans for Boca Raton were curtailed, his impact was seen in jobs, buildings, visitors, permanent residents, and national attention. He set the stage for future development, and his grand vision for the "Golden City of the Florida East Coast" eventually became a reality.

In 1928 Clarence Geist, a one-time railway brakeman from Indiana who made a fortune in utilities and was one of Mizner's original investors, successfully bid on the assets of the failed corporation. Geist hired golf-course architects Toomey and Flynn to reconstruct the hotel's two courses and also proceeded to greatly expand the Cloister Inn. Two years and $8 million later, he reopened it as the Boca Raton Club, one of the world's finest "gentlemen's clubs."

Although never fiscally profitable, the Club was kept flourishing by its exclusive membership. Private railroad cars and yachts brought in such notables as Herbert Hoover, several du Ponts, Jacob Raskob, and many other celebrities. Geist subsidized the perennial Club deficit through the Depression and even after his death, by which time the property had grown to four times its original size.

A Second World War service roster replaced the guest book when the government commandeered the resort in 1942. Army Air Corps officers referred to their quarters as "the most elegant barracks in history." After the war, hotel, theater, and real estate magnate J. Myer Schine bought the resort for a paltry $3 million. Completely refurbished and modernized, the club reopened in 1945 as the Boca Raton Hotel and Club and became extremely popular. A 1947 *Saturday Evening Post* article said, "If you were looking for the prodigal public spot on the globe, there is little argument that you need to look no further than the Boca Raton Hotel and Club."

The resort's (and, in many ways, Boca Raton's) future was secured when Arthur Vining Davis, one of the founders of Alcoa, bought the property from Schine in 1956 for $22.5 million. At the time, it was the largest real estate deal in Florida's history. Davis's plans for the legendary hotel were to "preserve the atmosphere of quiet luxury." He succeeded, and so did successive owners after him, always improving on Mizner's original grand plans.

Arvida Corporation owned the resort until 1983, when it was purchased by VMS Realty Partners and the Boca Raton Hotel and Club Limited Partnership. A decade later, Boca Raton Management Company replaced VMS as the general partner for the now-renamed Boca Raton Resort & Club. Since then, ongoing multimillion-dollar renovations have taken place at the world-class property that is the symbol for a world-class city. In 1997, a group controlled by South Florida billionaire Wayne Huizenga purchased it. Continued improvments and innovations are expected throughout the resort.

Mizner's legacy lives and breathes on the property through its architecture, elegant furnishings, many Mizner touches, and even a **"Mizner Room"** just off the lobby, which is filled with memorabilia from those early Boca days. But you'll find Addison Mizner's influence throughout the city, with historic, modern, and often pink reminders seemingly around every Boca Raton corner.

After exploring the resort, head into Boca Raton proper, starting at famed **Mizner Park** (North Federal Highway, between Palmetto Park and Glades; 561–362–0606). This major Mizner attraction can actually be quite expensive if you're from the shop-till-you-drop school.

Downtown Boca's village-in-a-city, Mizner Park features dozens of shops, restaurants, and much more, all in pretty pink Mizner-influenced buildings set in a bustling village atmosphere. Drop your car off at the valet parking stand and then check out the huge selection at Liberties Fine Books & Music, designer duds at Nicole Miller, and one-of-a-kind gifts at Celebrations of Boca. With lots of pink (and mink), it's Boca at its best. The dining scene at Mizner Park (see below) is one of the most creative in the state. In many ways, lush Mizner Park defines the blending of Addison Mizner's original vision with today's ritzy Boca Raton results.

LUNCH: Mizner Park boasts many excellent restaurants, including creative South Florida cuisine at **Max's Grille** (Plaza Real; 561–368–0080; moderate). **Gigi's** (Plaza Real; 561–368–4488; moderate), a tavern, oyster bar, and cafe, with brasserie-style beer and Karl Alterman-created fare, is another good Mizner Park possibility.

Afternoon

Located just across the street from Mizner Park, **Town Hall** (71 North Federal Highway; 561–395–6766; no entrance fee) is a great place to further your exploration of Mizner's modern-day Boca Raton. Mizner envisioned an entire community that would reflect his Mediterranean Revival-style architecture, and he included the 1927 Town Hall in his plans. The building is now the headquarters of the Boca Raton Historical Society.

A visit reveals several Mizner nuances, like arched entrances and fanlight windows, tile and Dade County pine floors, and pecky cypress ceilings. There's also the Historical Society's library, which includes a permanent exhibit of historic maps, photographs, documents, and Mizner memories. This Historical Society also presents special exhibits and traveling exhibits, but visitors will be especially interested in their scheduled **"Guided City Tour"** (Town Hall, 71 North Federal Highway; 561–395–6766; tour charges) on a trolley and historical tours of the Boca Raton Resort & Club as well as other even more extensive tours.

Just down the street, get directions and a map for a free driving tour of the **Old Floresta Historic District** (Boca Raton Historical Society, Town Hall, 71 North Federal Highway; 561–395–6766; no entrance fee). Just several blocks in size, this small residential area is filled with Mizner-designed and -influenced homes that provide wonderfully varied examples of his unique style. Keep in mind, however, that these are private residences. Nearby, the **Boca Raton Museum of Art** (801 West Palmetto Park Road; 561–241–7432; entrance fee) and the **Children's Museum** (498 Crawford Boulevard; 561–368–6875; entrance fee) are both popular stops.

Of course, there's more to modern Boca than swanky shopping and housing. Located in a large pink Mizner-style building on the edge of Mizner Park, the **International Museum of Cartoon Art** (Mizner Park, 201 Plaza Real, 561–391–2200; entrance fee) provides much more than a good laugh. After twenty years in metropolitan New York, the new location is now open in Boca Raton.

Founded by Mort Walker, creator of *Beetle Bailey,* the mammoth museum's permanent collection, which is the largest in the world, includes more than 160,000 original drawings, 10,000 books, and more than 1,000 hours of video and film dating back to the first efforts to create animation. Through permanent galleries, changing exhibitions, and special events, visitors can experience the nostalgic pleasure of being with old and new friends in comic strips,

The International Museum of Cartoon Art in Boca Raton provides much more than a good laugh.

comic books, and animation, including Mickey Mouse, Flash Gordon, Batman, Dumbo, Little Orphan Annie, Beetle Bailey, Superman, Popeye, Garfield, and many others.

DINNER: To keep with the Mizner theme, head to **Addison's** (2 East Camino Real; 561–391–9800; moderate to expensive). Located in Mizner's beautiful old administration office complex, the cuisine is continental and the atmosphere is distinctly Mizner.

LODGING: Boca Raton Resort & Club.

Evening

As could be expected, the cultural scene in Boca Raton is quite strong. Depending on the season, evening entertainment possibilities include: **Musicana**

Supper Club (2200 NW 2nd Avenue; 561–361–9704); **Little Palm Theatre** (154 NW 16th Street; 561–394–0206); **Caldwell Theatre Company** (7873 North Federal Highway; 561–241–7432); **Boca Pops** (100 NE 1st Avenue; 561–393–7677 or 800–876–POPS); and **Jan McArt's Royal Palm Dinner Theatre** (303 SE Mizner Boulevard; 561–392–3755).

DAY 3

Morning

BREAKFAST: Again, **The Patio** at the resort.

Pursuits right at the resort include golf, tennis, watersports and marina facilities, several fitness centers, five pools, biking, croquet, and several popular children's activities. Of course, the private Boca Beach Club is always a relaxing option.

LUNCH: If you head over to the Boca Beach Club, enjoy lunch at **The Cabana** (501 East Camino Real; 561–447–3000; moderate) with a tropical beach setting and a wide variety of a la carte and buffet selections, including fresh seafood, pasta, and salads. The Cabana Terrace serves light oceanside patio fare.

Afternoon

Before heading back to the Miami area, the **Gumbo Limbo Environmental Complex** (1801 North Ocean Boulevard; 561–338–1473; entrance fee) provides a unique diversion. This 20-acre facility includes a coastal dune, a sabal palm hammock, and mangrove wetlands. Interesting faunal species include a variety of mammals, birds, reptiles, and fish. Rare and endangered species like the manatee, the brown pelican, the osprey, and sea turtles are often seen. Facilities include indoor and outdoor classrooms, interpretive displays, aquariums, visual presentations, a 40-foot-high observation tower, and an elevated boardwalk through the hammock and mangrove communities.

If you didn't get your fill of shopping at Mizner Park, **Town Center at Boca Raton** (Glades Road, between I–95 and the Florida Turnpike; 561–368–6000) provides more upscale shopping and dining. It's a convenient stop before heading back south.

Take I–95 or the Florida Turnpike back south to the Miami area.

THERE'S MORE

Other sightseeing attractions: The Sports Immortals Museum (6830 North Federal Highway; 561–997–2575; entrance fee) has exhibits concerning many famous sports figures. **Boomer's Family Recreation Center** (3100 Airport Road; 561–347–1888; entrance fee) features go-karts, bumper boats, miniature golf, arcade games, pool tables, a snack bar, and much more. **Loxahatchee Everglades Tours** (15490 Loxahatchee Road; 407–482–6107 or 800–683–5873; tour fees) offers convenient and interesting airboat tours of the famed Everglades. Farther afield, the rest of Palm Beach County, as well as Fort Lauderdale, are all within easy day-trip distance. Up in nearby Delray Beach, the **Morikami Museum and Japanese Gardens** (4000 Morikami Park Road, Delray Beach; 561–495–0233; admission fee) includes a huge Japanese garden, a bonsai collection, and a museum of Japanese culture.

Polo: For something really unique and definitely "Boca," the **Royal Palm Polo Sports Club** (6300 Old Clint Moore Road; 954–994–1876; entrance fee for most games) has polo games on weekends and weekdays from January to April each year.

SPECIAL EVENTS

January. Fotofusion, Palm Beach Photographic Center in Delrary Beach. Annual photography convention, exhibition, and learning experience; (954) 276–9797.

February. Historic Home Tour, Old Floresta area; (954) 395–6766.

The Fiesta of Arts, on the City Hall grounds. Evening entertainment and dining; (954) 393–7806.

Annual Antiques Show and Sale, hosted by the Delray Beach Historical Society. Includes lecture series and luncheon cafe; (954) 243–0223.

Boca Raton Art Festival. One of the top arts events in the nation; (954) 392–2500.

March. Meet Me Downtown art-and-craft show, Boca Raton. Also features children's rides, festivities, and food; (954) 395–4433.

Spring Fling, Boca Raton's Mizner Park Amphitheater. Games, arts and crafts, food, rides, and contests; (954) 393–7806.

April. The Delray Affair. One of Florida's largest and oldest art festivals; (954) 278–0424.

Art/Music in the Park Series, Mizner Park Amphitheater; (954) 393–7806.

May. Sea Turtle Watches, Boca Raton beaches; (954) 338–1473.

August. Boca Festival Days. Wine tastings and other festivities throughout the month; (954) 395–4433.

Bon Festival, Delray Beach. Annual Japanese festival, with folk dancers, taiko drummers, and a street fair at Morikami Park.

December. The Annual Holiday Street Parade, Boca Raton. Federal Highway from Southeast Eighth Street to Mizner Park; (954) 393–7806.

OTHER RECOMMENDED RESTAURANTS AND LODGINGS

On the dining front, another splurge is possible at **La Vielle Maison** (770 East Palmetto Park Road; 561–391–6701; expensive), with fine French cooking and decor (try the escargot to start and one of the lamb entrees). On the other end of the spectrum, if you're looking for some good down-home barbecue, head to **Tom's Place** (7251 North Federal Highway; 561–997–0920; moderate), where you'll find tasty country cooking, plastic tablecloths, and the hospitality of Tom and Helen Wright. Out at Town Center,

If the Boca Raton Resort & Club is full or a bit too pricey, other excellent accommodations include Town Center's **Boca Raton Marriott** (5150 Town Center Circle; 561–392–4600 or 800–228–9290; moderate); family-run and oceanfront **Shore Edge Motel** (425 North Ocean Boulevard; 561–395–4491; inexpensive to moderate); and suites at **Radisson Suites Hotel** (7920 Glades Road; 561–483–3600 or 800–333–3333; moderate).

FOR MORE INFORMATION

Palm Beach County Convention & Visitors Bureau, 1555 Palm Beach Lakes Boulevard, Suite 204, West Palm Beach, FL 33401. (561) 471–3995 or (800) 554–PALM.

Lake Okeechobee

A RIDE AROUND A BIG LAKE

2 NIGHTS

Lake activities • Clewiston Inn

Okeechobee is Seminole for "big waters," and this name is truly fitting. At more than 700 square miles in size, Lake Okeechobee is the largest lake in the state and the second largest freshwater lake in the United States. A fun 150-mile drive will take you around this famed Florida lake, including lots of great views, watersports possibilities, food, and a unique lodging option. You should plan to spend two nights in Clewiston, using it as a base for a drive around the lake on the middle day, pursuing activities along the way or planning them for your next day.

DAY 1

Afternoon

Set out in the late afternoon for the start of your drive, planning to arrive in Clewiston in time for dinner. You can take US 27 all the way out of Miami or take I–95 north to I–595 west and join US 27 west of Fort Lauderdale. Either way, this interesting drive starts as soon as you get north of I–595.

It's about 40 miles up to Lake Okeechobee. Though you're less than a half hour from the urbanism of South Florida, you're in a world of agriculture here. Sugarcane and other crops replace skyscrapers and malls for as far as the eye can see. You'll likely see agricultural workers and machinery in the field, but little else. U.S. Sugar, the nation's largest sugar company, is the area's biggest

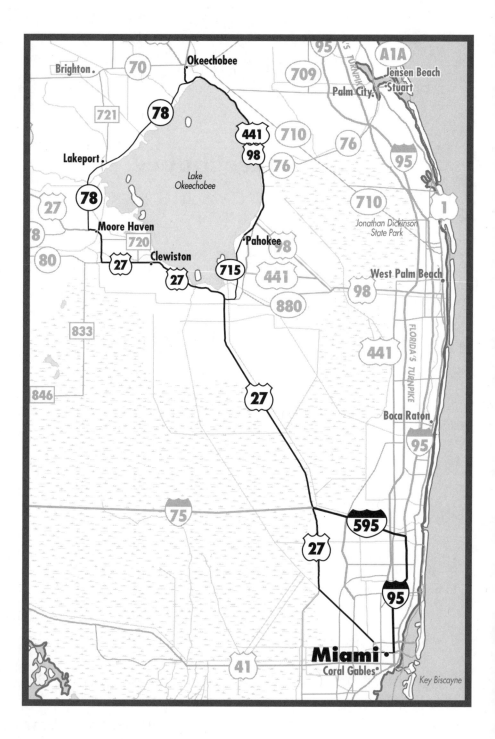

employer. There aren't any towns until you reach Okeelanta and then South Bay, where you'll turn left and continue north along US 27.

As you begin to drive around the lake, it will be on your right, and you'll see that it is surrounded by the 40-foot-high Herbert Hoover Dike, which was built to help control flooding. The hurricanes of 1926, 1928, and 1947, as well as other flood-provoking storms, caused the U.S. Army Corps of Engineers to build this dike and a series of canals and other dikes to control the flooding. However, this manmade control has also had a negative effect on the ecosystem found around the lake, the Everglades (which are fed by the lake), and the rest of South Florida. A new series of programs is attempting to reverse the damage.

US 27 passes through tiny Lake Harbor, which was the location of land speculation in the 1920s, when visitors from the north actually bought Lake Okeechobee swampland. Though the acreage was supposed to be drained, the real estate boom (and their investments) ended with the hurricanes.

US 27 continues on into Clewiston, and the city limits sign proudly tells drivers that they've reached the "Sweetest Little Town in America" (thanks to the sugar industry and the friendly people). The road runs right through town, and you can't miss the Clewiston Inn on your right. Check into this interesting hotel and then head out to dinner.

DINNER: During your stay in Clewiston, you have to have at least one meal at **Sonny's BBQ** (1388 East Sugarland Highway, US 27; 863–983–4171; inexpensive to moderate). This Southern ranch–style restaurant is famed in the region for barbecue chicken, pork, and other meats. This is a great place to immerse yourself in the lake- and agriculture-oriented lifestyle in and around Clewiston.

LODGING: The **Clewiston Inn** (108 Royal Palm Avenue; 863–983–8151; inexpensive) is a Lake Okeechobee landmark. It was built back in 1938 by U.S. Sugar as a plantation-style guesthouse for high-level employees and other visitors. The lobby (note the animal mural from 1945), lounge, restaurant, and rooms are a throwback to the 1940s. The friendly staff, clean surroundings, and quiet atmosphere make this a unique place to stay in Florida.

Evening

Because of Lake Okeechobee's rural setting, there isn't much to do in the evening.

The Clewiston Inn was built in 1938 and is a great Lake Okeechobee base.

DAY 2

Morning

BREAKFAST: The Clewiston Inn offers a fresh Southern-style breakfast (as well as lunch and dinner) in its quaint dining room.

Head out of the Clewiston Inn and turn right onto US 27. The road leads away from Lake Okeechobee for a bit, making its way up to Moore Haven. This small town features a huge old courthouse that survived the massive 1926 hurricane that killed more than 200 people in Moore Haven.

Just west of Moore Haven, turn right onto County Road 78, which heads northeast and takes you back along the lake. Don't blink, or you'll miss the tiny town of Lakeport, which was once a bustling town full of Polish and Belgian immigrants before the 1926 hurricane.

County Road 78 runs right along the edge of Lake Okeechobee, where

there are many Dike Access roads that offer good parking and views of the massive lake. There are a total of thirty-nine of these roads and parks around the lake. This area is also the home of the Brighton Seminole Indian Reservation.

For a short detour, take State Road 60 3 miles north up to the town of Okeechobee. This quiet town was developed during the Flagler railroad building boom. South Park Street features a pretty 1917 courthouse, a museum located in an old Cracker-style schoolhouse, and a nice Main Street boulevard with shops and dining.

LUNCH: **Gladys'** (511 West South Park Street; 863–763–9985; inexpensive) serves great local cooking, including fresh catfish right from Lake Okeechobee.

Afternoon

Head back down to the lake and join US 98/441 to continue the drive. This road hugs the lake to your right, with many more dike access possibilities. Besides lake views and tiny fishing camps and communities, there's not much else to see for 40 miles until you get to Pahokee.

Palm-lined Pahokee was settled after World War I and features a number of nice stately homes and other buildings. Along with Clewiston and Okee-chobee, Pahokee is a popular fishing and watersports base. The dike access area includes a marina, picnic tables, and lakefront camping.

Rejoin US 27 in Belle Glade and take a one-lane wooden bridge into town. This fishing community is another good base for lake activities. Take US 27 back to Clewiston to complete your round trip.

DINNER: The best restaurant in the area is actually right in **The Clewiston Inn** (108 Royal Palm Avenue; 941–983–8151; moderate). Dinner features include local catfish and hush puppies, seafood, fried chicken, and prime rib.

LODGING: The Clewiston Inn.

DAY 3

Morning

BREAKFAST: For a serious Southern-style breakfast with the locals, head to **Robbie's** (711 East Sugarland Highway; 863–783–7001; inexpensive). You'll find grits, biscuits, gravy, and lots of hungry fishermen and truckers.

Now that you've seen what Lake Okeechobee has to offer, use this day to enjoy one or more water-oriented pursuits, including fishing or boating (see below).

LUNCH: Most fishing and boating excursions include lunch or can provide provisions for a picnic lunch.

Afternoon

Continue to explore Lake Okeechobee on land or on the water, then take US 27 back to the Miami area.

THERE'S MORE

Fishing and boating: Clewiston's **Roland Martin** complex (920 East Del Monte; 863–983–3151 or 800–473–6766) is the mecca for Lake Okeechobee boaters and fishermen. You can rent a boat, hire a captain or guide, buy supplies, or arrange any type of specific boating or fishing outing. Roland is a world-renowned bass fisherman. Other options include **Captain JP's Boat Charters** (P.O. Box 642, Pahokee Marina; 561–924–2100 or 800–845–7411) in Pahokee and **Angler's Marina** (910 Okeechobee Boulevard; 863–983–BASS or 800–741–3141) in Clewiston.

Skydiving: Because of the lack of air traffic and development, the Lake Okeechobee region is an ideal skydiving venue. Clewiston's **Air Adventures** (Airglades Airport; 863–983–6151 or 800–533–6151) is a famed full-service operation that offers introductory tandem dives (with an instructor attached) and lots of courses and other programs.

SPECIAL EVENTS

January. Big Cypress-Sawgrass Festival & Rodeo; (863) 983–8923.

March. Hendry County Fair, Clewiston; (863) 983–9282.

April. Sugar Festival, Clewiston; (863) 983–7979.

May. Brown Sugar Festival, Clewiston; (863) 983–7507.

OTHER RECOMMENDED LODGINGS AND RESTAURANTS

Along with having great boating and fishing opportunities, Clewiston's huge **Roland Martin** complex (920 East Del Monte; 863–983–3151 or 800–473–6766; inexpensive) includes varied hotel rooms, apartments, and camping, all evoking a simple and clean fishing camp style. Camping is popular all the way around Lake Okeechobee, with the options including **KOA Clewiston** (Highway 27, Clewiston; 863–983–7078 or 877–983–7078; inexpensive) and **Okeechobee Landings** (420 Holiday Boulevard, Clewiston; 863–983–4144; inexpensive).

One other local dining choice is **Pinky's On the Green** (US 27 East; 863–983–8464; inexpensive).

FOR MORE INFORMATION

Clewiston Chamber of Commerce, 544 West Sugarland Highway, Clewiston, FL 33440. (863) 983–7979.

Pahokee Chamber of Commerce, 115 East Main Street, Pahokee, FL 33476. (561) 924–5579.

The Palm Beaches

PALMS, BEACHES, AND THE BREAKERS

2 NIGHTS

The Breakers • Palm Beaches culture • Outdoor activities

When many people think of high-class Florida, they think of the Palm Beaches. But the Palm Beaches lifestyle isn't just for the rich and famous. Anyone can arrange a Palm Beaches escape on almost any budget.

The Palm Beaches in general, and Palm Beach specifically, are historically known as the winter base for the likes of the Kennedys, Donald Trump, and Rockefeller heirs, but visitors can enjoy the same lifestyle thanks to several luxury accommodations options. When you're not staying in the lap of luxury, other possible activities include shopping along storied Worth Avenue, visiting or just gawking at some huge homes, and exploring the surprising outdoor activities in north Palm Beach County.

DAY 1

Afternoon

Take I–95 or the Florida Turnpike north to Okeechobee (US 704) and head east over to Palm Beach.

Palm Beach is the perfect base for exploring the entire area. Head straight to your chosen accommodations to get settled in for a luxurious escape.

DINNER AND LODGING: There are several excellent accommodations possibilities in the Palm Beach area, but **The Breakers** (1 South County Road; 561–655–6611 or 800–833–3141; expensive) is definitely the most legendary.

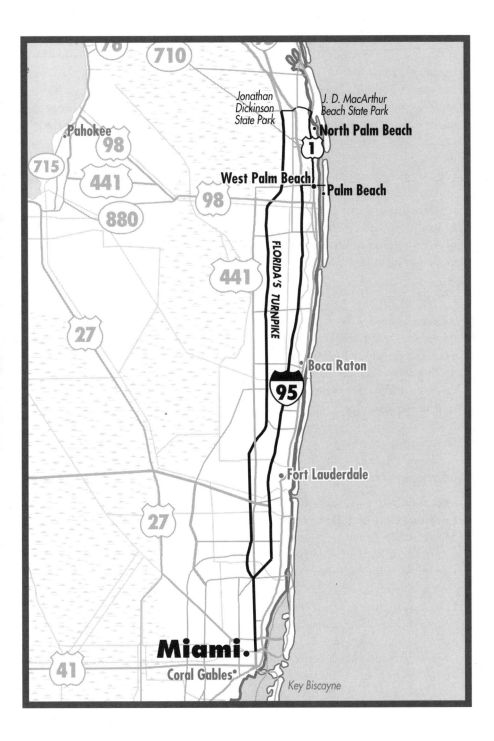

Built in 1895 by railroad mogul Henry Flagler, the huge twin towers of The Breakers have stood for Palm Beach opulence for more than 100 years. The 572-room hotel has become a tourist attraction in its own right, with daily tours a popular offering. No matter where you choose to stay, be sure to explore this resort during your visit. The phenomenal fountain out front, the palatial lobby, and the courtyard are among many highlights. Though guests may expect the resort to be old and stodgy, families are more than welcome and are offered a variety of programs. For a true splurge, try to book an ocean-front or concierge-level room.

For an appropriately extravagant meal, make reservations at The Breakers' **Florentine Dining Room** (1 South County Road; 561–659–8488; expensive), an upscale Italian restaurant. If the price is a bit too steep, other more moderate restaurants are listed below.

Evening

Be sure to have at least one drink in **The Tapestry Bar** (1 South County Road; 561–659–8488), the living room-style bar located in The Breakers. The sixteenth-century tapestries that give the bar its name are part of a collection on display throughout the hotel. The ornately carved vintage mahogany bar was constructed from the original turn-of-the-century mantel from Caxton Hall in London.

DAY 2

Morning

BREAKFAST: If you want to eat with a wide range of locals, walk over to **Green's Pharmacy** (151 North County Road; 561–832–0304; inexpensive). This bustling drugstore also features a diner with small tables and a busy counter. The standard breakfasts are right off the griddle, but you come for the interesting mix of people as much as the food.

Along with The Breakers, there are several interesting attractions right in Palm Beach proper. **The Henry Morrison Flagler Museum** (1 Whitehall Way; 561–655–2833; entrance fee) is one of the area's best sightseeing attractions. Oil, railroad, and real estate gave Henry Flagler the money to build this huge waterfront winter home in 1901. The fifty-five-room mansion includes a huge drawing room, fourteen bedrooms, lots of family artifacts and antiques, and even Flagler's old railroad car. The tours are excellent.

The Breakers was built in 1895 and is the traditional Palm Beach base.

Nearby, the **Society for the Four Arts** (2 Four Arts Plaza; 561–655–7226; entrance fee) features year-round programs of art, literature, drama, and music (the "four arts") in stunning architectural and garden settings. It's best to call for current offerings.

LUNCH: Again, follow the lead of the locals and eat lunch at **Toojay's** (313 Royal Poinciana Plaza; 561–659–7232; moderate). This upscale sandwich shop offers huge and creative takes on almost anything that will fit between two slices of bread.

Afternoon

Be sure to budget (time and money) for at least one afternoon of shopping and strolling along famed **Worth Avenue** (Worth Avenue Association; 561–659–6909), right in the heart (and soul) of Palm Beach. Running right off the beach and South Ocean Boulevard 4 blocks to Cocanut Row, you'll find unbelievable designer shops, art galleries, dining, expensive cars, and well-dressed and -jeweled people. Quite simply one of the world's most exclusive shopping areas, Worth Avenue will give you more than 200 fancy options from which to choose. Some of the numerous possibilities include Saks Fifth Avenue, Cartier, Chanel, Giorgio Armani, Louis Vuitton, Tiffany & Co., Calvin Klein, and many small and unique local shops.

DINNER: You can stay right at The Breakers and enjoy one of the hotel's many other varied dining experiences. In addition to the Mediterranean ambience and cuisine at the elegant **Florentine Dining Room,** the possibilities include huge steaks and chops at **Flagler's Steakhouse/The Terrace Grill,** pub grub at **Henry's Place,** an oceanfront raw bar and fresh fish at **The Seafood Bar,** and casual oceanfront dining and South Florida cooking at **The Beach Club and Patio.** If you want to venture further afield on Palm Beach or into West Palm Beach, try one of the recommendations listed here for Royal Poinciana Way, Worth Avenue, or Clematis Avenue.

LODGING: The Breakers.

Evening

For an interesting mix of locals and nightlife, head to **E. R. Bradley's Saloon** (104 Clematis; 561–833–3520; moderate), a 1920s gambling hall that's now a popular watering hole.

DAY 3

Morning

BREAKFAST/BRUNCH: Enjoy a Sunday Breakers brunch at **The Beach Club and Patio** (1 South County Road; 561–655–6611; expensive) or head back to **Green's Pharmacy** (151 North County Road; 561–832–0304; inexpensive) for a different kind of breakfast experience.

North Palm Beach County is surprisingly outdoors-oriented. **John D. MacArthur Beach State Park** (10900 State Road 703; 561–624–6950; entrance fee) provides a perfect introduction to the possibilities. This protected patch of Florida coastline includes a nature center (with guided tours), exhibits, a hiking trail, and a boardwalk through a lovely lagoon to 8,000 feet of dune-lined oceanfront beach.

Afternoon

Your morning will give you a taste for the outdoors of North Palm Beach County and an afternoon further north at **Jonathan Dickinson State Park** (16450 South Federal Highway; 561–546–2771; entrance fee) will be even more fulfilling. The highlights of the park are several varied hiking trails, ranging from a few hundred yards to 13 miles. Other possibilities include an observation tower, camping, cabins, boat trips, and excellent canoeing.

After your day in the outdoors, take I–95 or Florida's Turnpike back to the Miami area.

THERE'S MORE

Other sightseeing attractions: Lion Country Safari (Southern Boulevard; 561–793–1084; entrance fee) is an excellent outing for all ages, with more than 1,300 animals featured throughout the 500-acre park and a driving tour through the varied preserve. The **Mounts Horticultural Learning Center** (531 North Military Trail; 561–233–1749; no entrance fee) is no less wild, with more than 500 examples of Florida flora. The **Palm Beach Polo and Country Club** (11809 Polo Club Road; 561–798–7000; entrance fee) has frequent matches from January to April at one of the nation's best polo facilities.

SPECIAL EVENTS

January. Palm Beach Polo and Country Club. Season opens; (561) 798–7000.

South Florida Fairgrounds, Palm Beach County. Celebrity entertainment, a carnival midway, and native foods; (561) 793–0333.

March. Annual Palm Beach Seafood Festival, Bryant Park. Seafood, entertainment, rides, crafts, and children's activities; (561) 832–6397.

Easter Sunday Brunch, The Breakers. Includes egg hunt; (954) 659–8465.

April. SunFest, West Palm Beach. Jazz, blues, and pop entertainers; a juried art show; water events; food; a youth park; and a fireworks display.

May. Seafare, Jupiter Inlet Lighthouse. Seafood, arts and crafts, and entertainment; (954) 747–6639.

June. Tropical Fruit Festival, Mounts Building Auditorium; (954) 233–1759.

October. Trick-or-Treat on Worth Avenue. Includes candy collection and a costume contest; (954) 659–6909.

November. Holiday Promenade, Worth Avenue. Refreshments, late store hours, a visit by Santa Claus, and the traditional tree lighting.

December. Art Week at the Armory Art Center, West Palm Beach. Artists Ball, seminars, master workshops, an art auction, an art walk, and an open-house studio tour.

OTHER RECOMMENDED LODGINGS AND RESTAURANTS

Palm Beach

Along with The Breakers, there are two other AAA Five Diamond hotels in the city, making it the only area with three Five Diamond properties in the nation. The other two elegant options are **The Ritz-Carlton** (100 South Ocean Boulevard; 561–533–6000 or 800–241–3333; expensive) and the **Four Seasons Resort Palm Beach** (2800 South Ocean Boulevard; 561–582–2800 or 800–432–2335; expensive). More moderate Palm Beach options include the **Chesterfield Hotel** (363 Cocanut Row; 561–659–5800 or 800–243–7871; moderate to expensive); the **Palm Beach Historic Inn** (365 South County Road; 561–832–4009; moderate); and the **Plaza Inn** (215 Brazilian Avenue; 561–832–8666; moderate).

Due to its creative continental cuisine, **Ta-boo** (221 Worth Avenue; 561–835–3500; expensive) is an ever-popular Worth Avenue choice. On Royal Poinciana Way, near The Breakers, try the varied international menus at **Testa's Restaurants** (221 Royal Poinciana Way; 561–832–0992; moderate to expensive); consistently strong continental cuisine at **Chuck & Harold's** (207 Royal Poinciana Way; 561–659–1440; moderate to expensive); or Italian fare at **Cucina dell' Arte** (257 Royal Poinciana Way; 561–655–0770; moderate to expensive).

West Palm Beach

If bed-and-breakfasts are more your style, try the **West Palm Beach Bed & Breakfast** (419 32nd Street; 561–848–4064 or 800–736–4064; inexpensive to

moderate) or the **Hibiscus House** (501 30th Street; 561–863–5633; inexpensive to moderate).

Clematis Street has become a hotbed for evening dining and entertainment. Some of the most creative possibilities include **Big City Tavern** (224 Clematis Street; 561–659–1853; moderate to expensive); **Sforza Ristorante** (223 Clematis Street; 561–832–8819; moderate to expensive); and **My Martini** (225 Clematis Street; 561–832–8333; moderate to expensive).

FOR MORE INFORMATION

Palm Beach Convention and Visitors Bureau, 1555 Palm Beach Lakes Boulevard, Suite 204, West Palm Beach, FL 33401. (561) 471–3995 or (800) 554–PALM.

Bimini, Bahamas
THE COMPLETE ESCAPE

2 NIGHTS

Seaplane trip • Hemingway legacies
Bahamian Out Island life

Though you often hear the Bimini Islands called simply "Bimini," they are really a group of several islands and cays stretching for almost 30 miles, with northernmost North Bimini and South Bimini being the destinations for most visitors. It's common to use the term "Biminis" or "Bimini" when referring to the area.

A seemingly perfect blend of the development of more major islands and the seclusion of other less-developed Out Islands, the Biminis are and will always be an ideal Bahamian getaway. Just 50 miles and a short and scenic flight from Miami, Bimini is another world away from bustling South Florida life.

Historically, the Biminis have been a world-famous destination for anglers. More recently, excellent diving has become a big lure. But those who don't fish or dive are now coming as well, thanks to the friendliness of the people, the charm of Alice Town and the rest of the Biminis, and decades-long tourism experience that helps every visitor enjoy the islands.

DAY 1

Afternoon

Unless you have your own boat or charter one, by far the most enjoyable and convenient way to reach Bimini is with **Chalk's Ocean Airways** (MacArthur Causeway; 305–371–8628 or 800–4–CHALKS) and one of their

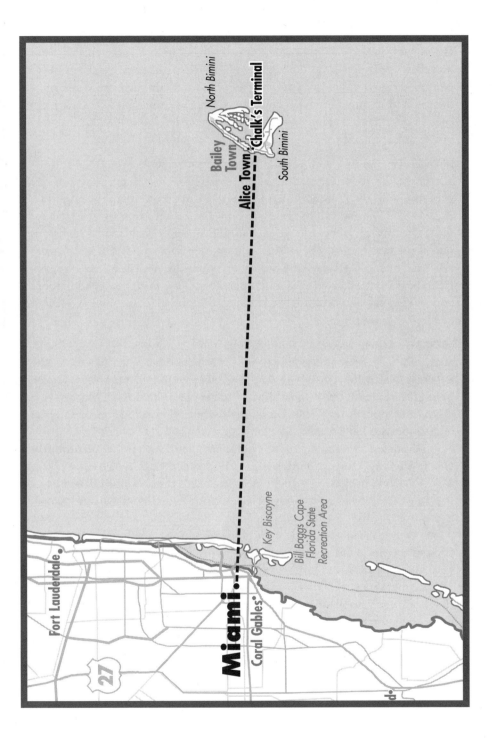

Grumman Mallard G-73 seaplanes (often called a "Goose"). You take off from downtown Miami next to the huge and looming cruise ships. You wear headphones as the pilot provides a low-flying view and narrative, or you listen to the music of Benny Goodman and others from an earlier era. It's like a flight back in time. Within twenty minutes or so, you've left busy Miami and landed in the water near Alice Town. It's a great way to arrive in Bimini.

DINNER: One of the most popular places for native cooking in Alice Town is just down the street (virtually everything is within walking distance in this pedestrian-oriented town). **The Red Lion Pub** (King's Highway; 242–347–3259; moderate) features friendly service and large servings of local food. The Shrimp Delight (large shrimp stuffed with conch and native fish) is one of the best meals on the island. Prepared out back, the barbecued ribs are also a tasty choice. Most entrees are served with peas 'n' rice, corn on the cob, green beans, and other side orders. There's a bar in the front and a dining room overlooking the harbor in the back, where the ribs are cooked on an ancient open brick grill.

LODGING: Though most accommodations in the Biminis are relatively simple, many offer more amenities than you'll find on other Out Islands in the Bahamas. No matter where you stay, you'll soon become a part of the family. If you plan to be in the Biminis during one of the many fishing tournaments during the summer (especially on summer weekends), you may need to make reservations well in advance.

The biggest and most popular choice in Alice Town is the **Bimini Big Game Fishing Club & Hotel** (King's Highway, P.O. Box 669, Alice Town; 242–347–3391 or 800–737–1007; moderate). This resort is one of the best in the Out Islands, with a full array of amenities. Owned by the Bacardi International rum folks, the complex has thirty-five regular hotel rooms on two floors, twelve first-floor cottages and four third-floor penthouse apartments. Each of the simply furnished hotel-like rooms has two beds, a television, and a balcony or patio overlooking the pool or marina and harbor. The cottages and penthouse apartments have refrigerators and kitchens, but cooking isn't allowed. There's ample storage space for fishing and diving gear near each front door. The resort has hosted anglers and many famous guests for more than fifty years, and veteran manager Curtis Carroll gives it a small club-like feel. They offer a wide range of fishing and diving packages, including flights with Chalk's Ocean Airways.

DAY 2

Morning

BREAKFAST: Owned and operated by famed (and Hall of Fame) fishing captain Bob Smith, **Capt. Bob's Restaurant** (King's Highway; 242–347–3260; inexpensive) features hearty breakfast fare and local lunches for hungry anglers heading out at the crack of dawn or waking up late after a night on the town celebrating the big one that didn't get away. For breakfast, the fish and eggs or fish omelette are both excellent, as is the famous French toast using fresh Bimini bread. The lunch fare is simple Bahamian and American cooking. This friendly local restaurant often boasts the wahoo and grouper that Captain Bob catches. Capt. Bob's serves breakfast and lunch only.

Before the sun gets too high in the sky, take a walking tour of Alice Town. Before or during your walk, be sure to stop by the busy **Bimini Ministry of Tourism** office (King's Highway; 242–347–3529). Along with providing specific information and brochures, they can also arrange a People-to-People experience on the island. However, with the friendly Bimini locals, you'll have a "people" experience every day.

For a unique walking tour of Alice Town, you should contact **Ashley Saunders** through the Ministry of Tourism. Ashley is a fascinating Bimini historian, author, and poet who has written two books concerning the history of Bimini as well as several books of poetry. The history books also provide insight about herbal medicine, fishing, vegetation, genealogy, and much more. His walks include historic sights, anecdotes, shops, and dining. It's also a great way to be introduced to lots of interesting locals. Any of the taxi drivers will also show you around the island for a modest fee.

Located on the southern end of North Bimini, Alice Town is mainly made up of two narrow streets, with King's Highway running parallel to the harbor and Queen's Highway up on the hill running in the same direction along the ocean and the surprisingly pretty beach. Most of the action is along King's Highway.

It takes just five minutes or so to walk the length of Alice Town, starting with the seaplane airport in the south. Overlooking the airport are the gutted remains of a three-story hotel.

Just south of this building, ask a local to show you the remains of the **Bimini Bay Rod and Gun Club.** Now in ruins and well overgrown, this 100-room hotel was built in 1919 and was a popular Prohibition-era getaway until it was destroyed by a hurricane in 1926. You can still find the large wind-

Located just 50 miles from Miami, Bimini is "the Gateway to the Bahamas."

ing staircase, once-lavish ballroom, tennis court, and huge pool with faded tilework.

Heading north along King's Highway and into town, the street is usually alive with locals (depending on the day of week, the time of day, and the season). Many of them will greet you. You'll quickly fall into the habit of greeting everyone as you pass them in the street. Within a day of walking around town, you will seemingly have said hello to almost everyone in Alice Town at least once.

Look for a white arch on your right, which proclaims the Biminis as "The Gateway to the Bahamas." You'll next pass a small straw market on both sides of the street, where you can buy straw goods or other souvenirs and chat with the friendly salespeople. Be sure to buy at least one loaf of famous and fresh Bimini bread from Nathle Thompson or someone else in town.

Located in All My Children Hotel, the **Bimini Fishing Hall of Fame** (King's Highway; 242–347–3334; no entrance fee) pays tribute to the many men (so far) who have made Bimini fishing famous. Ever since S. Kip Far-rington Jr. caught the island's first blue marlin back in 1933, fishing has been the backbone of Bimini's economy and the base for many legendary anglers. Members of the Hall of Fame include Farrington, Ernest Hemingway, Mike Lerner, Bimini promoter and developer Neville Stuart, and fishing captains and guides Eric Sawyer, Manny Rolle, Bob Smith, and Sammy Ellis. The displays include historic pictures and articles.

Farther along, you'll reach the **Compleat Angler Hotel** (King's Highway; 242–347–3122; no entrance fee) on your left. By far the most famous sight in the Biminis, it includes a museum room devoted completely to Ernest Hemingway's time on Bimini. Overlooking King's Highway, the well-maintained museum room was where Hemingway often wrote while he was in town. He completed much of *To Have and Have Not* here. The museum features dozens of good black-and-white photos documenting Hemingway's fishing exploits, with many locals also highlighted. There's also a photo of Cuban fisherman Angelmo Hernandez, who was the model for Hemingway's hero in *The Old Man and the Sea*. Hemingway also took on all comers in boxing matches nearby.

Running parallel with King's Highway, Queen's Highway has none of the limited commercialism of the lower street, but it does have a peaceful beach that you'll often have to yourself. You might want to stop by **Atlantis Spring** (Queen's Highway; 242–347–2787; no entrance fee), the island's crystal-clear water distributor, where they'll be happy to give you a tour of the Queen's Highway facilities, of which they're rightfully proud. (Be sure to call in advance.) Heading out of town, there are also several pretty local churches overlooking the sea.

You'll probably still have time to explore the rest of North Bimini in the morning. It's easy to rent a golf cart in town or hire a taxi driver to drive you around the rest of the island. **Capt. Pat's Island Golf Cart Rentals** (King's Highway; 242–347–3477) is a good contact. **Bimini Undersea Adventures** (King's Highway; 242–347–3089) also offers bike rentals.

King's Highway leads out of Alice Town and runs along the water through the small and nondescript villages of Bailey Town and Porgy Bay. It's easy to stop almost anywhere along King's Highway to strike up a conversation with locals.

The road turns to dirt and leads through shady Australian pines out to Paradise Point, where you'll find the "steps" to the lost continent of Atlantis, which is a popular diving and snorkeling site. These huge limestone slabs are thought to be more than 5,000 years old, and some believe they were once part of a sacred site, possibly the fabled Atlantis. There's a nice 2-mile beach here, overlooking crystal-clear waters. This is literally the end of the road for North Bimini, and it's a short ride back into Alice Town.

LUNCH: If you like hanging out with local anglers after they're back from a morning of fishing, as well as eating the bounty they've caught, then **Fisherman's Paradise** (King's Highway; 242–347–3220; moderate) will be your paradise. The steamed grouper, the varieties of conch, and other selections of the sea make this another good King's Highway choice overlooking the water. Owned by a Bahamian couple, Oswald and Chloe Smith, and managed by their daughter Desni, this is a popular spot for all three meals.

Afternoon

Out in the harbor, between North and South Bimini, bonefishing fanatics can be seen stalking the gray ghosts. There are also waterways running through the peaceful mangroves across the harbor that are just starting to be explored by sea kayakers and others in small boats.

Down one of the more narrow waterways, local guides can take you to the quiet spot they call the "Healing Hole," where an underground spring releases clear "healing" water to just a foot under the murky surface. Bonefishing guide **Ansil Saunders** (King's Highway; 242–347–2178 or 242–347–3098) is one of the best people to take you there, thanks to his special experience and stories.

Ansil has been a fishing guide in the Biminis for more than three decades and is also a talented fifth-generation boatbuilder (his ancestors were some of the original settlers). He has guided anglers to bonefishing world records, built several beautiful boats, staged a forty-two-day sit-in for equal rights, and even taken Martin Luther King Jr. out to the quiet mangroves, where King wrote much of his Nobel Peace Prize acceptance speech. On that day, Ansil recited a poem he had written for King and will be happy to recite it to guests he takes out now. Even if you don't break a world record or go fishing at all, a morning on the water with Ansil provides great insight into the Biminis from a very special islander.

DINNER: On the western side of Alice Town overlooking the sea, the **Anchorage Dining Room** (Queen's Highway; 242–347–3166; moderate) is Bimini Blue Water's hotel restaurant, and it's a good one. The views at sunset from the large wood-paneled dining room make this location a special treat, and the many lobster, conch, and seafood specials are all good choices. After dinner, take a stroll on quiet Queen's Highway or the beach below.

LODGING: Though it's most convenient just to stay another night at the Bimini Big Game Fishing Club and Hotel, it's also easy to switch to another lodging option in Alice Town for a different flavor.

Evening

King's Highway generally comes alive after sunset, with visitors and locals roaming the street between bars and restaurants. Of course, Hemingway's drinking legacy lives at the **Compleat Angler Hotel** (King's Highway; 242–347–3122), where fishing and Papa memorabilia hang everywhere, and tourists and locals hang out. Ask to see the famous photo of Gary Hart and Donna Rice when they were at the bar. There are two inside bars and an outside bar that overlooks King's Highway. A calypso band plays on many evenings, and this is a great place to start or finish a night on the town. Though popular manager Ossie Brown passed away in 1996, this wonderfully historic Bimini bar is still in the Brown family and shouldn't be missed.

Next up for drinks should be the **End of the World Bar** (King's Highway; no phone), which is also called "Sand Bar," thanks to the sand floor. Overlooking the harbor in the back, this tiny place's other claim to fame is the plethora of underwear from around the world adorning the walls. Dozens of men's and women's underpants (and a few bras) make this friendly bar an unusual place for a fun drink or two. Sarah Lee Pinder and many other family members will usually welcome you like you're part of the family. The Sand Bar was the late New York congressman Adam Clayton Powell Jr.'s favorite watering hole.

DAY 3

Morning

BREAKFAST: Located at the Bimini Big Game Fishing Club & Hotel, the **Gulf Stream Restaurant** (King's Highway; 242–347–3391; moderate) is a good choice for a quiet Sunday morning breakfast. Overlooking the pool, this continental restaurant is also excellent for a more formal dinner choice.

If you think North Bimini is low-key, just wait until a morning of exploring South Bimini. The ferry for South Bimini leaves from both marinas. South Bimini is even quieter, but does have an airport, the popular Bimini Beach Club & Marina, the wreck of the *Sapona,* the Bimini Biological Field Station, and the well that Ponce de León thought might have been the Fountain of Youth.

You travel between North and South Bimini by **T.S.L. Water Taxi** (VHF radio channel 68). T.S.L. also provides taxi service and tours on South Bimini, making for a good day-trip if you're staying on North Bimini. The ferry deposits visitors at the small dock, where a taxi can be called for in advance from the boat. A basic tour of the island just takes an hour or so, depending on your interests.

The *Sapona,* lying partially submerged off the island's southern shore, was a concrete troop ship built by Henry Ford in the early 1900s. It sank, blew onto the reef, and was used as target practice during World War II. It's now a popular diving and snorkeling site.

The **Bimini Biological Field Station** (BBFS, no phone) is the fascinating undertaking of University of Miami professor and biologist Dr. Samuel H. Gruber. Its mission is evenly divided between education and research, with most of the focus on sharks and especially on lemon sharks. Along with courses at secondary and university levels, there are also Earthwatch trips and many other possibilities for short or extended research and volunteer stays. Visitors are definitely welcome, but it helps to call Dr. Gruber's Miami office (305–274–0628) in advance.

Though it hasn't yet been developed as a tourist destination, the rock-lined well that Ponce de León found is marked by a small sign. It still attracts New Age and mystical-oriented visitors, who say the site still has special spiritual and healing powers.

The rest of South Bimini is completely deserted, save for some older houses along the canal near the Bimini Beach Club & Marina and a condominium and marina development (Bimini Sands, 242–347–3500) that is drawing many U.S. buyers looking for their own piece of an island in the stream. The ferry back to North Bimini leaves frequently, so just head back to the dock.

LUNCH: Also located at Bimini Big Game Fishing Club & Hotel, the casual second-floor **Big Game Sports Bar** (King's Highway; 242–347–3391; moderate) overlooks the marina. This is a popular spot for a cold drink and "pub grub" after a morning of activity. Along with many appetizers and entrees of conch or other seafood, the sandwich selection gets rave reviews from hungry visitors.

Afternoon

Since the last Chalk's International flight back to Miami doesn't leave until late afternoon, you have time for some more exploration of Alice Town, including finding a perfect souvenir. Many of the shops are open on Sunday afternoon. Bimini is by no stretch a shopping destination. King's Highway has a few small shops where you can buy T-shirts and such, as well as a small straw market. The Bimini Big Game Fishing Club & Hotel's **Logo Shop** (King's Highway; 242–347–3391) has a wide range of hotel- and Bimini-logoed products to wear as a reminder of your time in the Biminis. All-purpose **Chic Store** (King's Highway; 242–347–3184) has sold a little bit of everything, from souvenirs to shampoo, since 1935. The perfume selection and the smiling salespeople make the **Perfume Bar** (King's Highway; 242–347–3517) a fragrant and friendly shopping stop. King's Highway is also the place to find the famed and fresh Bimini bread, sold at several stands and shops.

The flight back on the seaplane is just as short and sweet, landing conveniently between downtown Miami and Miami Beach.

THERE'S MORE

Fishing: These "Islands in the Stream" were made famous by Hemingway for offering some of the finest big game fishing in the world. Along with Ernest, other anglers avidly seeking world-record deep-sea catches have included the likes of Howard Hughes and Richard Nixon. This is true world-record territory for a wide variety of big game fish, from marlin to tuna. The Gulf Stream basically flows right through the Biminis.

The various hotels and marinas can help arrange boats, guides, tackle, and anything else you may need. From spring to fall, there seems to be a tournament almost every weekend. Recommended charter fishing boats and captains include **Captain Bob Smith** (*Miss Bonita II,* 242–347–2367); **Captain Jerome Stuart** (*Miss Bonita,* 242–347–2081); **Captain Alfred Sweeting** (*Nuttin Honey,* 242–347–3447); and **Captain Frank Hinzey** (*Nina,* 242–347–3072). For smaller catch, like snappers and grunts, **Elvis Saunders** (242–347–3055) comes highly touted.

If you have your own boat and just want an expert local guide, contact one of the following: **William Pinder** (242–347–3391); **Captain Benjamin Frances** (242–347–2630); **Captain Leo Levarity** (242–347–2346); or **Mack Rolle** (242–347–2462).

Bonefishing is also big business on Bimini, with bonefish caught year-round on the flats right in the harbor area. Recommended bonefish guides include **Ansil Saunders** (242–347–2178 or 242–347–3098); **Cordell Rolle** (242–347–2576); **Tommy Sewell** (242–347–3234); **Ebbie David** (242–347–2053); **Johnny David** (242–347–2198); **Rudy Dames** (242–347–2266); **George David** (242–347–2198); **Jackson Ellis** (242–347–2315); and **Sam Ellis** (242–347–2087).

Boating: Though the islands are known for fishing, boating is naturally popular as well. Boaters typically dock in North Bimini, South Bimini, Gun Cay or Cat Cay, all of which offer nice cruising grounds. For all of your boating needs (including guides and rentals), contact the **Bimini Big Game Fishing Club & Hotel** (242–347–2391), **Bimini Blue Water Marina** (242–347–3166), **Brown's Marina** (242–347–3227), or **Weech's Bimini Dock** (242–347–3028). **Charlie Weech** (242–347–3290) also has a variety of self-guided boats for rent.

Scuba Diving and Snorkeling: Bimini actually has some very good scuba diving. The oldest dive shop in the Biminis, popular **Bill & Nowdla Keefe's Bimini Undersea,** (King's Highway; 242–347–3089 or 800–348–4644), offers packages with most major hotels. Bill and Nowdla Keefe will make the entire experience personalized and enjoyable. Their dive boats are just across the street from their second-floor King's Highway shop. If you have your own boat and certification card (c-card), you can just get air fills for your own diving. Many South Florida divers swear by these Bimini dive packages, rather than heading to the Florida Keys. Bill & Nowdla Keefe's Bimini Undersea also rents sea kayaks (the mangroves are great for exploration) and windsurfers on a limited basis.

Over on South Bimini at the Bimini Beach Club, **Scuba Bimini** (South Bimini; 800–848–4073) offers packages at prices that keep dedicated divers returning for years. Most packages include round-trip airfare from Fort Lauderdale to South Bimini, ground transportation to and from the resort, hotel accommodations, two dives on the day of arrival, three dives each day of your stay, one dive on the day of departure, unlimited shore diving, and free breakfast and lunch. As with those at Bill & Nowdla Keefe's Bimini Undersea, many South Florida divers prefer these Bimini dive packages to heading to the Florida Keys. Bahama Island Adventures also has an operation in the Biminis on Chub Cay.

The *Sapona* is probably the most famous dive in the Biminis. This 300-foot concrete ship sits partially submerged in less than 20 feet of water. Since it has been underwater so long, the coral, sponge, and fish life are very colorful and active. Because the ship was used for target practice during World War II, it has many holes for divers to swim through. This is a great site for novice divers, but veterans also enjoy returning to the *Sapona* often. Other popular wreck dives include *Bimini Barge,* a 150-foot ocean barge in 85 feet of water, and *Bimini Trader,* a 90-foot freighter.

Reef diving is just as good. Shallow Rainbow Reef provides colorful coral, lots of fish, and frequent nurse sharks. Between North and South Bimini, Eagle Ray Run features spotted eagle rays in large numbers. You can even dive the "steps" to Atlantis. Cat Cay Wall starts at 70 feet and drops straight down more than 2,000 feet. Shark Reef features "pet" Caribbean reef sharks, nurse sharks, and Orson, a huge black grouper.

Lying along the warm currents of the Gulf Stream, Bimini also has some unusual snorkeling sites. Jean-Michel Cousteau's **"Out Islands Snorkeling Adventures,"** is a great way to experience Family Islands snorkeling. Bimini Big Game Fishing Club & Hotel (King's Highway; 809–347–3391 or 800–737–1007) participates in the program.

Popular snorkeling sites include the *Sapona;* Rainbow Reef (lots of colorful fish along a coral ridge); Stingray Hole (hand-fed stingrays); and Eagle Ray Run (dozens of eagle rays swimming in formation). As with most Bahamian islands, Bimini's shoreline also offers some great snorkeling sites.

One recent snorkeling development that everyone should consider pursuing is the "Wild Dolphin Excursions" offered by Bimini Undersea Adventures. These are wild spotted dolphins that, when found, seek interaction with humans. The adventures usually last three to five hours, depending on how long it takes to locate the dolphins (they have an 80 percent success rate in finding them). Once there, the dolphins typically allow people to swim and interact with them at will (sometimes for as much as an hour). It's truly a once-in-a-lifetime "wild" experience.

SPECIAL EVENTS

Call (800) 4–BAHAMAS for further information.

March. The Annual Bacardi Billfish Tournament. Big prizes for the biggest fish. Hemingway Billfish Tournament.

April. Bimini Break & Blue Marlin Tournament.

May. Annual Bimini Festival. Local events, food, and fun, including another popular fishing tournament.

June. Saltwater Sportsman Fishing Tournament.

August. Big Game Club Family Fishing Tournament and Bimini Native Fishing Tournament.

September. Big Game Small B.O.A.T. Tournament. For fishermen with small boats in search of big fish.

OTHER RECOMMENDED RESTAURANTS AND LODGINGS

A resort-like experience can also be found at **Bimini Blue Water Resort** (King's Highway; 242–347–3166; moderate). The resort stretches from east to west across the island; there's a pool and marina on one side and a variety of accommodations on the ocean side. The main hotel building has ten standard hotel rooms and two suites, which all have balconies overlooking the water. In addition, the Marlin Cottage is an ideal choice for families or small groups. Overlooking the water, with plenty of balcony space, it has three bedrooms and bathrooms and a huge living room. This was once the home of Mike Lerner, who hosted Hemingway on several occasions, and it is the setting for *Islands in the Stream*. The pioneering Brown family owns this resort, along with the Compleat Angler.

If you want to stay on Bimini like Hemingway, then the **Compleat Angler Hotel** (King's Highway; 242–347–3122; inexpensive) should be your choice. Located above the famed bar and Hemingway hangout, the small hotel offers six simple rooms on the second floor and six more on the third, with balconies overlooking King's Highway. Hemingway stayed in Room 1 on the second floor. The pine and layers of varnish throughout give this legendary hotel the feel of an old ship. Keep in mind these are very plain rooms and that the crowd and music can be loud late into the night. But you'll be following in famed Papa's famous footsteps.

Just north of "downtown" Alice Town, try **Dun's Bayfront Apartments** (King's Highway; 242–347–2093; inexpensive) for an inexpensive housekeeping holiday. Situated on King's Highway and overlooking the harbor across the street, it offers five simply furnished one-bedroom and efficiency apartments, all with a full kitchen, living room area, and television. The rooms open onto a shared balcony overlooking the water. This is a great place to get into local life, away from the tourist hubbub of Alice Town. The beach is just a short walk over the hill to the other side of the island.

A little to the north, **King Brown's Apartments** (King's Highway; 242–347–2620; moderate) has three very modern apartments overlooking the harbor from the second floor. All similar in layout and with the best furnishings of any lodging on the island, each apartment has a huge living room, a large kitchen, a master bedroom overlooking the water, and a second bedroom overlooking King's Highway. Larry Brown owns the general store next door and lives nearby, making this a family-like housekeeping stay within the lap of luxury.

A bit farther out of town is **Ellis' On-The-Bay** (King's Highway; 242–347–2258; moderate), for those seeking even more peace and quiet. Clarence Ellis has three simply furnished cottages for rent that are perfect for small families. Santa Maria, the largest, has a huge master bedroom, a smaller bedroom, a large living room, kitchen, and two bathrooms (one with whirlpool tub). It overlooks the boat docks. Also overlooking the docks, the Nina has a large single bedroom and a kitchen. Located just behind the Santa Maria, the Pinta is similar to the Nina. All three cottages have pullout sofas for additional guests.

Over on South Bimini, the **Bimini Beach Club** (South Bimini; 242–247–3500; moderate) is a secluded choice that was once known only by divers. Now word is getting out that this is a convenient getaway for anyone interested in a quiet commune with the outdoors in simple surroundings. The two-story hotel facility has forty simple but updated rooms overlooking the water with shared balconies. There's also a pool that's a popular gathering place after diving and other activities. Two dive operators are based right outside the door at the full-service marina. Diving and fishing packages are a surprisingly excellent value at this friendly property.

On the dining front, **Opal's Restaurant** (King's Highway; 242–347–3082; inexpensive to moderate), located across the street from the Big Game Fishing Club, has been owned and operated by Opal Duncombe for almost fifty years. Her son, Webster, is the bartender and waiter. Opal's turtle dish with peas 'n' rice is legendary.

FOR MORE INFORMATION

Bahamas Ministry of Tourism, 150 East 52nd Street, New York, NY 10022. (212) 758–2777 or (800) 4–BAHAMAS.

Bahamas Out Islands Promotion Board, 1 Turnberry Place, 19495 Biscayne Boulevard, Suite 809, Aventura, FL 33180. (305) 931–6612 or (800) OUT–ISLANDS.

Bimini Ministry of Tourism, King's Highway, Alice Town, Bimini, Bahamas. (242) 347–3529.

ORLANDO
ESCAPES

ORLANDO

The Treasure Coast
INDIAN RIVER COUNTRY

2 NIGHTS

Small-town Florida • Resort activities

Unlike much of Florida's southeast Atlantic coastline, the Treasure Coast is made up of several small towns, quiet ocean and intracoastal shoreline, and a wide variety of nonglitzy resorts and hotels. It's still the way much of Florida's coastline was back in the 1960s. For many escapees, it's a true Florida treasure.

Basically running from Jupiter in the south to Sebastian in the north, the Treasure Coast is small-town Atlantic coast Florida at its best. There's a great combination of historic pursuits and outdoor activities as well as just enough tourism facilities to make for a perfect escape from the busier parts of Florida and elsewhere.

DAY 1

Afternoon

Head south from Orlando on the Florida Turnpike to exit 133 in Palm City. Follow Martin Downs Boulevard and the signs for South Hutchinson Island and "Beaches" to A1A, which crosses over the Indian River and takes you right into Indian River Plantation, on your right.

DINNER: Depending on your time of arrival, you can eat at one of many resorts. However, a very pretty coastal drive along A1A north takes you right to one of the area's most interesting restaurants. It's a perfect first-night outing. Located right at the north end of South Hutchinson Island, **Theo**

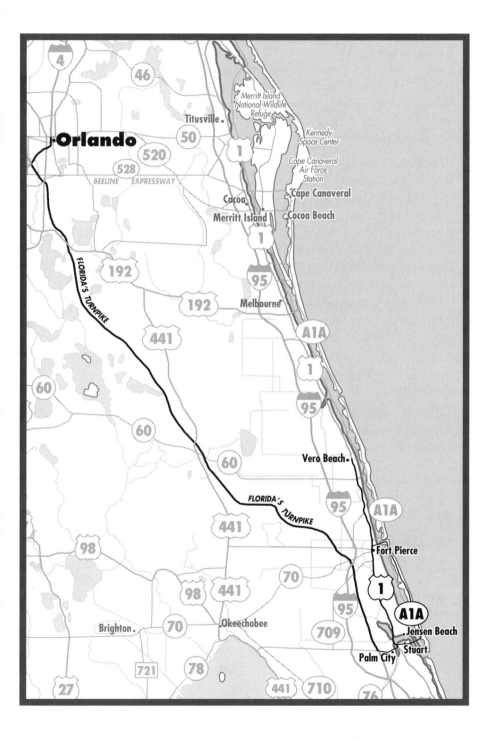

Thudpucker's (2025 Seaway Drive; 561–465–1078; moderate) is one of those classic casual chowder houses that dot Florida's coastline. You may have to wait at the bar for a table (or you can eat right at the bar with the locals), but the various freshly prepared chowders and stews, as well as excellent sandwiches and entrees, make it well worth it. This restaurant is a fitting introduction to the low-key Treasure Coast.

LODGING: With 200 acres on the Atlantic Ocean and Indian River, **Indian River Plantation Marriott Resort** (555 NE Ocean Boulevard; 561–225–3700; moderate to expensive) is the perfect Treasure Coast base for your Indian River escape. Even though it's the area's largest resort community, it has a small-Florida-resort feel and is located close to many area attractions. The range of accommodations includes modern hotel rooms; one- and two-bedroom oceanfront suites with kitchens and private balconies; and villas for long-term and seasonal rentals. Activities abound, with three distinct golf courses, an award-winning tennis center, fishing and boating, four pools and the Atlantic ocean, four restaurants, and Pineapple Express trolley transportation throughout the resort and around the area. It's as if you've moved into a small and self-contained beach village.

Evening

Indian River Plantation and the rest of the area are pretty quiet at night. Located adjacent to Scalawags and overlooking the marina, **Scalawags Lounge** features live entertainment on weekend nights.

DAY 2

Morning

BREAKFAST: Indian River Plantation (**The Emporium Café** offers light fare all day, opening early for breakfast and remaining open into the late evening).

After an unhurried morning, take the time to explore Indian River Plantation. It's easy to walk, drive, or take the shuttle to many places of interest. Some highlights include the marina along the Indian River, the golf courses, and the stunning oceanfront. It makes for a nice introduction to your options.

Head back across A1A into downtown Stuart by mid- to late morning. You'll want to take several hours before and after lunch to explore this fascinating throwback to an earlier Florida.

The UDT-SEAL Museum on North Hutchinson Island highlights the Navy's most elite sailors.

Once a bustling commercial downtown district in the 1920s, Stuart is part of the successful Main Street program for revitalizing historic downtown areas. Several blocks of shopping and dining have returned to their former charm, with a definite European feel to the cityscape along Osceola and Seminole Streets. There are several excellent art galleries, bookstores, bakeries, and cafes. A few blocks away, the **Stuart Feed Store** (161 SW Flagler Avenue; 561–220–4600; no entrance fee) is an early-century general store and small museum.

LUNCH: There are many fine restaurants from which to choose in downtown Stuart. Several feature outside dining along the lively street. **The Jolly Sailor** (1 SW Osceola Street; 561–221–1111; moderate) is definitely a local favorite. This British-style pub and restaurant is owned and operated by a former seaman. With several British Isles beers on draft and lots of filling pub grub on the menu, you'll love eating outside on the sidewalk, inside at the restaurant, or right at the bar. One of the highlights of a meal or drink at The Jolly Sailor is the huge amount of Cunard cruise ship memorabilia that is seemingly everywhere. Just pick up your pint and wander around.

Afternoon

Finish exploring downtown Stuart, then take US 1 or I–95 up to the Fort Pierce area, a river-oriented city that features several interesting museums and sightseeing opportunities. Right on US 1, the **Harbor Branch Oceano-graphic Institution** (5600 US 1 North; 561–465–2400; entrance fee) is a huge facility that provides a great tour of its J. Seward Johnson Marine Education Center and the Aqua-Culture Farming Center. Highlights include research submersibles, aquariums, and a saltwater reef.

Next, take the causeway to North Hutchinson Island, following A1A to the fascinating **UDT-SEAL Museum** (3300 North A1A; 561–462–3597; entrance fee). This oceanside museum highlights the life and times of the Navy's most elite sailors. The Navy used the area for World War II landing training, so there's lots of equipment and memorabilia from this time.

Go back into Fort Pierce and then head across the causeway (A1A, Seaway Drive) over to South Hutchinson Island, looking for the left-hand turn for the **St. Lucie Historical Museum** (414 Seaway Drive; 561–462–1795; entrance fee) about halfway across. The museum features a re-creation of the garrison at old Fort Pierce, early photographs of the area, shipwreck and Native American artifacts, and the restored 1907 Gardner House.

Follow Seaway Drive (A1A) on into South Hutchinson Island and take the peaceful ocean and riverfront drive back down to Indian River Plantation. If you didn't eat there your first night in the area, be sure to stop by **Theo Thudpucker's** (2025 Seaway Drive; 561–465–1078; moderate) for a drink or bowl of chowder with the locals.

DINNER: A visit to the Treasure Coast wouldn't be complete without a meal at **Conchy Joe's Seafood** (3945 NE Indian River Drive; 561–334–1130; moderate) in Jensen Beach. Situated right on the Indian River, with great outdoor and rustic indoor dining, Conchy Joe's features fresh seafood, friendly service, and one of the coast's best atmospheres. The appetizer platter of oysters, clams, shrimp, crab legs, smoked fish, and smoked fish dip is simply outstanding.

LODGING: Indian River Plantation.

Evening

Conchy Joe's is definitely one of the area's best spots for live weekend entertainment.

DAY 3

Morning

BRUNCH: The Sunday brunch at Indian River Plantation's **Scalawags** (555 NE Ocean Boulevard; 561–225–3700; expensive) is legendary with locals and repeat guests.

Head out of Indian River Plantation and take either A1A, US 1, or I–95 up to the Vero Beach area. The Vero Beach vicinity is more developed than its neighbors to the south, with premier shopping, dining, and accommodations along the Ocean Drive area.

LUNCH: You cannot visit Vero Beach without having at least one meal or drink at **Waldo's** (3150 Ocean Drive; 561–231–7091; moderate). Part of the appropriately named and equally legendary Driftwood Resort, Waldo's features an oceanfront location that is simply awesome. Sandwiches and simple entrees provide only slight diversions from the view.

Afternoon

Along with a vibrant oceanfront and downtown area, Vero Beach also features the **Indian River Citrus Museum** (2140 14th Avenue; 561–770–2263; entrance fee/donation). This small museum highlights the history and quality of Indian River oranges and grapefruit, which are considered among the world's finest. The museum's gift shop and several other local shops offer fruit that's ready for shipping.

Take US 60 west out of Vero Beach. It intersects with Florida's Turnpike at Yeehaw Junction, about 30 miles out of town.

THERE'S MORE

Other sightseeing attractions: The Stuart area has many other sightseeing possibilities, including Hutchinson Island's **Elliott Museum** (825 NE Ocean Boulevard; 561–225–1961; entrance fee) of early American history and the county's oldest structure, **Gilbert House of Refuge Museum**

(301 SE MacArthur Boulevard; 561–225–1875; entrance fee), which served as a refuge for shipwrecked sailors. Up in the Vero Beach and Sebastian area, one of the most interesting possibilities is **Mel Fisher's Treasure Museum** (1322 US 1; 561–589–9874; entrance fee).

SPECIAL EVENTS

March. ArtsFest Juried Art Show, Court House Cultural Center; (561) 288–2542.

September. Florida Craftsmen competition. Award-winning artists from the area south to the Keys; (561) 287–6676.

OTHER RECOMMENDED RESTAURANTS AND LODGINGS

If you don't want the resort experience of Indian River Plantation, the Stuart area has several other options, including **Harborfront Inn Bed & Breakfast** (310 Atlanta Avenue; 561–288–7289 or 800–294–1703; inexpensive to moderate); and the **Hutchinson Inn** (9750 South Ocean Drive; 561–229–2000; inexpensive to moderate).

Other dining in and around Stuart includes regional seafood at **The Black Marlin** (53 West Osceola Street; 561–286–3126; moderate); **Eleven Maple Street** (11 Maple Street, Jensen Beach; 561–334–7714; moderate to expensive); and **Jan's Place** (1897 Jensen Beach Boulevard, Jensen Beach; 561–334–9598; inexpensive).

FOR MORE INFORMATION

Stuart/Martin County Chamber of Commerce, 1650 South Kanner Highway, Stuart, FL 34994. (561) 287–1088 or (800) 524–9704 in Florida.

Indian River County Chamber of Commerce, 1215 21st Street, Vero Beach, FL 32961. (561) 567–3491.

Central Atlantic Coast

THE SPACE COAST—
A GALAXY OF OPTIONS

2 NIGHTS

Kennedy Space Center • Cocoa Beach • Ron Jon Surf Shop

From moon walks to walks on dunes, there is a galaxy of options along Florida's Space Coast. This 72-mile stretch of Atlantic shoreline, space-age attractions, and protected wildlife refuges provides a plethora of options at down-to-earth prices.

Highlights of a Space Coast escape include the Kennedy Space Center Visitor Complex, where visitors can view actual launch pads, astronaut training centers, a rocket garden, and other spin-offs from space. Surrounding the Space Center, the 220-square-mile Merritt Island National Wildlife Refuge serves as the home of more federally endangered species than any other refuge in the United States. For beach lovers, Cocoa Beach provides a throwback to early Florida beaches.

DAY 1

Afternoon

The best way to reach the Space Coast is by the Beeline Expressway (SR 528), but you can also take US 50 for a more leisurely drive. Follow the signs for Cocoa Beach off I–95.

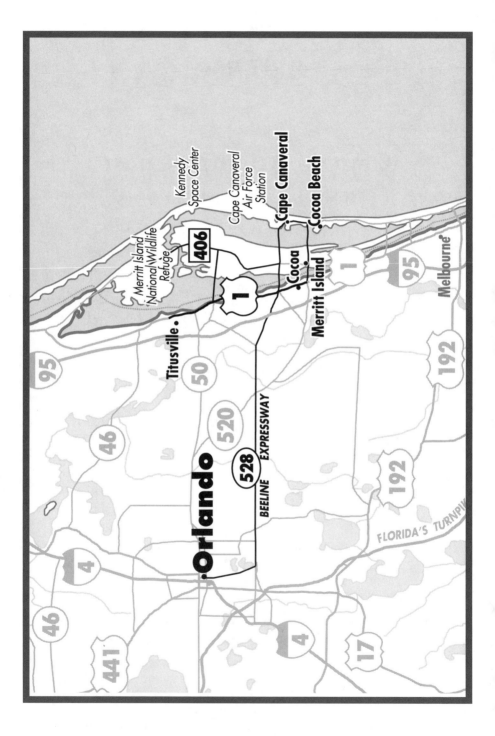

DINNER: To get you immediately into a Cocoa Beach mentality, head straight to the Cocoa Beach Pier and **Pier Restaurant** (401 Meade Avenue; 321–783–7549; moderate). Located right over the water, this casual restaurant specializes in fresh seafood.

LODGING: Because it's such a huge tourist attraction, the Space Coast, particularly Cocoa Beach, has a large number of tourist accommodations. Along with the numerous modern oceanfront chain possibilities, the individually decorated rooms and friendly personal attention at **The Inn at Cocoa Beach Bed & Breakfast** (4300 Ocean Beach Boulevard; 321–799–3460 or 800–343–5307; inexpensive to moderate) make your visit more special.

Evening

Cocoa Beach has several lively nightlife possibilities. Some of the best bets are the restaurants, lounges, and raw bars on and near the famed **Cocoa Beach Pier** (401 Meade Avenue; 321–783–7549; no entrance fee for dining areas).

DAY 2

Morning

BREAKFAST: Try The Inn at Cocoa Beach or get up for sunrise and head back to the **Pier Restaurant** for an early breakfast with the fishermen.

You can't come to the Space Coast without going to the **Kennedy Space Center Visitor Complex** (US 405; 321–452–2121; entrance fees for tours and films) and the other space-oriented attractions in the same vicinity. Depending on your interests, this can easily be an all-day or multiday affair.

From Cocoa Beach, it's easiest to reach the Kennedy Space Center area by following SR 401 north, rather than heading back out to US 1 or I–95. The signs make it a snap.

Open daily at 9:00 A.M. (only closed on Christmas Day), the Kennedy Space Center Visitor Complex provides an unbelievable number of touring options. You start at the large Visitor Center, where you should try to arrive early to review the day's schedule of events. The Visitor Center includes Information Central, shopping, and indoor and outdoor exhibits (including actual space vehicles).

Two different two-hour tours are available, and many people choose to pursue one tour in the morning and one in the afternoon. The **Red Tour** includes a simulated Apollo 11 moon launch; a Saturn V rocket, the huge

Cocoa Beach's pier is one of many Space Coast attractions.

Vehicle Assembly Building (one of the world's largest buildings), the massive six-million-pound crawler transporters that carry the space shuttles to their launch pads; and the actual pads where all Apollo moon and space shuttle missions are launched.

LUNCH: Standard fast-food fare at **The Lunch Pad, Orbit Cafeteria,** and many smaller food and drink stands are your best bet during your day at Kennedy Space Center Visitor Complex.

Afternoon

The **Blue Tour** includes the Cape Canaveral Air Force Station and the Air Force Space Museum, the Mercury and Gemini launching stations, and other launch pads for various scientific, commercial, and military missions.

In addition, the facility includes two 5½-story **IMAX** screens that show three feature films: *The Dream Is Alive,* which astronauts say is as close as most

people will get to riding in a space shuttle; *Blue Planet,* an awesome display of our planet's beauty and fury; and *Destiny In Space,* providing an overview of our future in space.

If that isn't enough to get you spaced out, the nearby **U.S. Astronaut Hall of Fame** (6225 Vectorspace Boulevard; 321–269–6100; entrance fee) includes a G Force Trainer, a virtual reality gravity-free exhibit, a shuttle simulator, a flight simulator, and a multimedia space flight aboard the space shuttle replica. The actual Hall of Fame honors those who journey into space and includes Buzz Aldrin's grade-school report card and Gus Grissom's Mercury spacesuit.

The U.S. Astronaut Hall of Fame is also the home of **Space Camp Florida** (P.O. Box 070015, Huntsville, AL 35807-7015; 800–63–SPACE; tuition fees), which provides a wide range of programs for children and adults to learn lots more about space sciences and exploration. The popular possibilities include realistic astronaut training, propulsion exercises, an in-depth NASA tour, simulated shuttle missions, films, and much more. Space Camp programs range from three to eight days and must be arranged in advance. There's also a similar Space Camp in Alabama.

You can also call to check on current launches (321–452–2121) while you're in the area. Tickets are sold for attending launches on government property, but you can also see most of them from the beach (at a distance).

You should definitely visit **Merritt Island National Wildlife Refuge** (US 406; 321–861–0067; no entrance fee) and the **Canaveral National Seashore** (US 406; 321–428–3384; no entrance fee). Famed for its birding, varied ecosystems, and a large number of endangered and threatened species, the refuge includes a Visitor Center, many hiking trails, and Black Point Wildlife Drive. The 25-mile protected seashore includes empty beaches and windswept dunes that are popular with surfers and campers.

Before heading back to the Cocoa Beach area, you might enjoy the short drive up US 1 to Titusville for one more space-oriented stop and dinner. Located right on the Indian River, Titusville is one of those Atlantic Coast fishing towns that seems forgotten by time (except during a launch).

Titusville's **U.S. Space Walk of Fame** (downtown Titusville; 321–267–7241; no entrance fee) edges the Indian River and overlooks Kennedy Space Center. It is the only riverwalk in the United States that preserves America's history in space through a progressive maze of memorabilia, interpretive plaques, public art, sculptures, and bronze markers. The waterfront terrace is a favorite viewing spot for launches.

Titusville is also a great place for another fresh seafood dinner, where you'll literally find dockside prices and freshness.

DINNER: For something really local on the Space Coast, head to **Dixie Crossroads** (1475 Garden Street; 321–268–5000; moderate) in Titusville. Nicknamed "Home to the Rock Shrimp" and run by a fifth generation Florida native, this incredible place serves 2,000–3,000 plates a night (including lots of local rock shrimp)!

LODGING: The Inn at Cocoa Beach.

DAY 3

Morning

BRUNCH: For an excellent Sunday brunch or a la carte breakfast on Cocoa Beach, head to **Coconuts on the Beach** (2 Minutemen Causeway; 321–784–1422; moderate).

A quiet morning is a perfect time to take a stroll on the beach or check out what they're catching from the pier. After that, anytime is the right time to visit one of Florida's commercial landmarks, **Ron Jon Surf Shop** (4151 North Atlantic Avenue; 321–799–8888). Open 24 hours a day, 365 days a year, Ron Jon Surf Shop is a cult with a wide variety of surfers and shoppers. This huge and brightly painted store, located just a block from Cocoa Beach's famed surfing waves, sells virtually every product associated with beach life. Next to the space-oriented attractions, it's definitely the area's biggest draw, with more than 52,000 square feet of swimwear, active wear, beach gear, watersports equipment, Ron Jon logo wear, and lots of bikes, in-line skates, surfboards, and boogie boards for rent. You can't come to the Space Coast without visiting Ron Jon Surf Shop.

Afternoon

On your way back to Orlando, make time to stop in historic **Olde Cocoa Village,** which is located in Cocoa proper on the mainland. The town center area features small shops, art galleries, frequent arts and crafts shows, and the Village Playhouse, an old vaudeville theater that's been restored for live productions.

From Merritt Island or the Canaveral National Seashore, take US 405 and then the Beeline Expressway (SR 528) or US 50 back to the Orlando area.

THERE'S MORE

Other sightseeing attractions: Melbourne's **Space Coast Stadium** (321–633–9200; entrance fee) hosts the Florida Marlins for major league spring training in March and the Brevard Manatees for Class A minor league baseball from April to September. The only zoo between Jacksonville and West Palm Beach, Melbourne's **Brevard Zoo** (North Wickham Road; 321–254–WILD; entrance fee) features a variety of Latin American animals, including jet black jaguars, 600-pound tapirs, a giant anteater, and two-toed sloths as well as a tropical boardwalk, a "Paws On" interactive learning area, and up-close "Animal Encounters." Melbourne's **Brevard Museum of Art and Science** (1463 North Highland; 321–242–0737) and the Brevard **Museum of History and Natural Science** (2201 Michigan Avenue; 321–632–1830; entrance fee) are great rainy-day attractions. Fighting planes from WWI to the present are on display at the TICO Space Center Airport's **Warbird Air Museum** (SR 405; 321–268–1941; entrance fee).

Additional natural attractions: Running parallel with the ocean for 160 miles, **Indian River Lagoon** (1900 South Harbor City Boulevard; 321–722–5363; entrance fee) is one of the most diversified estuaries in the nation, with more than 4,000 species of plants and animals, including the precious Florida manatee. Palm Bay's **Sebastian Inlet State Recreation Area** (Palm Bay; 321–984–4852; entrance fee) has more fish species than anywhere else in the world and is also the top surfing spot in Florida, with a dramatic stone pier, natural jetties, and crashing waves. Palm Bay's **Turtle Creek Sanctuary** (Palm Bay; 321–952–3433; entrance fee) features a 4,000-foot boardwalk that twists and turns along a bass-filled blackwater creek that is surrounded by sand pines, saw palmettos, and live oaks emerging from ancient sand dunes.

SPECIAL EVENTS

February. Grant Seafood Festival, Melbourne. Seafood specialties along the banks of Indian River Lagoon; (321) 723–8687.

March. Easter Surfing Festival, Cocoa Beach; (321) 452–5352.

Valiant Air Command Warbird Air Show, TICO Space Center Airport.

Biggest air spectacle in the area, with historic and modern warbirds; (321) 268–1941.

April. Melbourne Beach Arts and Crafts Show. More than 275 Florida and regional exhibitors; (321) 722–1964.

July. Space Week Celebration, Titusville. Science fairs, outer-space art exhibits, a space station settlement design, and other galactic adventure programs; (321) 267–3036.

October. Seminole Indian and Florida Pioneer Festival, Cocoa. Indian dancing, high-speed airboat rides, and authentic Seminole samples of food and cultural events; (321) 459–2200.

November. Brevard County Fair, Cocoa Beach. Ten days of arts and crafts shows, chili cookoffs, petting zoos, thrill rides, and music; (321) 459–2200.

Space Coast Art Festival, Cocoa Beach. More than 500 artists show; (321) 784–3322.

December. Christmas Boat Parade, Cocoa. Up to 12,000 twinkling lights on boats along the Indian River; (321) 690–6819.

OTHER RECOMMENDED RESTAURANTS AND LODGINGS

Cocoa Beach/Cocoa

There are a number of chain hotels scattered along the beach, including **Days Inn at Cocoa Beach** (5500 North Atlantic Avenue; 321–784–2550 or 800–245–5225; moderate); **Cocoa Beach Hilton** (1550 North Atlantic Avenue; 321–799–0003 or 800–526–2609; moderate to expensive); **Comfort Inn & Suite Resort** (3901 North Atlantic Avenue; 321–783–2221 or 800–247–2221; moderate); **Best Western Oceanfront** (5600 North Atlantic Avenue; 321–783–7621 or 800–962–0028; moderate); **Holiday Inn Cocoa Beach Resort** (1300 North Atlantic Avenue; 321–783–2271 or 800–206–2747; moderate); and **DoubleTree Cocoa Beach Hotel** (2080 North Atlantic Avenue; 321–783–9222 or 800–552–3224; moderate). Some smaller inns or suite/condo possibilities include: **Econolodge Resort Cocoa Beach** (1275 North Atlantic Avenue; 321–783–2252; moderate); **Cocoa Beach Oceanside Inn** (One Hendry Avenue; 321–784–3126; inexpensive to moderate); and **Ocean Suite Hotel** (5500 Ocean Beach Boulevard; 321–784–4343 or 800–367–1223; moderate).

Other dining options in the area include barbecue at **Sonny's Real Pit Bar-b-que** (2005 North Atlantic Avenue; 321–868–1000; moderate); German fare and fun at **Heidelberg Restaurant** (7 North Orlando Avenue; 321–783–6806; moderate); and still more seafood at **Bernard's Surf** (2 South Atlantic Avenue; 321–783–2401; moderate), **Gregory's Steak and Seafood Grille** (900 North Atlantic Avenue; 321–799–2557; moderate), **Old Fish House** (520 and A1A, White Rose Center; 321–799–9190; moderate).

Melbourne

The county seat of Melbourne is another good base for inexpensive Space Coast accommodations. The options include **Radisson Suite Hotel Oceanfront** (3101 North Florida A1A; 321–773–9260 or 800–333–3333; inexpensive to moderate); **Melbourne Hilton at Rialto Place** (200 Rialto Place; 321–768–0200 or 800–437–8010; moderate); and the **Best Western Harbor View** (964 South Harbour City Boulevard; 321–724–4422 or 888–329–8901; inexpensive to moderate).

Merritt Island / Titusville

If you want to be based right next to the Kennedy Space Center, try the **Ramada Inn Kennedy Space Center** (3500 Cheney Highway; 321–269–5510; inexpensive), **Indian River Bed & Breakfast** (3810 South Washington Avenue, 321–269–5945 or 888–420–3044; inexpensive), or the **Holiday Inn Titusville** (4951 South Washington Avenue; 321–269–2121 or 800–HOLIDAY; inexpensive).

FOR MORE INFORMATION

Florida's Space Coast Office of Tourism, 8810 Astronaut Boulevard, Suite 102, Cape Canaveral, FL 32920. (321) 868–1126 or (800) USA–1969.

Daytona Beach

START YOUR ENGINES

2 NIGHTS

Beach • Daytona International Speedway complex

When many people think of Florida, they think of Daytona Beach and auto travel (and racing). The wide beach allows cars and drivers on its broad expanse, and, to the west, the Daytona International Speedway complex gives auto enthusiasts an inside look at auto racing, whether or not there happens to be a race that day. It all makes for an interesting beach getaway right in the middle of Florida's east coast.

DAY 1

Afternoon

Take I–4 east out of Orlando and follow Daytona Beach signs to I–95 north and US 92 east.

For an introduction to the area, you may want to stop by the **Halifax Historical Museum** (252 South Beach Street; 386–255–6976; entrance fee), which is housed in a 1912 bank building. Exhibits include lots of Native American artifacts, a model of the old Ormond Hotel, and many model cars.

DINNER: Frappes North (123 West Granada Boulevard, Ormond Beach; 386–615–4888; moderate) is the top choice here for creative American cuisine. Chef Bobby Frappier is known throughout Florida for his unique approach to fresh local ingredients. The restaurant's decor reflects his style, contemporary and casual.

LODGING: When you visit Daytona Beach, you must stay on the ocean. One of the best places is friendly and family-run **Perry's Ocean Edge Resort** (2209 South Atlantic Avenue; 386–255–0581 or 800–447–0002; inexpensive to moderate). Three-fourths of the rooms overlook the palm-fringed beach, and many of them have kitchens and sitting areas. It's the perfect Daytona Beach base.

Evening

The nightlife in Daytona Beach isn't quite as lively as it was when the city was the most popular college spring-break destination in the world, but there are still lots of possibilities. For dance club fans, **Razzles** (611 Seabreeze Boulevard; 386–257–6236) is a good option. A bit quieter, **Frappes North** (123 West Granada Boulevard; 386–615–4888) is popular for late-night piano jazz, dessert, after-dinner drinks, and cigar smoking.

DAY 2

Morning

BREAKFAST: Perry's Ocean Edge Resort provides a complimentary continental breakfast to its guests, which includes famous freshly baked doughnuts.

Use your first morning to explore all or part of the more than 23 miles of Daytona Beach's famed beach. You can drive and park directly on parts of the beach here, but there's a small access charge from February to November. The north and south ends tend to be less crowded, but the beach is generally wide enough to accommodate everyone easily.

Along with walking and driving on the beach, the **Main Street Pier** (Main Street and Ocean Avenue; 386–253–1212) and **Sun Glow Fishing Pier** (3701 South Atlantic Avenue, Daytona Beach Shores; 386–756–4219) provide nice diversions and views of the Daytona Beach expanse. Fishing is permissible.

The **Ponce de Leon Inlet Lighthouse Museum** (4931 South Peninsula Drive, Ponce Inlet; 386–761–1821; entrance fee) is also an interesting stop on the way to lunch. Rebuilt in 1982, it's 203 steps to the top for great views of the area. At the base, the museum includes an interesting re-creation of a lighthouse keeper's house in the 1890s, a lighthouse lens exhibit, and lots of lighthouse displays.

LUNCH: In keeping with your water-oriented morning, head down to Ponce Inlet and **Down the Hatch** (4894 Front Street; 386–761–4831; inexpensive to moderate) for lunch. Located right on the Halifax River, this fishing-camp-style restaurant features fresh seafood and fine views in a very casual atmosphere. The shrimp boat docked outside means the shrimp can't get any fresher than this.

Afternoon

Plan to spend the entire afternoon at the **Daytona International Speedway complex** (1801 West International Speedway Boulevard; 386–947–6800 for information and 904–253–RACE for tickets; entrance fees for certain attractions). Auto racing began in the Daytona Beach area way back in 1902, when cars began racing on the hard-packed sand of the wide beach. Many land-speed world records were set there, and it became so popular that the Daytona Speedway opened in 1959. This huge complex now hosts at least eight major racing events each year, including the famed Daytona 500 each February.

Highlights at the speedway include the mile-long, 160,000-plus-seat grandstand and the actual racetrack, which is also often used for car testing. You'll want to start at the **World Center of Auto Racing Visitors' Center,** which includes excellent audio and video presentations outlining the history of auto racing worldwide and in the Daytona Beach area, a Gallery of Legends tribute to some of racing's best drivers, and the departure point for excellent twenty-five-minute tours of the entire facility. Be sure to take the tour. Opened in 1997, the 50,000-square-foot **Daytona USA** attraction allows visitors to see a NASCAR pit stop in action, drive a car by computer, "talk" to legendary drivers, announce the finish of a race, and much more.

Serious auto aficionados will also want to visit **Klassix Auto Attraction** (2909 West International Speedway Boulevard; 386–252–3800; entrance fee). This interesting museum features every Corvette model since 1953 as well as other collector cars, historic Daytona racing cars, and other memorabilia.

DINNER: For another local treat, **Aunt Catfish's** (4009 Halifax Drive, Port Orange; 386–767–4768; inexpensive to moderate) is a great find. This Southern-style restaurant, which overlooks the Halifax River, serves huge portions of country cooking. Each entree comes with cinnamon rolls, hush puppies, a slice of watermelon, a huge salad bar, and friendly service. You'll like it so much you may want to come back for the popular Sunday brunch.

LODGING: Perry's Ocean Edge Resort.

Daytona USA is a Daytona Beach highlight with exhibits and hands-on displays.

Evening

Daytona Beach has an active cultural scene, with shows often taking place at the **Oceanfront Bandshell** (Main Street and Beach Drive; 386–673–8698), **Ocean Center** (101 North Alantic Avenue; 386–254–4545 or 800–858–6444), **SMT Downtown** (176 North Beach Street; 386–252–6200 or 800–854–5592), and **Peabody Auditorium** (600 Auditorium Boulevard; 386–254–4545 or 800–858–6444).

DAY 3

Morning

BREAKFAST: Perry's Ocean Edge Resort.

There's more to Daytona Beach than the beach and auto racing. The peaceful **Sugar Mill Botanical Gardens** (Old Sugar Mill Road;

386–767–1735; no entrance fee) opens at dawn each morning and welcomes curious visitors with a huge garden of native plants and marshlands as well as incongruous concrete dinosaurs dotting the grounds (the remains from Bongoland, an old theme park on the property).

LUNCH: For casual California cusisine, head to **Dancing Avocado Kitchen** (110 South Beach Street; 386–947–2022; moderate).

Afternoon

The large **Museum of Arts and Sciences** (1040 Museum Boulevard; 386–255–0285; entrance fee) contains an eclectic collection, including the huge donations of Cuban dictator Fulgencio Batista in the Cuban museum, lots of American and African art, and an interesting science museum that's popular with kids.

Before you leave town, you'll want to buy that Daytona Beach T-shirt at one of several shopping attractions. Along Beach Street, between Bay Street and Orange Avenue, Daytona's antiques row has become a popular strolling and buying area for antiques fans. In addition, there are more than fifty antiques stalls at **House of Gamble** (1102 State Avenue; 386–258–2889) and a much more eclectic collection of vendors at the **Daytona Flea and Farmer's Market** (I–95 and U.S. 92; 386–252–6484).

Take US 92 west and then I–4 south back to the Orlando area.

THERE'S MORE

Other sightseeing attractions: You can watch the greyhound races at the **Daytona Beach Kennel Club** (2201 West International Speedway Boulevard; 386–252–6484; entrance fee), which is also a popular sightseeing and dining venue.

Fishing: Daytona Beach has justifiably popular fishing right off the famed beach, including from the **Main Street Pier** (Main Street and Ocean Avenue; 386–253–1212) and **Sun Glow Fishing Pier** (3701 South Atlantic Avenue; 386–756–4219), as well as through **Critter Fleet** (4950 South Peninsula Drive; 386–767–7676) and **Sea Love Marina** (4884 Front Street; 386–767–3406) down in Ponce Inlet.

SPECIAL EVENTS

February. Rolex 24 at Daytona, Daytona International Speedway; (386) 253–RACE. Daytona 500, Daytona International Speedway; (386) 253–RACE.

Bike Week, Daytona Beach. Celebrates motorcycles; (386) 255–0415 or (800) 854–1234.

March. Spring Car Show and Swap Meet, Daytona International Speedway. Wide range of exhibits and events for car-racing fans; (386) 253–RACE.

July. Pepsi 400; (386) 253–RACE.

October. Four-day Biketoberfest, Daytona Beach. Motorcycle events; (386) 255–0415 or (800) 854–1234.

November. Annual Turkey Run Car Show and Swap Meet, Daytona International Speedway; (386) 255–7355.

Birthplace of Speed Celebration, Ormond Beach; (386) 677–3454.

OTHER RECOMMENDED RESTAURANTS AND LODGINGS

Other non-chain options in the Daytona Beach area include the twenty-six-suite **Beach Quarters Resort** (3711 South Atlantic Avenue; 386–767–3119 or 800–332–3119; moderate) and the B&B style of the **Coquina Inn** (544 South Palmetto Avenue; 386–254–4969 or 800–805–7533; inexpensive to moderate) or **Live Oak Inn** (444–448 South Beach Drive; 386–252–4667; inexpensive). Part of the varied nonchain group of oceanfront **Ocean Resorts** (2025 South Atlantic Avenue; 386–257–1950 or 800–874–7420; inexpensive to expensive), **Bahama House** (2001 South Atlantic Avenue; 386–248–2001 or 800–571–2001; moderate) features modern oceanfront accommodations and resortlike amenities.

Other seafood-oriented restaurants include **The Chart House** (1100 Marina Point Drive; 386–255–9022; moderate to expensive) and **The Lighthouse Landing** (4940 South Peninsula Drive; 386–761–9271; moderate).

FOR MORE INFORMATION

Daytona Beach Area Convention & Visitors Bureau, 126 East Orange Avenue, Daytona Beach, FL 32115. (386) 255–0415 or (800) 854–1234.

ORLANDO

Tampa

CITY BY THE BAY

2 NIGHTS

Busch Gardens Tampa Bay • Ybor City

Just an hour from the Orlando area, the Tampa Bay area is a completely different style of city. Though it has several excellent theme parks and sightseeing attractions, Tampa Bay is not entirely tourist-oriented. The refurbished historic, dining, and entertainment area of Ybor City, an old cigar manufacturing hub, draws visitors to the downtown area, while the beaches, Busch Gardens, and the Florida Aquarium keep them busy nearby. It's a good combination.

DAY 1

Afternoon

Take I–4 west to the Tampa Bay area, having dinner downtown and establishing your base at one of the modern hotels located there or heading a bit north on I–75 to Saddlebrook Resort, a Tampa Bay area landmark that is a destination in its own right but also serves as a countryside base for forays into Tampa proper.

DINNER: While in the Tampa Bay area, you have to have at least one meal at famed **Bern's Steak House** (1208 South Howard Avenue; 813–251–2421; expensive), which is consistently rated one of the best steak restaurants in the United States. Reservations are generally a requirement at this establishment, where aged steaks are grilled to your exact specifications and served with onion soup, salad, and much more. The dessert room is virtually a tourist attraction.

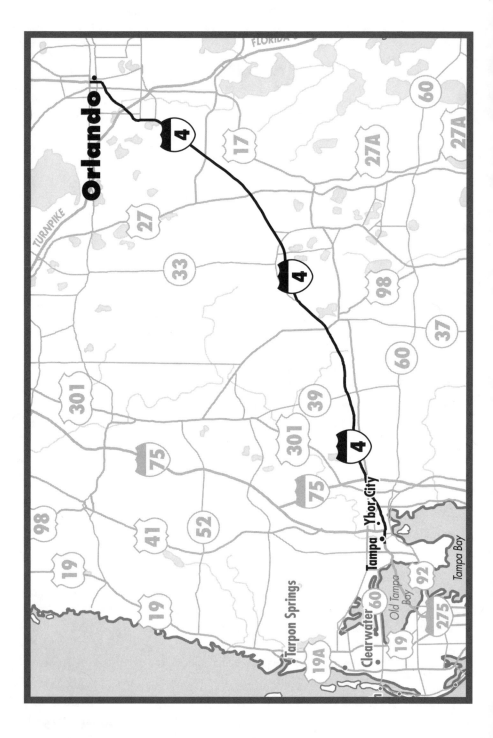

LODGING: A quick escape in its own right, **Saddlebrook Resort** (5700 Saddlebrook Way, Wesley Chapel; 813–973–1111 or 800–729–8383; moderate to expensive) is a 480-acre retreat that you may not want to leave to head into Tampa. Golf and tennis reign supreme here, but the countryside setting, huge pool, spa and fitness center, and much more make this a Southeast U.S. gem. It's just twenty minutes or so to downtown Tampa, and the resort offers lots of help for Tampa Bay exploration. The downtown Tampa area has several large and modern chain hotels that work well if you want to stay right in town.

Evening

Saddlebrook's lounge often has live entertainment on weekends.

DAY 2

Morning

BREAKFAST: Saddlebrook Resort.

After exploring Saddlebrook Resort, head into Tampa Bay proper to begin your investigation of this fascinating city and surrounding area.

Many people escape to Tampa just for **Busch Gardens Tampa Bay** (3000 East Busch Boulevard; 813–987–5171; entrance fee). This huge African-oriented theme park features a wide range of rides, entertainment, animal attractions and exhibits, shopping, and dining. More than 3,000 animals can be viewed, providing an experience officials rightfully claim can only be repeated on an African safari. The natural setting in the various themed areas is well done and the rides provide nice interludes from animal viewing. You'll want to spend at least a half-day here. If you have kids, you might also enjoy adjacent **Adventure Island** (4545 Bougainvillea Avenue; 813–987–5600; entrance fee), a water-oriented theme park with many pools, slides, and other children's attractions.

LUNCH: Busch Gardens.

Afternoon

Plan to head to the **Ybor City** area in the late afternoon, which will allow you time to quietly explore the historic sites before hordes of people descend on the area later at night. For an overview of the area, be sure to stop by the **Ybor City State Museum** (1818 9th Avenue; 813–247–6323; entrance fee).

This fascinating museum has a wide variety of exhibits depicting the area's earlier life as a cigar and social center, including old cigar memorabilia, factory pictures, and a renovated cigar worker's cottage. You can walk around the old tobacco warehouses (now shops and restaurants) on your own or explore more thoroughly with organized walking tours leaving from the museum.

DINNER: Ybor City's famed **Columbia Restaurant** (2117 East 7th Avenue; 813–248–4961; moderate to expensive) is the perfect place to eat. The Spanish scenery and cuisine (the paella is always popular) make this one of Ybor City's (and Tampa Bay's) best restaurants.

LODGING: Saddlebrook Resort.

Evening

Ybor City has become Tampa's most popular evening attraction because the main drag is closed to autos, allowing visitors to freely roam the streets. Along with many busy bars, **Frankie's Patio Bar & Grill** (1920 East 7th Avenue; 813–248–3337) is one of the best spots for live music.

DAY 3

Morning

BREAKFAST: Saddlebrook Resort.

Tampa Bay's nature theme continues at **The Florida Aquarium** (701 Channelside Drive; 813–273–4000; entrance fee). This huge aquarium features more than 5,000 examples of Florida flora and fauna, with highlights being the various ecosystem exhibits and the huge 14-foot-high aquarium viewing area. Plan on spending the entire morning wandering through the numerous exhibits.

LUNCH: Located conveniently near The Florida Aquarium and Old Hyde Park, **Cactus Club** (1601 Snow Avenue; 813–251–4089; inexpensive to moderate) provides an unusual lunch venue and menu. The Southwestern decor and cuisine are a perfect complement.

Afternoon

Old Hyde Park Village (1509 West Swann Avenue; 813–251–3500) is the ideal place to stroll around for a couple of hours after lunch, looking for that perfect Tampa Bay souvenir. With more than fifty varied shops, you're sure to find something perfect.

Spring training for the New York Yankees at Legends Field is one of many Tampa attractions.

Don't leave Tampa without visiting the **Henry B. Plant Museum** (401 West Kennedy Boulevard; 813–254–1891; entrance fee), just across the Hillsborough River. This huge Spanish-style building was originally the 511-room Tampa Bay Hotel, built by railroad mogul Henry Plant. It's now filled with memorabilia from his life and the early days of the hotel and tourist city.

Take I–4 east back to the Orlando area.

THERE'S MORE

Other sightseeing attractions: Tampa offers much more to see, including the large **Lowry Park Zoo** (7530 North Boulevard; 813–932–0245; entrance fee); the **Museum of Science and Industry** (4801 East Fowler Avenue; 813–987–6300; entrance fee), the largest of its kind in the Southeastern United States; and the eight-gallery **Tampa Museum of Art** (600 North Ashley Drive; 813–274–8130; entrance fee).

Boating: Thanks to all of the surrounding water, the Tampa Bay area has many excellent boating opportunities, including those through the tourist office's **Tampa Outdoor Adventures** (11 Madison Avenue; 813–223–2752 or 800–44–TAMPA, extension 6) and **Canoe Escape** (9335 East Fowler Avenue; 813–986–2067).

SPECIAL EVENTS

February. Gasparilla Pirate Fest, Hillsborough Bay. Pirate fun on boats and city streets, with lots of events, food, and music; (813) 272–1939.

March. New York Yankees, Legends Field. Spring training opens; (813) 875–7753.

October. Guavaween, Ybor City. A night of music and fun at Halloween; (813) 248–3712.

OTHER RECOMMENDED RESTAURANTS AND LODGINGS

The downtown Tampa area has several large and modern chain hotels that work well if you want to stay right in town. Some of the best options include **Hyatt Regency Tampa** (2 Tampa City Center; 813–225–1234 or 800–233–1234; moderate); **Hyatt Regency Westshore** (6200 Courtney Campbell Causeway; 813–874–1234 or 800–233–1234; moderate to expensive); **Radisson Bay Harbor Inn** (7700 Courtney Campbell Causeway; 813–281–8900 or 800–333–3333; inexpensive to moderate); **Wyndham Westshore** (4860 West Kennedy Boulevard; 813–286–4400 or 800–325–3535; moderate); **Wyndham Harbour Island Hotel** (725 South Harbour Island Boulevard; 813–229–5000 or 800–WYNDHAM; moderate to expensive). If you're looking for historic lodging, head a bit further afield over to Clearwater and **Belleview Biltmore Resort Hotel** (25 Belleview Boulevard, Clearwater; 727–442–6171 or 800–237–8947; moderate to expensive), built in 1897 and still the largest occupied wooden structure in the United States. The renovated old Victorian charmer is worth the drive.

The downtown Tampa Bay area has many excellent casual seafood restaurants, including **Crawdaddy's** (2500 Rocky Point Drive; 813–281–0407; moderate) and **Cafe Creole & Oyster Bar** (1330 East 9th Avenue, Ybor City; 813–247–6283; moderate).

FOR MORE INFORMATION

Tampa Bay Convention and Visitors Bureau, 400 North Tampa Street, Tampa, FL 33602–4706. (813) 223–2752 or (888) 44–TAMPA.

St. Petersburg/Clearwater
BIG CITY CULTURE AND HISTORY
AT THE BEACH

2 NIGHTS

Historic lodging • Beach • Seafood • Museums

In many ways, St. Petersburg/Clearwater is the "ideal" Florida escape. When it comes to an ideal Sunshine State getaway, most people think of sunshine, spacious and spotless beaches, unspoiled islands surrounded by gentle surf, and plenty or nothing to do. Major attractions, for which Florida is famous, are nearby but far enough away to escape the constant crowds. That all describes St. Petersburg/Clearwater.

Located on the west coast, bordered on the east by Tampa Bay and on the west by the Gulf of Mexico, the Pinellas County peninsula and its famous beaches are within minutes of Florida's popular attractions—Tampa's Busch Gardens (see Orlando Escape Four) is just thirty minutes away and Walt Disney World, Sea World, Universal Studios, and other central Florida sites are just ninety minutes from the area.

St. Petersburg/Clearwater offers 35 miles of white sand beaches on the Gulf of Mexico and 345 miles of shoreline around the peninsula, which encompasses the resort communities of Clearwater Beach, Dunedin, Indian Rocks Beach/Redington/Bellair Beach, Madeira Beach, St. Petersburg, St. Pete Beach, Tarpon Springs, and Treasure Island. Along with the beaches, visitors can enjoy historic lodgings like The Don CeSar Beach Resort & Spa; interesting culture, such as the Salvador Dali Museum; fresh seafood; and wonderful outings to small towns like Tarpon Springs and peaceful Fort DeSoto Park.

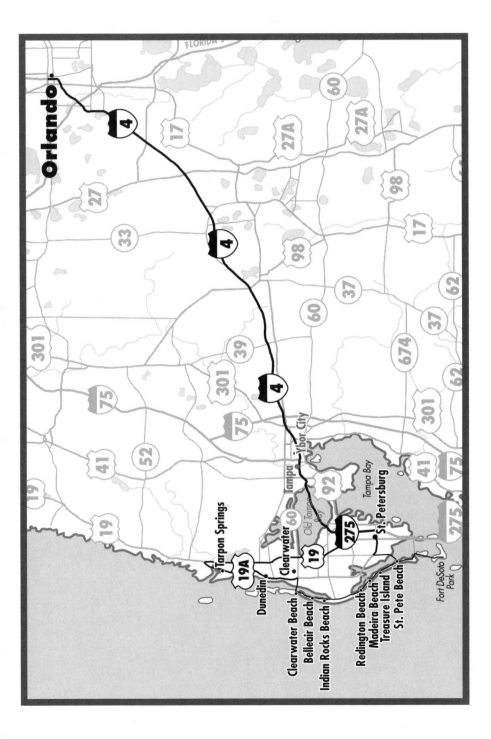

DAY 1

Afternoon

Try to head out of Orlando by mid- to late afternoon, so that you reach the coast (84 miles) before sunset. Take I–4 south to Tampa and then follow I–275 south to St. Petersburg. Take the Pinellas Bayway exit toward St. Pete Beach and follow the toll road until it ends at The Don CeSar Beach Resort & Spa, the ideal base for a St. Petersburg/Clearwater escape.

If you arrive before sunset, be sure to be somewhere on the beach for a normally spectacular end to daylight. **Sunsets,** right at The Don CeSar, is a popular spot to gather, as are several other bars and restaurants along the beach.

DINNER AND LODGING: The Don CeSar Beach Resort & Spa (3400 Gulf Boulevard; 727–360–1881 or 800–282–1116; moderate to expensive) is such a perfect base that you may never want to leave to explore the rest of St. Petersburg/Clearwater. Rising from the sugary Gulf shores, this romantic resort blends European grandeur, seaside elegance, and sweet sunsets with the enchantment of yesteryear. Known as Florida's "Legendary Pink Palace" since 1928, it is the only historic resort poised along the Gulf of Mexico from the Keys to the tip of Texas.

Referred to simply as "The Don" by generations of guests from around the world, the resort exemplifies the grandness of America's traditional beach resorts, charming its visitors with pampering, beach amenities, a modern spa, watersports, a children's program, superb shopping, evening entertainment, and completely renovated facilities throughout.

For your first night on the Gulf, it's easy to eat right at The Don CeSar. Depending on your mood, the two top choices include **Sea Porch Cafe,** a casual beachfront restaurant with a wide variety of fresh seafood and continental fare, and the more formal (but still casual) **Maritana Grille,** a popular restaurant that features "Floribbean" cuisine prepared over a pecan and cherry wood grill. For a unique experience, ask about dining at the Chef's Table, where you can eat with the chef and his staff back where the masterpieces are created.

The Don CeSar Resort & Spa, built in 1928, is one of Florida's top beach resorts.

DAY 2

Morning

BREAKFAST: Before heading into St. Petersburg, enjoy a leisurely breakfast at the resort's **Sea Porch Cafe.**

Head back across the Pinellas Bayway and take I–275 north and then I–175 right into downtown St. Petersburg. Follow the signs to the **Salvador Dali Museum** (1000 3rd Street South; 727–823–3767; entrance fee). This popular harborfront museum showcases the life and work of the strange Spanish surrealist painter. Five galleries display a selection of more than 90 oil paintings, 100 watercolors and drawings, and 1,300 graphics, sculptures, photos, and other works. The four huge masterworks and many other smaller canvases trace Dali's entire career. Depending on your tastes and interests, you'll

be entranced for hours or finished with the museum in less than thirty minutes. Either way, be sure to visit what has to be one of the best museum gift shops in the state.

If you're traveling with kids and your Dali Museum visit was cut short, now is the perfect time to head to **Great Explorations** (The Pier, 800 2nd Avenue; 727–821–8992; entrance fee). This hands-on museum lets everyone touch, move, and interact with exhibits that educate and entertain. Areas include Phenomenal Arts, Explore Galore, Exchange, Think Tank, Touch Tunnel, and Body Shop.

LUNCH: After the museum(s), head over to Fourth Street and up to the **Fourth Street Shrimp Store** (1006 4th Street North; 727–822–0325; inexpensive to moderate). Just north of downtown, this popular eatery sells shrimp and other fresh fish in the front shop and cooks and serves it in the expanded dining areas in the back. The sandwiches (including grouper), the shrimp, and many of the seafood entrees feature huge portions and come with friendly service in a Florida "fish house" atmosphere. If you can, top it off with some key lime pie.

Afternoon

Head back into the downtown area and follow the signs for parking at or near **The Pier** (800 2nd Avenue NE; 727–821–6164; no entrance fee). This lively complex out on the water features five floors of shopping, dining, boating tours, and an ongoing array of activities and live music.

From The Pier, you're close to a number of afternoon possibilities. Museum-goers have a choice of the **Museum of Fine Arts** (255 Beach Drive NE; 727–896–2667; entrance fee), which is noted for its collection of French Impressionist paintings and a collection of photographs by American master photographers; the **St. Petersburg Museum of History** (335 2nd Avenue NE; 727–894–1052; entrance fee), housing a permanent interactive exhibition of the chronology of St. Petersburg's history, filled with priceless artifacts, documents, and photographs (including a replica of the world's first scheduled commercial airliner, which flew from St. Petersburg to Tampa in 1914); and the **Florida International Museum** (100 2nd Street North; 727–822–3693; entrance fee), a Smithsonian affiliate with the largest collection of JFK memorabilia and ongoing temporary Smithsonian exhibits.

Depending on your timing, late afternoon is a great time to take a drive

up US 19 to **Tarpon Springs.** Located about 30 miles north of St. Petersburg, Tarpon Springs is known as the "sponge capital of the world," thanks to Greek immigrants who came to Tarpon Springs early in the century to make a living from sponging, fishing, and boating. Though sponges are still harvested and sold, many Greek descendants now make a living from the tourists who come to walk, shop, and dine along the Sponge Docks.

DINNER: If you stay at Tarpon Springs through early evening, there's a great place to have dinner before heading back south to The Don CeSar. The huge **Pappas Restaurant** (10 West Dodecanese Boulevard; 727–937–5101; inexpensive to moderate) is an appropriately Greek restaurant right off the Sponge Docks. Founded by Louis Pappamichaelopoulus in 1925, this family-owned and -operated restaurant has specialized in fresh seafood ever since. If you're already back down in the St. Petersburg area, other ideas are covered below.

LODGING: The Don CeSar Beach Resort & Spa.

DAY 3

Morning

BREAKFAST: Sleep in, read the *St. Petersburg Times*, and then head to The Don CeSar's famous **King Charles Brunch** (assuming you're there on Sunday). So popular that it must be served up in the fifth-floor King Charles Ballroom, the brunch includes more than 180 varied selections and is enhanced by spectacular Gulf views.

Most museums are closed on Sunday mornings, but one special "museum" is open daily, typically until dusk. The **Suncoast Seabird Sanctuary** (18328 Gulf Boulevard; 727–391–6211; no fee) is located just up Gulf Boulevard from The Don CeSar in Indian Shores. It's typically quiet on Sunday mornings (and most other times). This fascinating sanctuary is a haven for hundreds of sea and land birds and houses the largest wild-bird hospital in the United States.

Another good Sunday morning possibility is **Fort DeSoto Park** (Pinellas Bayway; 727–866–2662; entrance fee), which is located off the Pinellas Bayway. This barrier island fort was constructed for the Spanish-American War, though it never came under fire. The facilities now include the remains of the fort, camping, fishing, hiking, biking on a popular island-wide asphalt trail, and a stunning beach.

Afternoon

If you missed any museums that you still want to visit, most are open on Sunday afternoons. Sunday afternoons are also ideal times to shop for St. Petersburg area souvenirs, if you didn't buy anything at the Dali Museum or in Tarpon Springs. Some solid shopping possibilities include **John's Pass Village and Boardwalk** (12901 Gulf Boulevard; 727–391–7373; no entrance fee), a row of wooden structures on pilings that house shops and restaurants; **Haslam's** (2025 Central Avenue; 727–822–8616), a giant bookshop that is definitely one of the largest in the state; **P. Buckley Moss** (190 4th Avenue Northeast; 727–894–2899), a gallery specializing in the primitive works of the famous artist; and the **Florida Craftsmen Gallery** (501 Central Avenue; 727–831–7391), which showcases the work of more than 150 state artists and craftspeople.

THERE'S MORE

Other sightseeing attractions: Other possibilities include the **Clearwater Marine Aquarium** (249 Windward Passage; 727–447–0980; entrance fee), a small local spot on Clearwater Harbor that doesn't have the hype of many modern aquariums, and the **Tropicana Field** (1 Stadium Drive; 727–825–3250; no entrance fee for tours), the oddly shaped cable-supported dome that hosts Tampa Bay Devil Rays baseball and other events (tours are available). Nearby Tampa (see Orlando Escape Four) is also within easy reach for sightseeing.

Outdoor activities: The numerous possibilities include boating rentals through **Captain Dave's Watersports** (9540 Blind Pass Road; 727–367–4336); fishing with one of the **Queen Fleet headboats** (25 Causeway Boulevard, Clearwater Marina; 727–446–7666); or playing a round of golf at one of the area's many courses. There are also several sightseeing and gambling cruises offered in the area and seemingly advertised everywhere. Several excellent beach possibilities include the beach that runs all the way between Dunedin and St. Pete Beach; **Fort DeSoto Park** (see Day 3 above); **Caladesi Island State Park** (727–734–5263); and **Honeymoon Island State Recreation Area** (727–469–5942).

SPECIAL EVENTS

January. Outback Bowl, Raymond James Stadium. On New Year's Day, a premier college football bowl game, typically featuring two of the nation's top teams from the Big 10 and SEC; (727) 874–2695.

Greyhound racing, Derby Lane. Six-month season opens; (727) 812–3339.

Epiphany, Tarpon Springs. Day-long religious celebration by Greek Orthodox followers includes a morning service at the St. Nicholas Cathedral, a dive for the cross in Spring Bayou, release of a white dove of peace, Greek food, music, dancing, and lots of fun for locals and visitors; (727) 937–3540.

March. Spring training, St. Petersburg (Tampa Bay Devil Rays); Clearwater (Philadelphia Phillies); and Dunedin (Toronto Blue Jays); (727) 582–7892.

Renaissance Festival, Largo. Knights jousting, arts and crafts, entertainment, rides, and food; (800) 779–4910.

International Folk Fair, Tropicana Field. Cultural customs of more than forty countries and nationalities; (727) 551–3365.

April. Tarpon Springs Arts & Crafts Festival, Spring Bayou, Craig Park. Continuous entertainment; (727) 937–6109.

Highland Games and Festival, Dunedin. Celebrates the area's Scottish heritage; (727) 733–6240.

May. Mainsail Art Show, St. Petersburg's Straub Park. One of the Southeast's finest shows; (727) 892–5885.

June. Kid's Week, Clearwater Beach. A week of special events designed exclusively for kids, including marine and environmental programs, magic shows, beach activities, a fishing tournament, and a variety show; (727) 447–9532.

July. Caribbean Calypso Carnival, The Pier, St. Petersburg. Weekend of steel drum bands, authentic Caribbean food, limbo dancing, spectacular pageantry, and a host of other activities; (727) 821–6443.

September. Seaside Musicfest, St. Pete Beach. Live pop, jazz, and country music in a beachside setting; (727) 360–6961.

Florida Birding and Nature Festival. One of the largest bird-watching festivals in the United States; (800) 822–6461.

October. Annual Clearwater Jazz Holiday, Coachman Park. Top-name jazz musicians; (727) 461–5200.

Annual John's Pass Seafood Festival, Madeira Beach. Tons of fish, shrimp, crabs, and other seafood specialties, one of the largest seafood festivals in the state; (727) 391–7373.

November. Arts Alive!, St. Petersburg. Month-long tribute to the arts, with shows, gallery hopping, concerts, and more; (727) 821–4069.

Suncoast Dixieland Jazz Classic, Sheraton Sand Key Resort, Clearwater Beach; (727) 595–1611.

Snowfest & Holiday Fantasy, St. Petersburg. Month-long tradition of beautiful decorations, choirs of carolers, holiday entertainment, and a major Christmas parade; (727) 821–6443.

December. Lighted Boat Parade, The Pier, St. Petersburg. Boats of all sizes in lighted splendor; (727) 893–7494.

First Night, St. Petersburg. Entertainment and special events bring in the New Year in a nonalcoholic way; (727) 823–8906.

OTHER RECOMMENDED RESTAURANTS AND LODGINGS

If The Don CeSar is full or a bit too pricey, there are a number of other historic choices in the area.

St. Petersburg

Right downtown, the **Renassiance Vinoy Resort & Golf Club** (501 5th Avenue NE; 727–894–1000 or 800–HOTELS; moderate to expensive) has been stunningly restored to its former elegance. Originally built in 1925, the resort exudes history and elegance from another era. The Vinoy is convenient to many downtown attractions, and many rooms offer nice bay views.

There are also two excellent bed-and-breakfasts in St. Petersburg. **The Bay Gables Bed & Breakfast** (136 4th Avenue NE; 727–822–8855 or 800–822–8803; inexpensive to moderate), is an elegant Victorian house within walking distance of most downtown attractions that has nine rooms with separate bathrooms. **Bayboro Bed and Breakfast** (1719 Beach Drive SE; 727–823–4955; inexpensive to moderate) is a stunning Victorian inn with four rooms with individual bathrooms, a nice view of Tampa Bay, and a small beach.

Additional restaurant possibilities include the perfectly named **Ted Peters' Famous Smoked Fish** (350 Pasadena Avenue South; 727–381–7931; inexpensive to moderate) in St. Petersburg; rustic seafood at **Silas Dent's** (5501 Gulf Way; 727–360–6961; moderate) in St. Pete Beach; and famous grouper sandwiches and sunsets at **Hurricane** (807 Gulf Way; 727–360–9598; moderate), just south in Pass-a-Grille Beach.

Clearwater

Elsewhere in the area, historic hotel lovers would also enjoy Clearwater's **Belleview Biltmore Resort Hotel** (25 Belleview Boulevard; 727–442–6171 or 800–237–8947; moderate to expensive). Built in 1897, it's said to be the largest occupied wooden structure in the world. This Victorian charmer also has an excellent spa.

FOR MORE INFORMATION

St. Petersburg/Clearwater Area Convention & Visitors Bureau, 14450 46th Street North, Clearwater, FL 34622. (877) FLBEACH.

Mount Dora

A TOWN, A HILL, AND A LAKE

2 NIGHTS

Quaint Central Florida town • Lake Dora activities

Mount Dora is one of those charming central Florida towns that most visitors and residents don't associate with the Sunshine State. Set on a hill and over-looking a pretty lake, Mount Dora's active historic downtown area has made it a popular weekend escape for many people. Whenever you visit, you'll find Mount Dora's peaceful accommodations, dining, and shopping scene a welcome respite.

DAY 1

Afternoon

Take US 441 directly out of the Orlando area, leaving the bustling city quickly behind and entering farming, fishing, and boating country. State Route 46 east leads right into the downtown area and the Lakeside Inn.

DINNER AND LODGING: Lakeside Inn (100 North Alexander Street; 352–383–4101 or 800–556–5016; moderate) is the ideal Mount Dora base. Overlooking the sunsets of Lake Dora, the Lakeside Inn was built in 1883 as a ten-room inn and has developed into one of the state's most charming small hotels. The completely restored inn offers eighty-eight varied rooms, including garden parlors and lakefront chambers; an inviting ballroom lobby with a popular fireplace; sweeping verandas with paddle fans and colonial rockers; and a pool and watersports facilities. Owners James Barggren and Richard

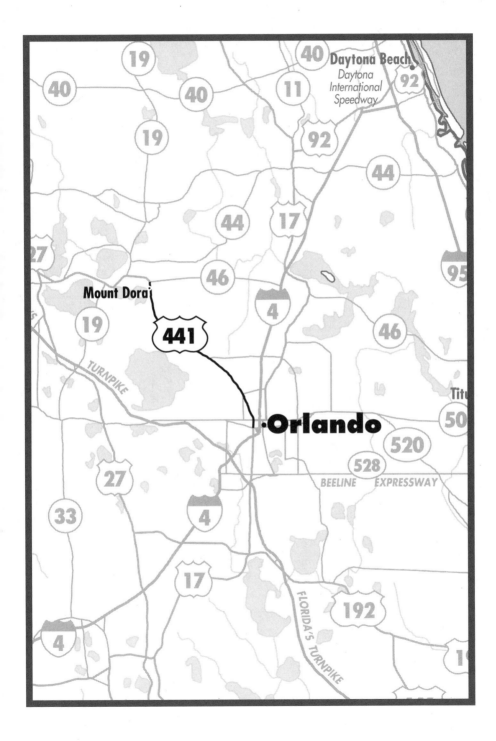

Dempsey, who specialize in historic properties, have turned this into an ideal retreat. **The Beauclaire Restaurant,** known for its American regional cuisine, is the perfect way to spend your first evening at the Lakeside Inn and Mount Dora.

Evening

The Lakeside Inn's 1920s **Tremain's Lounge** provides live "vintage music" on many nights.

DAY 2

Morning

BREAKFAST: The Lakeside Inn offers a complimentary breakfast.

Use your first morning in Mount Dora to slowly explore the grounds of the Lakeside Inn. Opened as "The Alexander House," the ten-room inn was originally a popular retreat for bird-watchers, fishermen, and boaters in the late 1800s and early 1900s. The Edgerton family expanded the successful hotel in the 1930s, with a two-wing addition dedicated by winter guest Calvin Coolidge. The new owners have returned the hotel to its original English Tudor splendor of the 1920s and 1930s, when the sultry air would ring with the sound of music and lakeside enjoyment. This is a good time to see some of the many (unoccupied) rooms and to arrange any specific lake-oriented outings at the full-service marina (e.g., fishing or boating).

Walk into downtown Mount Dora proper for lunch and further exploration. You may want to stop by the helpful **Mount Dora Chamber of Commerce** (341 North Alexander Street; 352–383–2165), located in the old train depot, for maps and specific help or recommendations.

LUNCH: Because Mount Dora is such a popular tourist destination, the town features a large array of dining options. Among the many lunch spots popular with local merchants and visitors, the **Palm Tree Grille** (351 North Donnelly Street; 352–735–1936; moderate) is among the best. Featuring Italian and continental cuisine in a casual atmosphere, the restaurant has seating that allows diners to overlook the bustling shopping atmosphere of Donnelly Street and Fourth Avenue.

Lakeside Inn is the ideal Mount Dora base.

Afternoon

Spend the afternoon strolling and shopping along Mount Dora's several blocks of old buildings. Some of the many interesting shopping stops include **Country Cottage Crafts** (334 North Donnelly Street; 352–735–2722); **Dickens-Reed Bookshop** (140 West 5th Avenue; 352–735–5950); **Double Creek Pottery** (112 East 5th Avenue; 352–735–5579); **When Pigs Fly** (121 Highland Street; 352–735–1555); and many, many others.

The Chamber of Commerce also offers an interesting self-guided historic tour map, with the addresses for a wide variety of interesting historic buildings, including the 1913 **Train Depot** (341 Alexander Street); the 1883 **Lakeside Inn** (100 North Alexander Street); the 1913 **Mount Dora Yacht Club** (351 West 4th Avenue); the 1929 **Community Building** (520 Baker Street); **City Hall** (510 Baker Street); the 1928 **Lawn Bowling Club** (at Donnelly Street and First Avenue); the 1893 **Donnelly House** (Donnelly Street between 5th and 6th Avenues); the 1920s **Princess Gallery Theatre**

(130 West 5th Avenue); the 1928 **Sears Roebuck House** (352 Alexander Street); and many other historic homes and other buildings. You'll easily spend the entire afternoon browsing around town.

DINNER: The **Gables Restaurant** (322 Alexander Street; 352–383–8993; moderate to expensive) is surely one of the county's and area's best gourmet restaurants. With a Victorian garden setting and traditional American fare, this restaurant on its own is worth the trip to Mount Dora.

LODGING: Lakeside Inn.

Evening

Contact the **IceHouse Theatre** (1100 North Unser Street; 352–383–4616) to see if they have any current shows.

DAY 3

Morning

BREAKFAST: Lakeside Inn.

There are many ways to enjoy the water part of the Mount Dora area. Lake and canal tour companies include **Lakeside Inn** (100 North Alexander Street; 352–383–4101 or 800–556–5016); **Dora Canal Tours and Heritage Lake Tours** (Palm Gardens, Tavares; 352–343–4337); and **Rusty Anchor** (400 West 4th Avenue; 352–383–3933).

LUNCH: For something very different, be sure to eat at least once at **Eduardo's Station** (100 East 4th Avenue; 352–735–1711; inexpensive to moderate). This Mexican-American cantina offers a casual open-air atmosphere as well as creative or traditional Mexican cuisine. The friendly staff make this a fun place to eat.

Afternoon

Whether or not you like to shop, you'll really enjoy **Renninger's Antique Center** (US 441 West; 352–383–8393). This 115-acre facility includes two separate air-conditioned structures. One building is a huge 40,000-square-foot Antique Center and the other one houses an active weekend Farmer's & Flea Market with more than 700 merchants. This is a popular regional weekend attraction.

Take US 441 back to the Orlando area.

THERE'S MORE

Other sightseeing attractions: History buffs will enjoy the small local museum at the **Royellou Museum** (450 Royellou Lane; 352–383–0006; entrance fee), while outdoors buffs will head for **Palm Island Park** (Tremain Street and Liberty Avenue; no phone) and **Wekiwa Springs State Park** (Wekiwa Springs Road, Apopka; 407–884–2009; entrance fee).

SPECIAL EVENTS

February. Annual Art Festival, sponsored by the Mount Dora Center for the Arts; (352) 383–0880.

April. Mount Dora Festival of Music and Literature; (352) 383–2165.

May. IceHouse Theater, summer season opens; (352) 383–4616.

June. Weekend antiques fairs, Renninger's Antique Center, runs through November; (352) 383–8393.

September. IceHouse Theater. Fall and winter season opens; (352) 383–4616.

October. Mount Dora Bicycle Festival. Celebrates everything on two wheels; (352) 383–2165.

Mount Dora Crafts Fair; (352) 383–2165.

December. Christmas festivities. Tree lighting, concert, walking tour, lighted boat parade, and home tours; (352) 383–2165.

OTHER RECOMMENDED RESTAURANTS AND LODGINGS

Along with the Lakeside Inn, the Mount Dora area features many smaller B&B-style accommodations options, including **Darst Victorian Manor** (495 West Old Highway 441; 352–383–4050; moderate); **Christopher's Inn** (539 Liberty Avenue; 352–383–2244; inexpensive); **Farnsworth House** (1029 East 5th Avenue; 352–735–1894; inexpensive); and **The Emerald Hill Inn** (27751 Lake Jem Road; 352–383–2777; inexpensive to moderate).

Other dining options in downtown Mount Dora include the **Park Bench Restaurant** (116 East 5th Avenue; 352–383–7004; moderate) and **Windsor Rose English Tea Room** (144 West 4th Avenue; 352–735–2551; inexpensive).

FOR MORE INFORMATION

Mount Dora Chamber of Commerce, 341 North Alexander Street, Mount Dora, FL 32757. (352) 383–2165.

ORLANDO

North Central Florida

THE ORIGINAL FLORIDA

2 NIGHTS

Quaint lodging • Antiquing • Outdoor activities • Driving tour

Much of north central Florida seems to have stopped in an earlier decade, and that's just fine with visitors and residents. This is certainly true in Micanopy and the surrounding area, providing a perfect base for antiquing, outdoors possibilities, or simply relaxing.

Whether you're visiting for a peaceful getaway or using Micanopy or another small town as a base to thoroughly explore what tourism officials (aptly) call "Original Florida," you'll find a perfect introduction to another side of the Sunshine State.

DAY 1

Afternoon

The quickest route to Micanopy and the Original Florida is to take the Florida Turnpike north to I–75. Head north to the Micanopy exit, just south of Gainesville. A prettier and more peaceful way, in keeping with this escape, is to take US 441 north all the way to Micanopy, passing through quaint towns like Mount Dora, Ocala, and many others along the way. This provides a perfect prelude to the escape.

DINNER: Just 8 miles south of Micanopy in Orange Lake, **Rocky's Villa** (US 441; 352–591–1809; moderate) provides an interesting culinary outing. The owner is Italian and the chef is Mexican, so the menu features an assortment

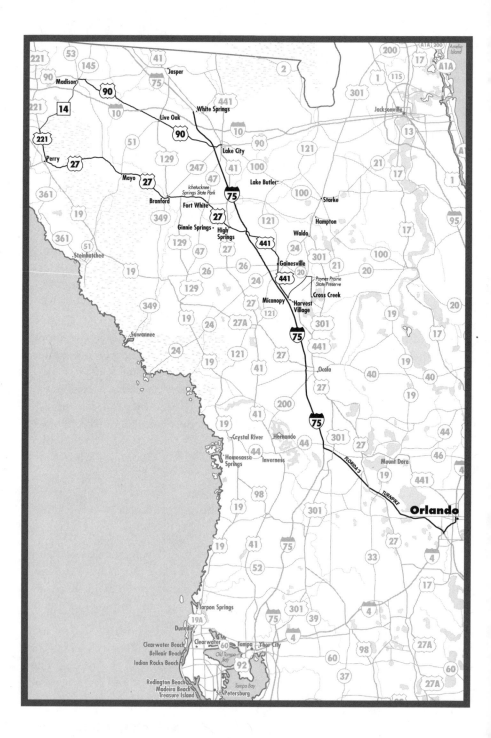

of creative (and ever-changing) dishes from both Italy and Mexico. It's a favorite for guests of The Herlong Mansion.

LODGING: The Herlong Mansion (Cholokka Boulevard; 352–466–3322; moderate) is a renovated oasis from an earlier era. The original two-story mid-Victorian house was built around 1845, with a detached kitchen connected to the house by a covered walkway. In 1910, this original structure was encased within a brick Classic Revival imitation of a Southern Colonial design. The history of the Herlong family can be found throughout the house. The rest is living history available for all to enjoy.

Four huge two-story Corinthian columns immediately draw the visitor into the warmth of the inn. The verandas on both floors, complete with rocking chairs and porch swings, are a further draw. Once inside, innkeeper Sonny Howard reminds guests that they should behave during their stay at The Herlong Mansion as if it were their own home or the home of a close friend. This truly is a side of "Original Florida" that you won't find in big cities or chain hotels.

Sonny completely renovated the house and the rooms, adding many modern amenities without changing the flavor of the building. He now offers twelve different accommodations possibilities. The Herlong Suite is typical with a king-size canopy bed, a fireplace with gas logs, a sitting room, a large original tile bathroom, and French doors opening onto the veranda.

Some of the other widely varied options include Amber's Suite (tub for two, fireplace, private porch); Mae's Room (king-size canopy bed); Pink's Room (two antique double cast-iron beds); Brother's Room (antique brass and copper bed, private rear sitting porch); Inez's Suite (elegant sitting area, hot tub in an alcove with leaded-glass windows); and several more moderately priced choices. Incredibly, Sonny has also renovated two nearby outbuildings as wonderful little cottages. Wherever you stay, you'll feel like you're home.

In keeping with the homelike atmosphere, complimentary refreshments are available in the huge kitchen refrigerator. Cookies and fruit await famished explorers on the buffet. In the evening, a complimentary after-dinner drink brings a pleasant end to the day. The rooms don't feature television, but there is a TV and VCR in the music room, where many visitors enjoy watching videos of *Cross Creek* and *Doc Hollywood*, which were both filmed in and around Micanopy.

The Herlong Mansion in Micanopy offers a perfect Central Florida base.

DAY 2

Morning

BREAKFAST: In the mornings, a gourmet breakfast is served in the dining room, where on any given morning you may have fresh fruit, crepes, warm muffins, and much more. Afterward, Sonny will happily tell historic stories about the house and Micanopy, including some about the mansion's resident ghost, Inez. You'll soon feel like you're part of the Herlong family.

Located just 12 miles south of bustling Gainesville and literally minutes from the speeding vehicles on I–75, Micanopy is the oldest inland town in Florida. It's located on the site of an old Timucuan Native American village, which was discovered by Hernando de Soto in 1539. The charming tree-lined

Cholokka Boulevard features more than a dozen friendly antiques shops, all located within easy walking distance of The Herlong Mansion. It's a great way to spend part or all of your first morning in the area.

Head back to US 441 and take it north toward Gainesville. Just north of Micanopy, you'll see the turnoff for **Paynes Prairie State Preserve** (Route 2, Box 41; 352–466–3397; fee to enter park grounds). This 21,000-acre preserve is mostly covered by marsh, wet prairie vegetation, and some open water. If you have time on your way to Gainesville or later in your stay, exploration opportunities include ranger-led walks and backpacking trips, a picnic area, horseback riding, biking, an observation tower, and wild herds of bison and horses. If you don't have time to visit the preserve, an observation platform is located north of the entrance just off US 441. You'll get a good overview of the area from here.

US 441 leads right into the college life and culture of Gainesville, home of the University of Florida. Depending on your interests, you may want to visit the **Florida Museum of Natural History** (Museum Road at Newell Drive; 352–392–1721; no entrance fee); the **Samuel P. Harn Museum of Art** (SW 34th Street and Hull Road; 352–392–9826; no entrance fee); bow-hunter Fred Bear's artifacts and trophies at the **Fred Bear Museum** (Fred Bear Drive; 352–376–2411; entrance fee); or the Kanapaha Botanical Gardens (4625 SW 63rd Boulevard; 352–372–4981; entrance fee); or walk around the Union Street area (revitalized shopping and dining), which is a great spot for lunch.

LUNCH: You'll find a variety of dining possibilities just by roaming around the Union Street area, including University Avenue, Main Street, and First and Second Avenues and Streets. For a throwback to downtown dining earlier in the century, head to **Wise's Drugstore** (239 West University Avenue; 352–372–4371; inexpensive). Owned and operated by the Wise family since the 1940s, the soda fountain is a popular place for local businesspeople, politicians, and college students. Grab a stool and order a bowl of homemade soup and a freshly prepared sandwich, topping it off with a milk shake.

Afternoon

Use the afternoon for exploring a little or a lot of the Original Florida. Taking the following driving route will introduce you to much of what the area has to offer, so you can decide where to return for a longer stay. US 441 heads out of Gainesville and up to High Springs, another of the typical towns found in this region.

Like Micanopy, in **High Springs** antique stores abound, but many out-doors enthusiasts also love it, with nearby canoeing, kayaking, hiking, fishing, and springs explorations.

If, like many passersby, you fall in love with High Springs, there are many B&Bs in the area. Outdoors types will also enjoy **Ichetucknee State Park** (Route 2, Fort White; 386–497–2511; entrance fee) for canoeing and tubing on a crystal-clear 13-mile river. In addition, Ginnie Springs is just ten minutes or so west of town.

Ginnie Springs is one of the best springs areas in a region filled with springs. If you're interested in scuba diving, snorkeling, canoeing, tubing, or hiking, head to **Ginnie Springs Resort** (7300 NE Ginnie Springs Road; 386–454–2202 or 800–874–8571; entrance fee) for the afternoon or much longer. The resort features a full-service dive center, rentals, instruction, snor-keling, other watersports and boating, and more than 2 miles of unlimited waterfront camping sites.

Back on US 441 (which connects with US 27 in High Springs), the dri-ving tour of the Original Florida continues northwest up through Branford and Mayo, where you'll find more small-town life and big-time springs. For springs exploration in the area, stop in Branford at **Steamboat Dive Inn** (corner of Routes 27 and 129; 386–935–2283) or **The Dive Shack** (386–935–0246).

Follow US 27 over to Perry, where the historic downtown area is under-going revitalization. Perry, a forestry town, is also the home of the **Forest Capital State Museum & Park** (US 19; 850–584–3227; entrance fee). Here, you'll find a fascinating overview of forestry and the role it has played in the area, as well as a sprawling re-creation of an old Florida-style Cracker home that was transported from a nearby site.

Take US 14 north out of Perry and then turn right on State Route 14 to Madison. The classically beautiful homes in Madison remind visitors that this was once a cotton plantation society. Be sure to visit the **Wardlaw Smith Mansion** (103 North Washington Street; 386–973–2288; entrance fee) to get a feel for life during this era. The town's **19th Century Steam Engine** (Range Street; 850–973–2788; no entrance fee) and the **T. J. Beggs Museum** (106 Range Street; 850–973–6163; no entrance fee) are also of interest.

You're now heading back to Micanopy, so take US 90 east to Live Oak. This small town holds interest because of the **Suwannee County Histori-cal Museum** (208 North Ohio Avenue; 386–362–1776; no entrance fee), which is located in the Old Train Depot. Farther along US 90, as you're heading into Lake City, be sure to stop by the **Florida Sports Hall of Fame** (601 Hall of Fame; 800–FLA–FAME; entrance fee). This unique museum features displays honoring a wide array of athletes associated with the state, including the likes of Chris Evert, Andre Dawson, Jack Nicklaus, Bobby Bowden, Steve Spurrier, and many others. The facility also houses the Florida Tourism Info Center, the state's largest government-operated tourist information center, where you can plan many more escapes throughout the state.

If you have the time and inclination, make the short 10-mile drive north on I–75 to White Springs, where you'll find the **Stephen Foster State Folk Culture Center** (P.O. Drawer G; 386–397–4331; entrance fee). Composer Stephen Foster immortalized Florida's Suwannee River in his 1851 song "Old Folks at Home," which is now the state song. The center contains a large museum, with dioramas depicting many of Foster's songs; the Carillon Tower, with bells playing famous Foster tunes; a Suwannee River Gazebo; a Craft Square; and camping.

You can get back to Micanopy quickly by taking I–75 or take the slow route along US 441 back through Gainesville and on into Micanopy and The Herlong Mansion.

DINNER: Along with The Cottage Cafe, Sonny highly recommends **Wild Flowers Cafe** (US 441; 386–754–1150; moderate), which is just north of Micanopy on US 441. Open for all three meals, the cafe's creative fare features Italian dishes, seafood, and grilled meats. The unusual chili and spaghetti, which is topped with cheese and onion, is one of many highlights.

LODGING: The Herlong Mansion.

DAY 3

Morning

BREAKFAST: The Herlong Mansion.

Midmorning, get directions over to nearby Cross Creek and the **Marjorie Kinnan Rawlings State Historic Site** (State 325; 352–466–3672; fee to enter house). Rawlings was the famed author of *The Yearling* and *Cross Creek,* which were both made into feature films. Her fascinating Cracker-style home and grounds are now open to the public, providing insight into her unique way of life. She lived in Cross Creek from 1928 until her death in 1953. Along with the house and many original furnishings, other highlights include a small orange grove and a short path through a hardwood hammock.

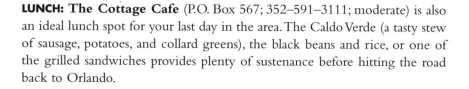

LUNCH: The Cottage Cafe (P.O. Box 567; 352–591–3111; moderate) is also an ideal lunch spot for your last day in the area. The Caldo Verde (a tasty stew of sausage, potatoes, and collard greens), the black beans and rice, or one of the grilled sandwiches provides plenty of sustenance before hitting the road back to Orlando.

Afternoon

Use this time for a more thorough visit to Paynes Prairie State Preserve, Cross Creek, Gainesville, or High Springs.

Take I–75 to the Florida Turnpike back to Orlando or, for a more leisurely pace, use US 441 for a slower drive back to a faster-paced Florida.

THERE'S MORE

Additional driving tour stops: If you have more than two days to explore the area, additional towns you might want to consider for your driving tour include Jasper, Lake Butler, Starke, Waldo, and Hampton.

SPECIAL EVENTS

January. Stephen Foster Day, Stephen Foster State Folk Culture Center, White Springs. Special music programs and carillon recitals; (386) 397–4331.

February. Olustee Battle Festival, Lake City, and Reenactment, Olustee. Commemorates Florida's only major Civil War battle; (386) 752–3690.

March. Gatornationals, Gainesville. Fastest dragsters in the world; (386) 336–7100.

April. Suwannee River Jam, Live Oak. Country music stars for four days; (386) 362–3071.

May. Florida Folk Festival, Stephen Foster State Folk Culture Center, White Springs. Annual three-day celebration of folk songs, music, dance, legends, crafts, and other forms of traditional expression; (386) 397–4331.

July. Independence Day Blow-Out, Jasper. Games, live entertainment, and fireworks; (386) 792–1300.

October. Suwannee River Jam, Fall Gospel Jubilee, and Fall Bluegrass Festival, all in Live Oak. Three of the state's best outdoor music festivals; (386) 362–3071.

Alligator Festival, Lake Festival. Honors Native American heritage; (386) 719–9887.

November. Rural Folklife Days, Stephen Foster State Folk Culture Center, White Springs. Four days of cane grinding, syrup making, lye soap making, quilting, and other farm traditions; (386) 397–4331.

Festival of Lights, Lake City. One of north Florida's most spectacular bazaars and light displays; (352) 758–1555.

OTHER RECOMMENDED RESTAURANTS AND LODGINGS

Micanopy

The **Shady Oak Bed & Breakfast** (203 Cholokka Boulevard; 352–466–3476; moderate) is an excellent Micanopy alternative to The Herlong Mansion. Innkeepers Candy and Mark Lancaster offer five suites in an Old Florida mansion-style house, complete with a screened second-story Florida Room nestled under a 400-year-old live oak.

Gainesville

If you want to use the larger city of Gainesville as your base, B&B-style accommodations can be found at the **Magnolia Plantation Inn** (309 Southeast 7th Street; 352–375–6653; moderate) or the **Sweetwater Branch Inn** (625 East University Avenue; 352–373–6760; moderate).

Other dining options in the revitalized Union Street area include British drink and fare at **Market Street Pub** (120 Southwest 1st Avenue; 352–377–2927; moderate).

High Springs

The staff at **The Great Outdoors Trading Co. & Cafe** (65 Main Street; 386–454–2900) can help with accommodations possibilities in the High Springs area (of course, they can also help with great food and outdoor clothing and gear). B&B possibilities include **The Rustic Inn** (3105 South Main Street; 386–454–1223; moderate) and **Grady House** (420 NW 1st Avenue;

386–454–2206). For house rentals try **Poe Springs River House** (P.O. Box 385; 386–375–8036; moderate).

FOR MORE INFORMATION

The Original Florida, P.O. Box 1300, Lake City, FL 32056-1300. (386) 758–1555.

Citrus County

MOTHER NATURE'S THEME PARK

2 NIGHTS

Outdoor activities • Springs • Scuba diving and snorkeling

They call Citrus County "Mother Nature's Theme Park" for good reason. In a state of famed theme parks, this naturally nature-oriented area is like a theme park and zoo without ticket booths or fences.

Located on the Gulf Coast just ninety minutes from Orlando or Tampa, you can glide along the area's pristine rivers by canoe or pontoon boat; snorkel or dive the crystal-clear springs with the gentle and endangered manatee; and hike, bike, or go horseback riding through lush and tranquil landscapes with birds, deer, and wildlife as your companions. If you just can't get enough of Florida parks, stunning Homosassa Springs State Park provides nature in a more organized setting.

DAY 1

Afternoon

Take Florida's Turnpike to I–75 north for one exit, following SR 44 into the Citrus County area.

DINNER: Fresh seafood reigns here, and there are many excellent choices for dining. For your first night, stay close to Crystal River by heading to either **Cracker's Bar & Grill** (502 NW 6th Street; 352–795–3999; inexpensive to moderate) or **Charlie's Fish House Restaurant** (224 NW US Highway 19;

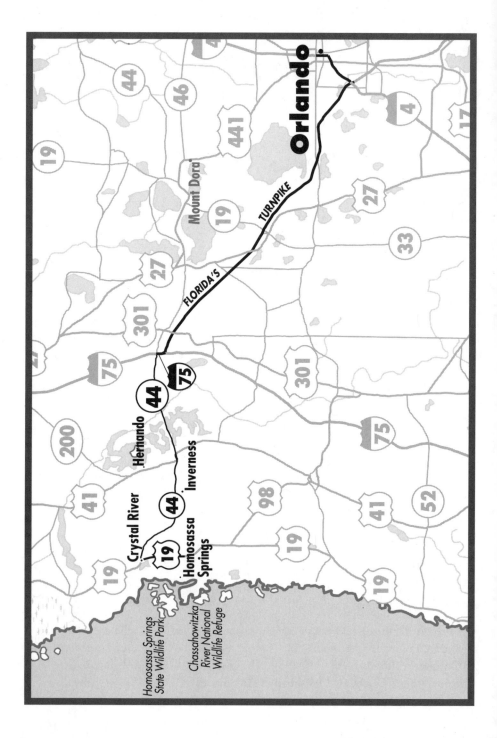

352–795–2468; inexpensive to moderate), both of which offer great seafood and views of the Crystal River. Cracker's is the more informal of the two, but everything is generally informal in Citrus County.

LODGING: Depending on your preferences, there is a wide range of accommodations options in Citrus County. **Plantation Inn and Golf Resort** (9301 West Fort Island Trail; 352–795–4211 or 800–632–6262; inexpensive to moderate) is a perfect example. Overlooking the Crystal River, it is reminiscent of a bygone era, with its Colonial architecture and Southern charm. Lodging choices range from standard double rooms to patio rooms, suites, and golf-course villas. The resort offers a wide range of outdoor activities on and off the property.

Evening

Residents and visitors rise early to enjoy the outdoors, so that means they generally go to bed early and there is relatively little nightlife. The Plantation Inn or one of the other area resorts may have live entertainment on weekends, so it's worth checking. Depending on the time of sunset, the Plantation Inn and other companies often offer evening and sunset boat tours.

DAY 2

Morning

BREAKFAST: Plantation Inn.

The Plantation Inn has its own diving and snorkeling outfitter at **Plantation Inn Marina** (9301 West Fort Island Trail; 352–795–5797), so you may want to stop by there or one of the other area dive shops to check on snorkeling or diving (if you're certified) opportunities in the Crystal River. Crystal County's crystal-clear spring-fed waters are constantly pleasant (around 70 degrees Fahrenheit) and often feature manatees. These aquatic giants love human interaction and will often nudge you for attention. They're most prevalent from fall to spring, when they're drawn by the warm and peaceful waters. Experienced divers will also enjoy exploring the spring cave systems through one of the many dive operators. Whether you dive or snorkel, it's the perfect introduction to "Nature's Theme Park."

Though US 19/98 in Crystal River may seem very commercialized, the historic downtown area is quite interesting. Stop by the **Citrus County Coastal Heritage Museum** (532 Citrus Avenue; 352–795–1755; entrance fee) in the old City Hall, which includes lots of interesting memorabilia and a diorama of the downtown area in 1927. A self-guided walking tour pamphlet will take you past late-1800s residences, the early-1900s depot, and 1920s commercial buildings.

LUNCH: Head down US 19/98 toward Homosassa Springs, turning right onto West Halls River Road just before town. Look for **K. C. Crump's** and **Ramshackle Cafe On The River** (3900 Hall's River Road; 352–628–1500; inexpensive to moderate) on the left. Located directly on the Homosassa River, this fine dining establishment and outdoor cafe is a great place to eat right on the river. This one-time fishing lodge has been renovated and expanded to become a very popular restaurant anytime of day. Though dinner here can be a special event, it's especially pleasant to enjoy Homosassa River activity outdoors, with a fresh grouper sandwich or other local fare an ideal choice.

Afternoon

Head back up West Halls River Road, taking a right toward the well-signed **Homosassa Springs State Wildlife Park** (4150 South Suncoast Boulevard; 352–628–2311; entrance fee). You can also park at the entrance out on US 19/98, taking an interesting introductory pontoon boat tour to the other park entrance. This state park is a showcase of native Florida wildlife, offering visitors a rare opportunity to view animals, birds, and plants in their natural setting. Visitors can stroll along unspoiled nature trails and see deer, bear, bobcats, otters, cougars, and birds at close range. Fascinating educational programs are offered daily on manatees, alligators, crocodiles, Florida snakes, and other wildlife. A huge spring, which features a popular floating observatory, is the showcase of the 166-acre park.

While in the southern part of Citrus County, you may also want to visit the **Chassahowitzka River Campground and Recreational Area** (8600 West Miss Maggie Drive; 352–382–2200; no entrance fee), which offers canoe and boat rentals for varied lengths of self-guided tours of the backcountry Chassahowitzka River. Situated near the Chassahowitzka National Wildlife Refuge, this well-managed park is typical of the outdoors opportunities available in the county.

DINNER: For a taste of local landscapes and food, head to **Peck's Old Port Cafe** (39 North Ozello Trail, Crystal River; 352–795–2806; inexpensive to moderate). Located between Crystal River and Homosassa Springs, 9 miles off US 19/98 on CR 494, Peck's Old Port Cafe is a typical riverfront eatery, with fresh local

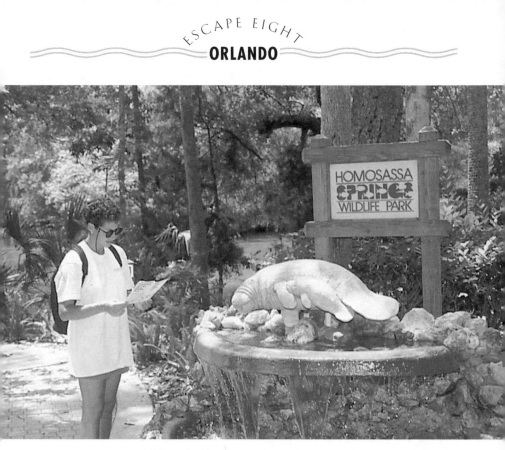

Homosassa Springs Wildlife Park offers an amazing variety of wildlife for your viewing.

seafood featured. Steamed blue crabs (often all-you-can-eat) and soft shell crabs are a specialty here and available all the time (because they farm their own). Other highlights include locally raised catfish, garlic crabs, shrimp, and very friendly service.

LODGING: Plantation Inn.

DAY 3

Morning

BREAKFAST: Plantation Inn.

Head up to the Hernando area and the Citrus Hills development to the fascinating **Ted Williams Museum & Hitters Hall of Fame** (2455 North Citrus Hills Boulevard; 352–527–6566; entrance fee). This fine museum is not only a tribute to the "Splendid Splinter," who now lives (and often fishes) in

Citrus Hills, but it also celebrates baseball and its greatest hitters. Eight galleries house a priceless collection from Ted's career and life, including his first Red Sox contract, actual Fenway Park seats, the largest collection of Ted Williams bats ever assembled in one place, and memorabilia from Ted's wartime and fishing adventures. The "Fenway green" museum is shaped like a baseball diamond and includes rafters like those used at Fenway. There are even life-size dugouts. A wing includes an ongoing tribute to the inductees of the museum's Hitters Hall of Fame.

Before heading back to the Orlando area, stop by Inverness for lunch and some further exploration.

LUNCH: The cute Main Street area around the old courthouse has several excellent restaurants, including seafood and other freshly prepared lunch items at **Stumpknockers** (110 West Main Street; 352–726–2212; inexpensive to moderate).

Afternoon

Historic Inverness is a typical small town and is worth several hours of exploration. The highlight of the downtown area is the 1912 **Old Citrus County Courthouse,** which is unique for its diagonal placement on Courthouse Square.

Inverness's **Fort Cooper State Park** (3100 South Old Floral City Road; 352–726–0315; entrance fee) was a fort built during the Second Seminole Indian War. Part of the palisade wall has been reconstructed, and a battle reenactment is staged during Fort Cooper Days each April. It's also a popular recreation site, with hiking along 5 miles of self-guided nature trails, lake swimming, and canoe rentals.

The **Withlacoochee State Trail** (12549 State Park Drive, Clermont; 352–394–2280; no entrance fee), a 46-mile linear state park under the Florida Rails-to-Trails program, also runs through Inverness, making it easy to try a short walk or bike ride. Hikers and cyclists use the concrete path, while horseback riders enjoy the adjacent trail. It's a great way to end your stay in "Nature's Theme Park."

Take US 44 back to I–10 and Florida's Turnpike into the Orlando area.

THERE'S MORE

Additional sightseeing attractions: The **Crystal River State Archaeological Site** (3400 North Museum Point; 352–795–3817; entrance fee) is the site of six Indian mounds believed to have been started by the Deptford culture and, at 1,600 years (200 B.C. to A.D. 1400), is considered one of the longest continually occupied sites in Florida. **Yulee Sugar Mill Ruins State Historic Site** (West Yulee Drive in Old Homosassa; 352–795–3817; no entrance fee) includes the preserved ruins of an original boiler, chimney, and mill machinery. Located across the street, the **Old Mill House Gallery and Printing Museum** (10466 West Yulee Drive; 352–628–1081; entrance fee) tells the story of printing from Gutenberg through the early 1900s.

Snorkeling and diving: American Pro Dive (821 SE US 19/98, Crystal River; 352–563–0041); **Birds Under Water** (320 NW Highway 19, Crystal River; 352–563–2763); **Crystal Lodge Dive Center** (525 NW 7th Avenue, Crystal River; 352–795–6798); **Crystal River Manatee Dive Tour** (267 NW 3rd Street, Crystal River; 352–795–1333); **Plantation Inn Marina** (9301 West Fort Island Trail, Crystal River; 352–795–5797); and **Port Hotel & Marina** (1610 SE Paradise Circle West, Crystal River; 352–795–7234).

Boating and fishing: Captain Mike's Fishing World (501 South Craig, Homosassa; 352–628–4207); **Chassahowitzka River Campground and Recreational Area** (8600 West Miss Maggie Drive; 352–382–2200); **Chassahowitzka River Tours** (P.O. Box 2455, Homosassa Springs; 352–382–0837); **Crystal Lodge Dive Center** (525 NW 7th Avenue, Crystal River; 352–795–6798); **Crystal River Manatee Dive Tour** (267 NW 3rd Street, Crystal River; 352–795–1333); **Larry Barnes Sportfishing** (5300 South Cherokee Way, Homosassa; 352–628–2922); **MacRae's of Homosassa** (5300 South Cherokee Way, Homosassa; 352–628–2922); **Manatee Campground Marina & Pub** (10175 West Fishbowl Drive, Homosassa; 352–628–5337); **Nature's Resort Marina** (10359 West Halls River Road, Homosassa; 352–628–4344); **Plantation Inn Marina** (9301 West Fort Island Trail, Crystal River; 352–795–5797); **Port Hotel & Marina** (1610 SE Paradise Circle West, Crystal River; 352–795–7234); **River Safaris** (P. O. Box 800, Homosassa; 352–628–5222); **The Last Resort** (10738 West

Halls River Road, Homosassa; 352–628–7117); and **Wild Bill's Airboat Tours** (12430 East Gulf to Lake Highway, Inverness; 352–726–6060).

Horseback riding: Clearview Farm (1150 East Allegrie Drive, Inverness; 352–344–1171); **Happy Tree Training Farm** (519 North O'Brien Point, Lecanto; 352–746–2016); and **Oak Isle Farm Incorporated** (7233 East Oak Isle Drive, Inverness; 352–637–4499).

SPECIAL EVENTS

Unless otherwise noted, for all events, call (352) 527–5222 or (800) 587–6667.

February. Florida Manatee Festival, Crystal River. Fine arts, crafts, entertainment, and seafood.

Homosassa Antique and Classic Car Show.

March. Citrus County Fair. Six days of prizes, rides, and entertainment.

Fort Cooper Days, Inverness. Reenactment of the skirmish between the First Georgia Battalion of Volunteers and the Seminole Indians that took place during the Second Seminole War; (352) 726–0315.

May. Olde Town Patriotic Evening, Inverness. Pre-July 4th celebration.

June. Homosassa River Raft Race. Anything that floats.

July. Family Freedom Festival, Crystal River.

August. Ramblin' River Raft Race, Crystal River. Naturally powered boats.

October. Heritage Village Scarecrow Festival, Crystal River. Fall celebration at shops and restaurants.

Fall Arts and Crafts Show, Homosassa Springs State Wildlife Park; (352) 628–2311.

November. Festival of the Arts, Courthouse Square, Inverness.

Homosassa Arts, Crafts, and Seafood Festival. One of the county's largest events.

December. Floral City Heritage Days. Celebrates the nineteenth-century birth of the town, and its citrus and phosphate history, with a parade, food, crafts, period costumes, and displays.

Christmas boat parades, Homosassa and Crystal River.

Celebration of Lights, Homosassa Springs State Wildlife Park. Popular lighting of the park; (352) 628–2311.

OTHER RECOMMENDED RESTAURANTS AND LODGINGS

If the Plantation Inn is full or you want a more traditional hotel option in Crystal River, the **Best Western Crystal River Resort** (614 NW US 19/98; 352–795–3171; inexpensive), also with its own dive shop and marina, is an ideal choice. Other Crystal River options include **Captain's Inn-Crystal River** (2380 NW US 19/98; 352–795–2111; inexpensive); **Kings Bay Lodge** (506 NW 1st Avenue; 352–795–2850; inexpensive); **Pirate's Cove Resort** (409 North Pirate Point; 904–563–2710; inexpensive); and **Port Paradise Resort** (1610 SE Paradise Circle; 352–795–3111 or 800–443–0875 {Florida only}; inexpensive).

Down in the Homosassa area, the **Howard Johnson Riverside Inn Resort** (5297 South Cherokee Way; 352–628–2474; inexpensive to moderate) is a perfect choice, overlooking the river and its own marina. Log cabin-style rooms and efficiencies on the Homosassa River are fun at **MacRae's of Homosassa** (5300 Cherokee Way; 352–628–2602; inexpensive).

Other Citrus County options include the Victorian-style **Crown Hotel** (109 North Seminole Avenue; 352–344–5555; inexpensive) in historic downtown Inverness and fishing camp cabins on Lake Henderson at **Watson's Fish Camp** (4195 East Parson's Point Road; 352–726–2225; inexpensive).

FOR MORE INFORMATION

Citrus County Tourist Development Council, 801 SE US 19, Crystal River, FL 34429. (352) 527–5222 or (800) 587–6667.

Steinhatchee

A NATURAL ESCAPE

2 NIGHTS

Steinhatchee Landing Resort • Quiet Gulf lifestyle
Outdoor activities

The northwest central Gulf Coast is a throwback to an earlier Florida, when fishing for seafood rather than tourists was (and is) a way of life. Called Florida's "Nature Coast" and "Original Florida," towns like Steinhatchee are quiet, friendly, and outdoors oriented. It's a far cry from the masses and mass-produced entertainment of some other areas in Florida.

Don't come here expecting bright lights and big cities. Small communities like Steinhatchee have a relaxed feel to them, where people have time to talk, walk, and enjoy the outdoors. Accommodations at Steinhatchee Landing Resort serve to enhance this feeling.

DAY 1

Afternoon

Take the Florida Turnpike out of Orlando to I–75 north. Then take US 27 Alternate north to US 19 north. The turnoff for Steinhatchee will be up about 40 miles on the left.

DINNER AND LODGING: Steinhatchee Landing Resort (P.O. Box 789; 352–498–3513; moderate to expensive) is reason enough to head to Steinhatchee for an escape to another Florida. This unique Victorian cottage community, developed by transplanted Georgian Dean Fowler, features unique

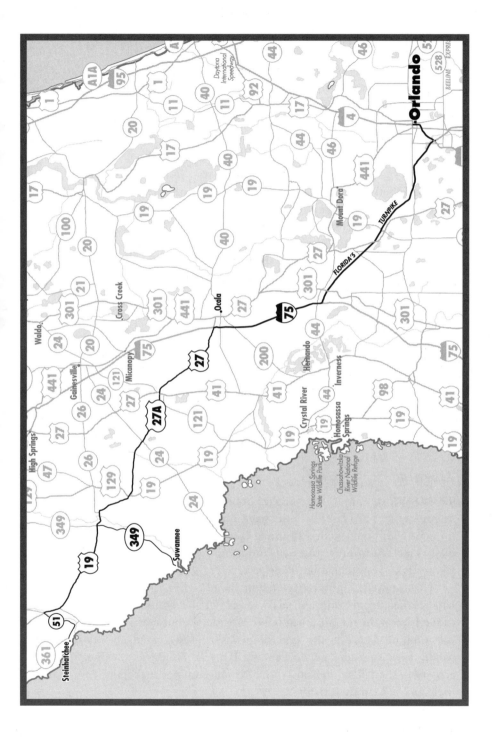

homelike accommodations throughout the property. Located on the peaceful Steinhatchee River, Steinhatchee Landing Resort offers a total of twenty-three one- and two-bedroom freestanding two-story houses; two-bedroom condominiums and townhouses; and three-bedroom houses (one of which former president Jimmy Carter and his family used as a retreat).

All of the cottage accommodations feature full kitchens and modern amenities. The quiet and slow pace is accentuated by a proliferation of screened porches, canoeing opportunities at your front door, bicycles, walking paths and footbridges, horses, several pools, and a health spa. Dean and his staff serve as friendly hosts and can help with any arrangements throughout the Steinhatchee area, including fishing, boating, bike trips, carriage rides, and much more.

For dinner on the first night, try **Fiddler's Restaurant** (Riverside Drive; 352–498–7427) for fresh seafood, steaks, spicy ribs, and more.

Evening

After dinner at Fiddler's, there's little to do in Steinhatchee beyond strolling around the resort and the area, enjoying the river, and sitting on your porch listening to the sounds of a night in the country. On this night or another night during your stay, be sure to arrange a trip out on the Steinhatchee Landing pontoon boat to enjoy a marvelous Gulf sunset.

DAY 2

Morning

BREAKFAST: Be sure to buy supplies from one of the local convenience stores so you can fix breakfast in your cottage. There's nothing better than sitting out on your own porch with a steaming cup of coffee. If your idea of a vacation doesn't include making your own coffee or breakfast, head up to the Welcome Center for a continental breakfast.

The outdoors options abound in Steinhatchee, and the staff at Steinhatchee Landing Resort can arrange any of the options outlined above. A canoe trip on the Steinhatchee River provides an outstanding introduction to the stunning nature in the area (drop-offs are easily arranged, and then you paddle back to Steinhatchee Landing Resort). Fishing is the most popular activity in the fall, winter, and spring. Come summer, scalloping reigns as the most enjoyed family activity.

Steinhatchee Landing Resort's cottages provide perfect accommodations.

LUNCH: Again, a freshly prepared meal back in your cottage is the most popular midday choice. You can also prepare a picnic to carry in your canoe, for enjoyment on the river.

Afternoon

A lazy afternoon on the river is an ideal way to spend time in Steinhatchee. Outdoors excursions or something as simple as reading a book are among the easy options. The Steinhatchee Landing Resort's staff can also recommend short excursion possibilities to other small towns, including Keaton Beach and Horseshoe Beach, where life is even simpler and quieter than "bustling" Steinhatchee.

DINNER: Steinhatchee's most popular local restaurant is called **Roy's Restaurant** (Highway 51; 352–498–5000; moderate). Roy's specializes in whatever seafood happens to be fresh as well as many other fish options. Entrees come with a good salad bar and lots of local flavor. A visit to Steinhatchee wouldn't be complete without a meal or two at Roy's (also open for breakfast and lunch).

LODGING: Steinhatchee Landing Resort.

Evening

Except for spectacular sunsets, evenings are quiet in this area.

DAY 3

Morning

BREAKFAST: In your cottage or up at the Welcome Center.

Use your last morning (if you're smart, you're staying for more than two nights) to simply enjoy the peace and quiet of this small river cottage community. There aren't too many places like this left in Florida. Before checking out, be sure to get directions down to Suwannee for a visit on the way back to Orlando.

Like Steinhatchee, Suwannee is another one of those quiet Gulf coastal towns. It's easily reached by taking US 19 back south to Old Town and then turning right on State 349 for the short drive out to Suwannee.

LUNCH: You'll probably arrive in this small fishing village around lunchtime, so head right to the **Salt Creek Shellfish Co.** (Highway 349; 352–542–7072; moderate). Located right on Salt Creek, with tables outside and inside, this local seafood spot offers huge fried combination dinners (choices of scallops, shrimp, oysters, gator tail, crab fingers, softshell crab, crab cakes, fish, and quail). Steamer pots of oysters, crabs, shrimp, or in-season stone crab claws are also popular. On a cool day, the oyster stew is hard to beat.

Afternoon

Take a drive around Suwannee. Of particular interest is **Miller's,** located right on the water. This bustling business includes unique houseboat rentals, fishing cabins, and camping. The houseboats are very popular, allowing up to eight people to explore and live on the Suwannee River. The 44-foot fully equipped houseboats allow you to cruise up to 70 miles up the Suwannee in style. Along with other accommodations options, the friendly staff at Miller's can help with any other fishing, boating, or outdoors pursuit you have in the Suwannee area.

Take State 349 back to US 19 south, which leads to US 27 to Ocala. At Ocala, take I–75 south to the Florida Turnpike and the short drive back to Orlando.

THERE'S MORE

Additional sightseeing attractions: Steinhatchee provides a good Gulf base for short excursions into the rest of the area. Some good day-trip destinations include the aforementioned Keaton Beach, Horseshoe Beach, and Suwannee; the Cedar Keys National Wildlife Refuge (16450 NW 31st Place, Chiefland, FL 32626; 352–493–0238); the inland historic towns of Perry or Live Oak; or any one of seven nearby state parks (upon request, Steinhatchee Landing provides free state park passes and guides).

SPECIAL EVENTS

Besides occasional special events at Steinhatchee Landing Resort, there aren't many major happenings in this quiet section of Florida.

OTHER RECOMMENDED RESTAURANTS AND LODGINGS

Steinhatchee

Also owned by Steinhatchee Landing Resort, the **Steinhatchee River Inn** (P.O. Box 828; 352–498–4049; inexpensive) provides a less expensive hotel-like experience right in town and across the street from the water. There are seventeen modern hotel suites.

Suwannee

Miller's (P.O. Box 280; 352–542–7349 or 800–458–BOAT; inexpensive to moderate), described above, provides houseboat rentals on the Suwannee River, fishing cabins, and camping. The houseboats provide a particularly unique option, and the Miller family serves as ideal hosts.

FOR MORE INFORMATION

The Original Florida, P.O. Box 1300, Lake City, FL 32056-1300. (352) 758-1555.

Tallahassee

A CAPITAL ESCAPE

2 NIGHTS

State and city history • Surrounding outdoor activities

Many people are surprised to learn that Tallahassee is the capital of the Sunshine State. Its northern location and size make the city a strange choice for the state's capital. But history shows us that Tallahassee was the logical choice in 1824 because it was located between the state's largest cities (at the time) of St. Augustine and Pensacola. This was before Orlando, Miami, and many other cities in South Florida were even a pinpoint on the map.

Today Tallahassee is a moderately sized city that is packed with Florida tradition and history. The city revolves around politics, FSU, and Florida A&M, but visitors can also enjoy many other diversions, including plantation homes, oak-canopied country roads, and lots of outdoor activities. In some ways, the city is a microcosm of what the entire state has to offer.

DAY 1

Afternoon

Take Florida's Turnpike out of Orlando and then head north on I–75 to I–10 west. A more leisurely drive can be found on US 19/98, which heads up the Gulf Coast to the capital.

DINNER: Thanks to the state legislature and other political matters, the historic downtown area offers many excellent dining options. Located along Adams Commons, the duo of **Andrew's Capital Grill and Bar** (228 South Adams

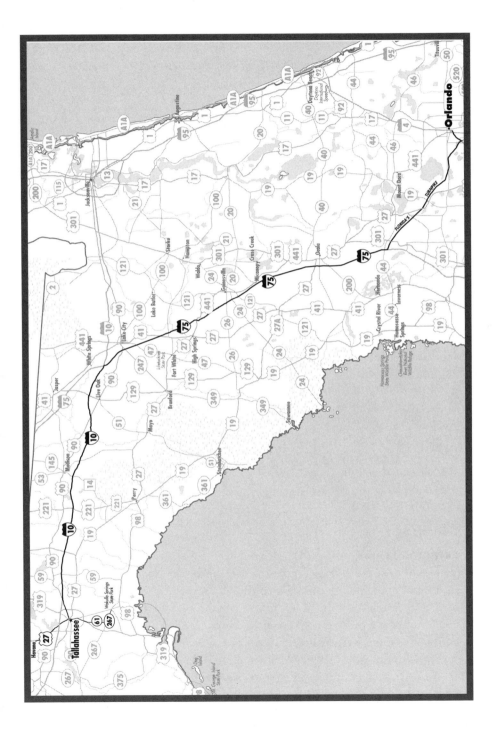

Street; 850–222–2759; moderate to expensive) and **Andrew's 2nd Act Cafe** (228 South Adams Street; 850–222–3444; inexpensive to moderate) have become Tallahassee dining traditions. The upscale 2nd Act features creative cuisine in an elegant atmosphere, while the Grill and Bar offers a wide variety of sandwiches, salads, and soups in a much more casual indoor and outdoor setting (lunch only).

LODGING: If you want to stay right in the heart of the city, **Governors Inn** (209 South Adams Street; 850–681–6855; moderate) on Adams Commons is the perfect choice. Part of the building was once a horse stable, but its present life is as an upscale hotel. Early evening cocktails and an elegantly presented continental breakfast are included in the price. For a treat, reserve one of the eight suites, which are each named for a Florida governor.

Evening

Because it's a college and government town, Tallahassee has a lively cultural and nightlife scene. There's often evening entertainment across Adams Commons at **Andrew's** (228 South Adams Street; 850–222–3444) as well as at the **Comedy Zone** (2900 North Monroe Street; 850–386–1027). For a bit more culture, call about scheduled events at the **Tallahassee Little Theatre** (1861 Thomasville Road; 850–224–8474); **FSU Mainstage** (Call and Copeland Streets, FSU; 850–644–6500); **Tallahassee Symphony Orchestra** (College Avenue and Copeland Street, FSU; 850–224–0462); or the **Tallahassee–Leon County Civic Center** (505 West Pensacola Street; 850–222–0400 or 800–322–3602).

DAY 2

Morning

BREAKFAST: Governors Inn.

Downtown Tallahassee's political and historical attractions are easy to explore on foot. There's a branch of the Tallahassee Area Convention and Visitors Bureau on the north side of the Capitol Complex to get you started. If you'd rather not walk much, the **Old Town Trolley** (850–891–5200) runs continuous loops in the historic downtown area.

The Capitol Complex (400 South Monroe Street) includes the Old Capitol and the New Capitol. Start your tour with the majestic **Old Capitol** (850–488–1673; no entrance fee), built in 1845 (with many changes,

additions, and subtractions since) near the site of the three log cabins that housed the original Florida state legislature in 1824. Excellent self-guided tours are available seven days a week, including a large exhibit outlining the state's history, the old governor's office suite, old House and Senate chambers, and the former Supreme Court chamber.

The contrastingly stark and tall **New Capitol** (850–413–9200; no entrance fee) includes the present House and Senate chambers (viewing galleries available when they're in session) an interesting chapel, and a twenty-second-floor observation deck that provides a great view of the city and surrounding countryside.

Located just across Monroe Street from the Old Capitol, the **Vietnam Memorial,** which honors more than 300,000 Floridians who served in the war, is definitely worth a visit.

It's a short drive or pleasant moderate walk out to the **Florida Governor's Mansion** (700 North Adams Street; 850–488–4661; no entrance fee), which features guided tours only in the spring from 10:00 A.M. to noon on Mondays, Wednesdays, and Fridays but is still worth a look at any time. The mansion was built in 1957 and was patterned after Andrew Jackson's Tennessee home, the Hermitage. The interesting forty-five-minute tours include the reception room, the dining room, guest bedroom, and gardens.

LUNCH: For lunch in the downtown area, head to **Po' Boys Creole Café** (224 East College Avenue; 850–681–9191; moderate) or **Uptown Café** (111 East College Avenue; 850–222–3253; moderate) for Creole cooking or fresh soups and sandwiches, respectively.

Afternoon

Spend the rest of the day exploring other attractions in the downtown area; the **Park Avenue Historic District** to the north features several historic houses and other buildings of note. The 1843 **Knott House Museum** (301 East Park Avenue; 850–922–2459; entrance fee) is open for tours. Other attractions on Park Avenue include the 1939 **Federal Courthouse** (110 West Park Avenue); **The Columns** (100 North Duval Street and Park Avenue), Tallahassee's oldest house, built in 1830; the 1838 **First Presbyterian Church** (110 North Adams Street and Park Avenue), which is the oldest continuously used church in the state; and the **Old City Cemetery,** which includes the remains of slaves, Civil War soldiers, and 1841 yellow fever victims.

Tallahassee's Governor's Mansion was built in 1957 and was modeled after Andrew Jackson's Tennessee home, the Hermitage.

In the late afternoon, plan a driving tour of one or more of Tallahassee's famed **"Canopy Roads,"** which are essentially oak-lined country roads that are sometimes overgrown so densely that the trees' branches connect to form dramatic canopies. The city's Convention and Visitors Bureau can provide a map of the possibilities, including Old Bainbridge Road, Centerville Road, Old St. Augustine Road, Meridian Road, and Miccosukee Road.

Driving out one of the northern Canopy Roads (e.g., Old Bainbridge Road or Centerville Road) is an ideal choice, in that they'll take you to several area attractions. Out Centerville Road, you'll find **Bradley's Country Store** (Centerville Road, about 8 miles north of I-10; 850-893-1647), an old country store that makes and sells its own sausage, grits, hams, and much more. It's a great place to find a tasty souvenir from your visit.

Located just 12 miles north of downtown Tallahassee on Old Bainbridge Road, the antiquing town of **Havana** is a fun excursion from the city. You'll find lots of shops, galleries, and friendly people. It's also a convenient stop before heading to one of the area's most popular dining choices, Nicholson's Farmhouse.

DINNER: Located on SR 12 just 3 miles out of Havana, **Nicholson's Farmhouse** (SR 12; 850–539–5931; moderate to expensive) is a north-central Florida landmark. This informal set of farmhouses and other buildings features famed huge steaks, chicken, seafood, and much more. When you sit down, you'll get a bowl of boiled peanuts for starters. There are wagon rides on weekends, when reservations are highly recommended.

LODGING: Governors Inn.

DAY 3

Morning

BREAKFAST: Governors Inn.

The area surrounding Tallahassee has a wide range of outdoors-oriented possibilities. One of the best outings is down to **Wakulla Springs State Park** (State Road 61 and 267; 850–922–3632; entrance fee), located just 12 miles south of the city. This lush 2,900-acre park includes a crystal-clear spring system, hiking, biking, swimming, and very interesting glass-bottom boat tours that typically feature alligators, birds, and lots of other tropical fauna and flora.

LUNCH: Wakulla Springs State Park also features the **Wakulla Springs Lodge** (1 Springs Drive; 850–224–5950; moderate), a Spanish-style lodge that has twenty-seven rooms and the large Ball Room restaurant, which serves Southern-style food in a spacious dining room that has a huge stone fireplace and nice views of the springs. There's also a cafe with a huge marble counter.

Afternoon

Other outdoors opportunities abound, including biking or in-line skating along the paved 16-mile **Tallahassee–St. Marks Historic State Trail** (904–656–0001) or canoeing and hiking in the **Apalachicola National Forest** (Route 6; 904–926–3561; no entrance fee).

Enjoy further Tallahassee outdoors opportunities before taking a drive down one of the other Canopy Roads as part of your drive out of town.

Rejoin I–10 or US 19/98 to I–75 and Florida's Turnpike for the drive back to the Orlando area.

THERE'S MORE

Other sightseeing attractions: The **Black Archives Research Center and Museum** (Martin Luther King Jr. Boulevard and Gamble Street; 850–599–3020; no entrance fee) includes one of the nation's best African-American cultural collections. Other museum possibilities include the **Florida State University Museum of Fine Arts** (Copeland and Call Streets; 850–644–6836; no entrance fee); **Mary Bragan Museum of Arts and Science** (350 South Duval Street; 850–513–0700); **Foster Tanner Arts Gallery** (Martin Luther King Jr. Boulevard at Osceola Street; 850–599–3161; no entrance fee); **Lemoyne Art Gallery** (125 North Gadsden Street; 850–222–8800; no entrance fee); the **Museum of Florida History** (500 South Bronough Street; 850–488–1484; no entrance fee); and the **Tallahassee Museum of History and Natural Science** (3945 Museum Drive; 850–576–1636; entrance fee).

Archaeological sites: The Tallahassee area was popular with Indians and early Spanish settlers, making it ideal for many archaeological finds and sites, including **San Luis Archaeological and Historic Site** (2020 Mission Road; 850–487–3711; no entrance fee); **DeSoto Archaeological and Historic Site** (1022 DeSoto Park Drive; 850–922–6007; no entrance fee); and **Lake Jackson Mounds State Archaeological Site** (3600 Indian Mounds Road; 850–922–6007; no entrance fee).

SPECIAL EVENTS

March. Annual reenactment, 1865 Natural Bridge battle, San Marcos de Apalache State Historic Site; (850) 922–6007.

Annual Jazz and Blues Festival, The Tallahassee Museum of History & Natural Science; (850) 576–2531.

Springtime Tallahassee. Four weeks of parades, festivals, contests, and crafts; (850) 224–5013.

April. Flying High Circus, Florida State University Big Top. America's first and most prestigious collegiate circus; (850) 644–4874.

July. World's "richest" vintage car race, downtown Tallahassee; (850) 413–9200.

September. Native American Heritage Festival, Tallahassee Museum of History & Natural Science. Canoe sculpting, roof thatching, native arts and crafts, and traditional Indian games; (850) 576–1636.

October. North Florida Fair, North Florida Fairgrounds, Tallahassee; (850) 878–3247.

November. Bradley's Fun Day, Bradley's Country Store, Centerville Road. Delicious homemade sausage, vintage car rides, country crafts, and more down-home fun; (850) 893–1647.

Market Days, North Florida Fairgrounds. More than 380 nationwide artists and craftspeople, live entertainment, and food; (850) 576–2531.

December. Winter on the Farm, Tallahassee Museum of History & Natural Science. Cane grinding, syrup making, and blacksmith demonstrations; (850) 576–1636.

Winter Festival, throughout Tallahassee. Celebration of Lights, twilight parade, Jingle Bell Run, fantasyland, and several stages offering musical and dramatic performances; (850) 891–3866.

OTHER RECOMMENDED RESTAURANTS AND LODGINGS

Other downtown Tallahassee hotel options include the elegant **Radisson Hotel** (415 North Monroe Street; 850–224–6000 or 800–333–3333; moderate) and the well-located **Holiday Inn Capitol Plaza** (850–224–5000 or 800–465–4329; inexpensive to moderate). B&B fans will love the quiet and personal **Calhoun Street Inn Bed and Breakfast** (525 North Calhoun Street; 850–425–5095; inexpensive). If you want to stay outside of town, try the **Killearn Country Club and Inn** (100 Tyron Circle; 850–893–2186; inexpensive) or the previously mentioned **Wakulla Springs Lodge** (1 Springs Drive; 850–224–5950; inexpensive).

Other downtown dining recommendations include French fare at **Chez Pierre** (1215 Thomasville Road; 850–222–0936; moderate); phenomenal lunch buffets and Thai dinner specialties at **Bahn Thai** (1319 South Monroe Street; 850–224–4765; inexpensive to moderate); and huge steaks at **Silver Slipper** (531 Scotty's Lane; 850–386–9366; moderate to expensive), the oldest family-run restaurant in the state. **The Wharf** (1480 Timberlane Road; 850–894–4443; moderate) features fresh seafood in a Florida fishing camp atmosphere; next door, **Mom and Dad's Italian Restaurant** (4175 Apalachee Parkway; 850–877–4518; inexpensive to moderate) features huge servings of Italian specialties and a friendly family atmosphere.

FOR MORE INFORMATION

Tallahassee Area Convention and Visitors Bureau, 106 East Jefferson Street, Tallahassee, FL 32301. (850) 413–9200 or (800) 628–2866.

Apalachicola

OYSTERS AND MORE

2 NIGHTS

Oysters and other fresh seafood • Quiet Gulf atmosphere

The Panhandle is a unique part of Florida, where life is generally quieter and more in tune with the surrounding water and land. Apalachicola and the nearby area provide a perfect introduction.

Apalachicola's claim to fame is the bountiful oyster harvest, but the town has a ton of history, and the nearby barrier islands have some of the best beaches in Florida. You can explore deserted beaches or quaint Gulf towns by day and enjoy perhaps the freshest seafood you'll ever eat at night.

DAY 1

Afternoon

Take Florida's Turnpike to I–75 north and I–10 west to Tallahassee. Then take US 319 and US 98/319 down to Apalachicola. Alternatively, for a more scenic route, take US 19/98 along the Gulf and then US 98 to Apalachicola.

DINNER: For a real introduction to the area, there's simply no better place to start than **Boss Oyster** (125 Water Street; 850–653–9364; moderate). Situated right on the water, this legendary old restaurant offers the most incredible menu of oysters anywhere. Of course, you can just get them raw, roasted (shuck 'em yourself), or steamed, but Boss Oyster also offers baked oysters with various toppings. Examples include Oyster Jalepeño (cheese and chopped jalepeños), Oyster Rockerfella (sauteed spinach, chopped onion,

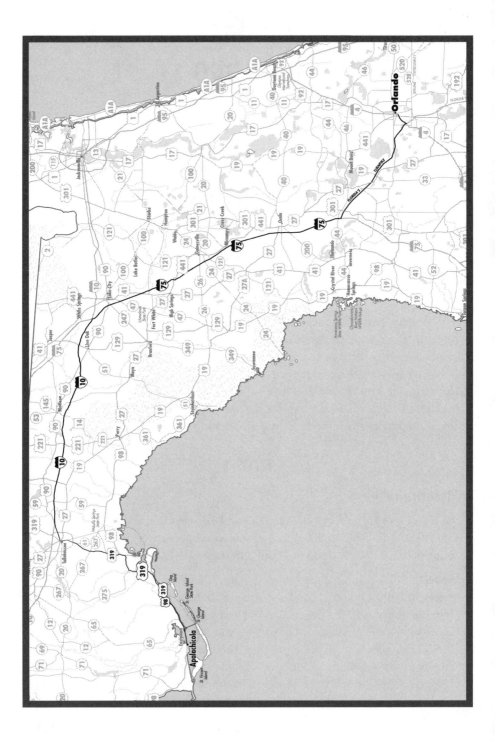

garlic, and cheese), Oyster St. George (asparagus, garlic, shallots, and cheese), Oyster St. Jacob (bay scallops, capers, bacon, and cheese), and many, many more. Other items on this delightful menu include steamed blue crabs, roasted garlic crabs, huge Gulf shrimp, crawfish, gumbo, oyster stew, grouper, platters, pizza (piled with seafood), steak, ribs, and yummy smoked fish dip. This is a tasty way to start your Apalachicola exploration.

LODGING: The **Gibson Inn** (51 Avenue C; 850–653–2191; inexpensive to moderate) is the perfect base for your stay in the Apalachicola area. The large Victorian structure was built in 1907 for visiting seamen. The wraparound porch, which is filled with rockers, leads to a large lobby. Each of the thirty-one rooms is unique in size, shape, color, and furnishings, but all have full baths and TV. The beds are either antique white iron or wooden four-posters.

Evening

In that it's still a working fishing town, Apalachicola is pretty quiet at night. The Gibson Inn has a pleasant bar, or you might want to try the sometimes lively **Roseate Spoonbill Lounge** (123 Water Street; 850–653–8139), located down on the river by Boss Oyster in the Apalachicola River Inn.

DAY 2

Morning

BREAKFAST: The Gibson Inn.

Use your first morning in the area to explore historic Apalachicola, much of which can be done on foot. **The Apalachicola Bay Chamber of Commerce** (99 Market Street; 850–653–9419) can provide an excellent tour map and other information about the area.

The town is filled with old buildings, many of which are now interesting shops and galleries. It's the perfect place for window-shopping or finding that special souvenir. Some shopping possibilities include **Market Street Emporium** (75 Market Street; 850–653–9889); and **Two Gulls** (54 Market Street; 850–653–2727).

For something unusual, the **John Gorrie State Museum** (Avenue D and 6th Street; 850–653–9347; entrance fee) memorializes the invention of an early air conditioner by Dr. John Gorrie, an Apalachicola physician attempting to keep his patient waiting room cool. A replica of that first "cooling machine" can be found in the museum, along with a diorama of the original

waiting room and other local historical items. Gorrie is buried across the street in Gorrie Square.

During your walk, you may also want to visit the **Apalachicola National Estuarine Research Reserve** (Estuarine Walk and Market Street; 850–653–8063; no entrance fee), which includes lots of aquariums with a wide variety of local animal life.

Elsewhere in town, be sure to take a look at the old **Sponge Exchange** building (Avenue D and Commerce Street), an old redbrick cotton warehouse (Avenue E and Water Street), the Greek Revival **Trinity Episcopal Church** (Avenue D and Sixth Street), shady and quiet **Lafayette Park** (Avenue A and Walnut Street), and **Chestnut Street Cemetery** (Avenue E, between 6th and 8th Streets), as well as all of the large old Victorian and Greek Revival houses, many of which have been restored.

LUNCH: Head toward **The Owl Café** (15 Avenue D; 850–653–9888), where seafood, steak, pasta, and an extensive wine list await.

Afternoon

A cruise on Apalachicola Bay is a great way to spend the afternoon, and the *Governor Stone* (71 Market Street; 850–653–8700) is the ideal boat for it. This 1877 Gulf schooner is the perfect setting for learning more about Apalachicola life yesterday and today. If you'd rather spend your time on a boat catching fish, contact **Boss Guide Services** (850–653–8139).

DINNER: For a truly special Apalachicola meal, look no further than the **Magnolia Grill** (Avenue E and 11th Street; 850–653–8000; moderate to expensive). Chef Eddie Cass has taken an 1800s local bungalow and turned it into one of the region's best restaurants. His creations feature fresh seafood and Cajun/Creole-inspired dishes. The seafood gumbo is popular for good reason.

LODGING: The Gibson Inn.

DAY 3

Morning

BREAKFAST: The Gibson Inn.

After a leisurely morning, check out of the Gibson Inn and head out to **St. George Island,** one of several area barrier islands that give the area its unique flavor. Once you reach the island, turn left on State Route 300 and drive past all of the stunning beach houses to **St. George Island State Park** (1900 East Gulf Drive; 850–927–2111; entrance fee). This classic seashore state park features a wonderful 6-mile drive along the Gulf, with high dunes, boardwalks, picnic and shower areas, and deserted beaches among the highlights. Besides one of the top state park campgrounds (which has a nice 5-mile bayside hiking trail), there's little else here, and visitors like it that way.

LUNCH: Back in the center of St. George Island, try the oceanfront **Blue Parrot Oceanside Café** (68 West Gorrie Drive; 850–927–2989; inexpensive to moderate), which, as you can guess, features lots of local seafood and great views. Alternatively, you can buy a pound of steamed shrimp from one of the local vendors or stores and take it down to the beach.

Afternoon

For a unique exploration of St. George Island and the surrounding water, visit **Jeanni's Journeys** (139 East Gorrie Drive; 850–927–3259). Local Jeanni McMillan offers a wide variety of outdoors options, including unique four-hour or eight-hour barrier island boat trips; guided canoe and kayak trips; adult and children's marine experiences; fishing trips; and kayak, canoe, and sailboard rentals. She's the perfect contact for exploring St. George Island.

From St. George Island, take US 98/319 and US 319 back to Tallahassee, joining I–10 to I–75 and Florida's Turnpike back to the Orlando area. Alternatively, for a more scenic route, take US 98 and US 19/98 along the Gulf, before joining I–75 and Florida's Turnpike back to Orlando.

THERE'S MORE

Other barrier islands: Two other barrier islands are now generally preserved as state or national parks. If you like Florida barrier island experiences, you'll love **St. Joseph Peninsula State Park** (County Road 30; 850–227–1327; entrance fee) and **St. Vincent National Wildlife Refuge** (County Road 30A; 850–653–8808; no entrance fee, but reached only by boat).

SPECIAL EVENTS

March. St. George Island Charity Chili Cookoff & Auction. Largest regional chili cookoff in the United States; (850) 927–2753.

St. George Island State Park is one of the finest seashore parks in Florida.

April. Panama City Gold Cup Antique Car Road Race. Finish line at Gibson Inn; (850) 234–2890.

May. Apalachicola's Historic Home Tour; (850) 653–9419.

June. Annual Waterfront Festival, Carrabelle. Arts and crafts booths, food, and entertainment; (850) 697–2585.

November. Florida Seafood Festival, Apalachicola. State's oldest and largest annual marine and seafood spectacle; (888) 653–8051.

OTHER RECOMMENDED RESTAURANTS AND LODGINGS

If the Gibson Inn is full or you'd like a smaller B&B experience, the renovated **Coombs House Inn** (80 6th Street; 850–653–9199; inexpensive to moderate) is another ideal choice. With eight Victorian-style rooms (the owner is an

interior decorator) and a wonderful parlor, this 1905 house provides another perfect Apalachicola base. **The Apalachicola River Inn** (123 Water Street; 850–653–8139; inexpensive) offers a simple and clean motel-like experience with pure Apalachicola friendliness.

If you want to stay out on St. George Island, contact the **St. George Inn** (Causeway Road; 850–927–2903 or 800–332–5196; moderate), where Jack and Barbara Vail offer eight B&B–style rooms that have French doors opening onto the balcony and views of the bay or gulf. If you want to rent a house for a longer stay, consider contacting **Gulf Coast Realty** (HCR Box 90, St. George Island; 850–927–2596 or 800–367–1680; inexpensive to moderate) or one of the other local realtors.

FOR MORE INFORMATION

Apalachicola Bay Chamber of Commerce, 99 Market Street, Apalachicola, FL 32320. (850) 653–9419.

Seaside

A COTTAGE BY THE SEA

2 NIGHTS

Seaside activities • Gulf beaches

Everyone dreams of a cottage by the sea, but too few of us find one. Unlike any other escape in the world, the very special Seaside makes your dream come true, if only for a few nights. This is an escape you have to experience to believe that such a place really exists.

Seaside is a time tunnel in Florida's western Panhandle. Memories of small towns past blend into the present in this small and colorful community of resident and rental cottages. Developed by Robert Davis and planned by famed Miami-based architects Andres Duany and Elizabeth Plater-Zyberk, Seaside was planned so all of the residences are within a quarter-mile of the central square and beach pavilions. Thus people tend to travel by foot or pedal power much more often.

From its first two cottages in 1981, Seaside has grown into the most visual of beachfront towns, with a palette of pastels and an architectural symphony of Victorian, Gothic, antebellum, and postmodern lines. Today there are more than 300 cottages, ranging in size from cozy bungalows to six-bedroom residences. Most of them are available for rental, and many have names (e.g., "Dreamweaver," "Precious," "Goodnight Moon," and "Sea for Two") that reflect their styles and owners' personalities. All are surrounded by white picket fences. Within walking distance, you'll find shopping, dining, and all the other advantages of small-town life.

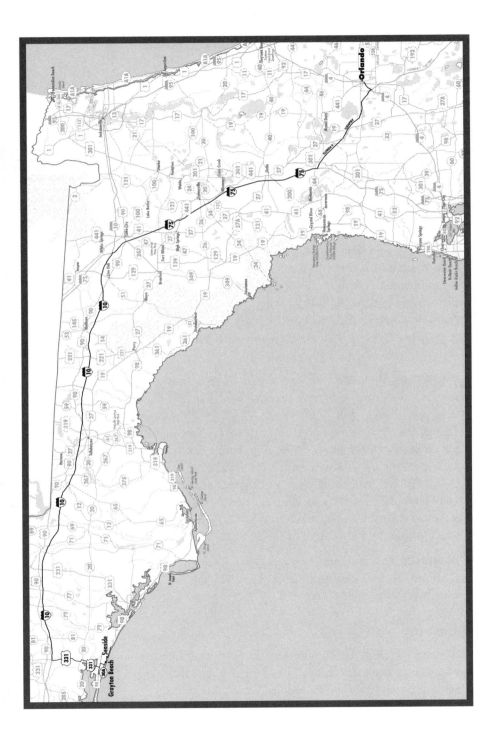

DAY 1

Afternoon

Take Florida's Turnpike out of Orlando to I–75 north and then I–10 west to US 331 south, which leads down to the Gulf Coast's Scenic Route 30A, with Seaside just a few miles to the east. Alternatively, you can take the leisurely route along the coast, utilizing US 19/98 to US 98.

Though the restaurants in Seaside and the surrounding area are excellent, you may want to have a meal or two in your cottage. Before or after check-in, stop by **Modica Market** (Central Square; 850–231–1214), where towering shelves stock every gourmet food imaginable as well as a wide variety of fresh fruits, vegetables, staples, and beverages. Even if you don't plan to use your cottage's kitchen, you'll still enjoy a visit to this market.

You should also rent a bike for your entire stay at Seaside, whether you plan to just cycle around the corner or all around the Panhandle. The **Bike Rentals office** (intersection of Savannah Street and Seaside Avenue; 850–231–2279) has a wide variety of rentals and rental rates, so stop by upon arrival or early the next morning.

DINNER: For the perfect introduction to Seaside dining, there's simply no better place than **Bud & Alley's** (Cinderella Circle; 850–231–5900; moderate to expensive). Opened in 1986, Bud & Alley's is still the landmark restaurant and one of the top dining spots in Florida. The spirit behind this beachfront restaurant is to serve creative food of uncompromising freshness and quality in an unpretentious setting. Hosts Dave Rauschkolb and Scott Witcoski change the menu seasonally and focus on ingredients in the peak of their season, embracing the region by seeking out the finest that local farmers and fishermen can offer. From appetizers and salads to dessert, this restaurant will put you in the right frame of mind for a Seaside stay.

LODGING: You can choose from a wide range of cottages through **Seaside Cottage Rental Agency** (P.O. Box 4730; 800–277–8696; moderate to expensive).

Evening

As can be expected, it's quite quiet in Seaside at night. You'll enjoy taking a bike ride or stroll through the various streets and many alleys, pausing to chat across a picket fence with a resident or another visitor.

Seaside's unique cottages are a highlight for all visitors.

DAY 2

Morning

BREAKFAST: In your cottage or at **Modica Market** (Central Square; 850–231–1214; moderate).

Seaside is a walking or leisurely biking town, so use your first morning to explore by foot or on two wheels. The architecture, beach, water, and other visual attractions soothe the senses in a way only small-town seaside living can. Along with using one of many town maps available, serious Seaside explorers will want to stop by **Sundog Books** (Central Square; 850–231–5481), which carries several excellent Seaside books with walking tour descriptions. This should take the better part of your morning, but if it doesn't, just head to the beach through one of many pavilion boardwalk passageways. **Cabana Man** (George's Gorge; 850–231–5046) rents beach chairs, umbrellas, kayaks, and more.

LUNCH: Walk or ride to lunch at **Cafe Spiazzia** (Obe District; 850–231–1297; inexpensive to moderate), an Italian-style neighborhood cafe with fresh subs, salads, pizza by the slice, gelato, and espresso, or **Shades** (Central Square; 850–231–1950; moderate), a casual neighborhood eatery right in the middle of things.

Afternoon

You'll probably want to spend more time just exploring the intricacies of Seaside life. Each street and footpath seems to lead to something special visually, but other diversions include **shopping** (Downtown Seaside Association; 850–231–5424) around Ruskin Place, Central Square, and across the street by the beach. Some of the many unique shopping possibilities include tropical watercolors and Seaside prints at **Cara Roy Artworks** (Ruskin Place; 850–231–2535); contemporary crafts at **Newbill Collection By The Sea** (Ruskin Place); Seaside memorabilia at **Sue Vaneer's of Seaside** (Four Corners; 850–231–2497); fun clothing and toys at **4KIDS** (Four Corners; 850–231–1733); original watercolors, prints, and notecards of Seaside and the area at **Artz by Donna Burgess** (Piazza Nancy Drew; 850–231–5781); and eclectic women's clothing at **Per-spi-cas-ity** (Open-Air Market; 850–231–5829).

DINNER: Take a short drive up to the small town of Grayton Beach, where another jewel of Gulf Coast dining awaits. Quite simply, **Picolo Restaurant & The Red Bar** (70 Holz Avenue, Grayton Beach; 850–231–1008; moderate) is one of the most creative restaurants in North Florida. Philippe Petit has fashioned an unusual setting, with lots of candlelight, red lights, posters, and much more. You have to see it to appreciate it, and the restaurant and bar's popularity attests to the attraction. The food doesn't play second fiddle to the atmosphere, however, with a small list of changing specials written simply on a blackboard. This restaurant is a real treat and well worth the short drive from Seaside.

LODGING: Seaside.

Evening

Picolo Restaurant & The Red Bar (70 Holz Avenue, Grayton Beach; 850–231–1008) features some sort of entertainment every night and is often open quite late for a widely varied crowd of locals and visitors.

DAY 3

Morning

BREAKFAST: Your Seaside cottage or **Studio 210** (Ruskin Square; 904–231–3720; moderate).

This morning ride your bike west on 30A or drive the short distance (less than a mile) to **Grayton Beach State Recreation Area** (Route 2, Box 6600, Grayton Beach; 904–231–4210; entrance fee). This fabulous 356-acre oceanfront park features several interesting hammock and dune nature trails, a spectacular beach, swimming, and canoe rentals on an inland lake. It's a great way to spend a quiet morning.

LUNCH: You can continue riding or driving back into the town of Grayton Beach, or you can simply walk about a half-mile west along the beach to reach it as well. Eating lunch upstairs (inside or outside) at **D & K's Corner Cafe** (63 Holz Avenue; 850–231–0455; moderate) is well worth the trek. With great views of town and the Gulf of Mexico, this Grayton Beach classic offers a wide array of fresh sandwiches, salads, and seafood.

Afternoon

Make your way back to Seaside for any additional walking, biking, or shopping you haven't been able to complete during your stay. It's all right outside your own cottage by the sea.

Take US 331 back north to I–10 east over to I–75 south and Florida's Turnpike back into the Orlando area. Alternatively, you can take the leisurely route along the coast, utilizing US 98 to US 19/98.

THERE'S MORE

Other sightseeing attractions: If exploring by foot and bike aren't quite your style, some excellent nearby outings include the lakefront Victorian town of **Defuniak Springs** (850–892–3191); the typical large beach resort activities of **Panama City Beach** (850–233–6503 or 800–PC–BEACH); and quieter beach towns around **Fort Walton Beach** and **Destin** (850–651–7131 or 800–322–3319).

SPECIAL EVENTS

Information for all Seaside events is available by calling the Downtown Seaside Association at (850) 231–5424.

April. Via Colori Italian Street Painting Festival. Adds even more color to the streets of Seaside.

March. Easter egg hunt and bunny visit, Village Green.

May. Spring Wine Festival. Special tastings, food, lectures, and entertainment. Memorial Day Concert.

June. Sunset Serenade Concert series, the Amphitheater. Continues through August.

Outdoor Summer Films series, the Amphitheater. Continues through August.

July. Parades, children's activities, and fireworks for July 4th.

September. Foreign Films series.

October. Foreign Films series.

Seaside Yard Sale, the Amphitheater.

November. Antique Car Show.

Fall Wine Festival. Tastings, food, lectures, and entertainment.

December. Christmas Parade and tree lighting ceremony, Cinderella Circle.

OTHER RECOMMENDED RESTAURANTS AND LODGINGS

Along with the renowned cottages, Seaside also features **Josephine's French Country Inn at Seaside** (101 Seaside Avenue; 850–231–1940 or 800–848–1840; moderate to expensive). Like a Southern seaside mansion with a French flair, this inn provides B&B–style accommodations and food in the lap of luxury. The seven "standard" rooms are luxuriously appointed and include a TV/VCR, bar, sink, refrigerator, microwave, coffeemaker, fireplace, and queen-size bed (two have twin beds or a king and no fireplace). The four suites include a living room, dining area, full kitchen, and a separate bedroom with a fireplace and queen-size bed. If you want more traditional accommodations in Seaside, rather than a cottage, this is the place.

The Seaside area has become somewhat of a Florida dining mecca. Other highly recommended options in the vicinity include creative continental cuisine and atmosphere at (**Cafe 30-A,** 3899 East County Highway 30-A; 850–231–2166; moderate) and Creole and Floribbean fare at **Criolla's** (170 East County Road 30A, Grayton Beach; 850–267–1267; moderate to expensive).

FOR MORE INFORMATION

Seaside Visitors Center and Cottage Rental Agency, P.O. Box 4730, Seaside, FL 32459. (850) 231–4224 or (800) 277–8696.

St. Augustine

A HISTORIC ESCAPE

2 NIGHTS

History and charm • Sightseeing attractions • B&Bs

Only people who haven't truly explored Florida say there's no history here. With the nation's oldest city and many other centuries- and decades-old historic attractions, the Sunshine State has much more than sun, beaches, and theme parks. St. Augustine is a living historic theme park, but it's also blessed with lots of sun and beaches.

Founded in 1565 by Spanish naval commander Pedro Menendez de Aviles, St. Augustine has had an interesting and varied history. Spain used the coastal city as an important port and defense for its shipping route and built a huge fort, Castillo de San Marcos, between 1672 and 1695 to solidify its hold on the area. Though the British attacked the fort several times, it stood strong (and still does).

In 1763, Spain ceded all of Florida to Britain, and most of the Spanish residents fled to Cuba. But Spain regained control of Florida in 1784, when most of the British citizens left St. Augustine and many Spanish residents returned. The United States bought Florida from Spain in 1821.

In the late 1800s and early 1900s, St. Augustine grew into a popular vacation destination, thanks to Henry Flagler's railroad. Three of his palatial hotels are still standing, but are now used for other purposes. The founding of the Historic St. Augustine Preservation Board in 1959 ensured that other historic sites, many that were centuries old, would remain for all to enjoy.

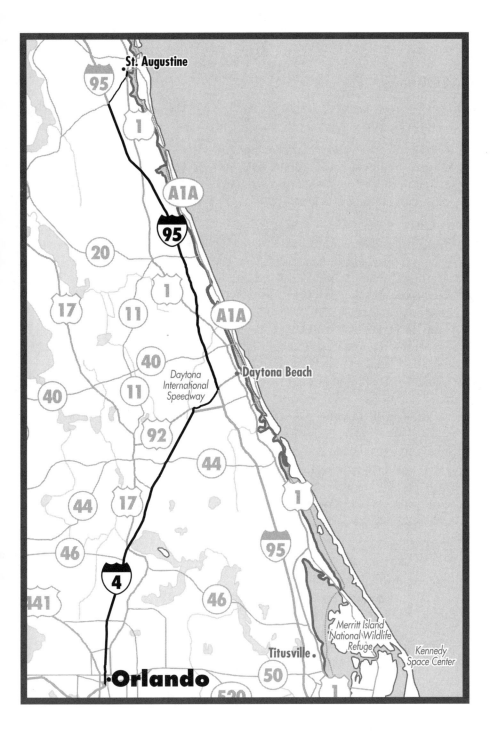

ESCAPE THIRTEEN

ORLANDO

DAY 1

Afternoon

Take I–4 east out of Orlando, joining I–95 at Daytona Beach for the trip north to St. Augustine. State Routes 207 or 16 both run right into the city.

DINNER: To start your stay on an appropriately historical note, go to **O. C. White's Seafood and Spirits** (118 Avenida Menendez; 904–824–0808), located in the 1791 Fort Worth Mansion, which overlooks the City Marina and features local seafood.

LODGING: St. Augustine's historic atmosphere is augmented by a wide range of quaint and often historic B&Bs (more than twenty-five and counting). Since there are a large number of good ones, your best bet is to contact the St. Johns County Visitors and Convention Bureau for specific information. Some recommended possibilities include **Carriage Way Bed and Breakfast** (70 Cuna Street; 904–829–2467 or 800–908–9832; inexpensive to moderate); **Casa de la Paz** (22 Avenida Menendez; 904–829–2915 or 800–929–2915; inexpensive to moderate); **Casa de Solana** (21 Aviles Street; 904–824–3555; moderate); **Casablanca Inn Bed & Breakfast** (24 Avenida Menendez; 904–829–0928 or 800–826–2626; inexpensive to moderate); **The Kenwood Inn** (38 Marine Street; 904–824–2116 or 800–824–8151; inexpensive to moderate); **Old Powder House Inn** (39 Cordova Street; 904–824–4149 or 800–447–4149; inexpensive to moderate); **Villas on the Bay** (105 Marine Street; 904–823–8885 or 800–826–2626; inexpensive to moderate weekly rentals); and **Whale's Tale Bed & Breakfast** (54 Charlotte Street; 904–829–5901 or 888–98–WHALE; inexpensive). If your tastes run toward more traditional hotel accommodations, see "Other Recommended Restaurants and Lodgings."

Evening

Because of the downtown tourist trade, St. Augustine has an active nightlife scene. The options include the historic **Milltop Tavern** (19½ St. George Street; 904–829–2329); **Waterfront Conch House** (57 Comares Avenue; 904–829–8646); and the cozy **Scarlett O'Hara's** (70 Hypolita Street; 904–824–6535).

DAY 2

Morning

BREAKFAST: At your B&B or hotel of choice.

To start your historical explorations, head straight to the Matanzas River and the **Castillo de San Marcos National Monument** (1 South Castillo Drive; 904–829–6506; entrance fee). This large fort, which took twenty-three years to build, is the nation's oldest masonry fort. The self-guided walking tours and occasional ranger or reenactment programs make for an interesting morning. Highlights include the 40-foot moat, the powder room, an old prison cell, and the chapel. Several of the storerooms feature exhibits about the fort.

LUNCH: For some great north Florida old-style cooking, try **Florida Cracker Cafe** (81 St. George Street; 904–829–0397; inexpensive to moderate).

Afternoon

History purists would say the true start of St. Augustine was out at the park called **Fountain of Youth** (11 Magnolia Avenue; 904–829–3168 or 800–356–8222; entrance fee). This pretty park was the site of a Native American village purportedly visited by Ponce de León when he was searching for the "Fountain of Youth." Visitors can take a drink from the park's spring fountain. There's also a Native American burial ground exhibit.

Your tour of St. Augustine's "oldest" is almost endless, but most of the sites are quite interesting and well presented. One of the best historic downtown area stops is the two-part **Authentic Old Jail** and the **Florida Heritage Museum** (167 San Marco Avenue; 904–829–3800; entrance fee). The 1890s jail was used until 1953 and includes excellent tours by costumed guides. Next door, the Florida Heritage Museum features artifacts and exhibits concerning the area's growth from Spanish rule through the Flagler boom times.

Next stop on the "oldest" tour is **The Oldest House** (14 St. Francis Street; 904–824–2872; entrance fee). The house dates from the early 1700s and is furnished to illustrate several periods in the history of the building. Visitors can also take in the small **Museum of Florida's Army** and **Manucy Museum of St. Augustine History** as part of the entrance price.

Continuing in the theme, **The Oldest Store Museum** (4 Artillery Lane; 904–829–9729; entrance fee) highlights the old C&F Hamblen General Store, which was open from 1835 to 1960. The museum basically presents the store as it appeared in the early 1900s, with more than 100,000 products on display. It's a fascinating throwback to an early version of a mall.

For your final themed stop of the afternoon, visit **The Oldest Wooden Schoolhouse in the USA** (14 St. George Street; 904–824–0192 or 800–OLD–SCHOOL; entrance fee). Built in the late 1700s, the small wooden structure features a typical classroom and lots of old artifacts from earlier education days. School was last in session in 1864.

DINNER: The dining tradition at **Oscar's Old Florida Grill** (614 Euclid Avenue; 904–829–3794; inexpensive to moderate) dates back to Henry Flagler's days, when he hosted oyster roasts at an old fishing camp here. Oscar's is located in an early-1900s roadhouse and still serves up oysters and other fresh seafood inside and outside. It's a great spot for dinner (or weekend lunch).

LODGING: St. Augustine B&B or hotel.

DAY 3

Morning

BREAKFAST: At your B&B or hotel of choice.

Plan an entire morning at the **Spanish Quarter Museum** complex (29 St. George Street; 904–825–6830; entrance fee), which includes several historic sites and many interesting reproductions. Guides dressed in eighteenth-century period costume interpret early St. Augustine life, starting at the **Florencia House** entrance and leading through the **Gallegos House** (an army sergeant and his family), the **Gomez House** (another soldier and his Native American wife), the **DeMesa–Sanchez House** (households from the late 1700s and mid-1800s), the **Gonzales House** (mid-1700s tavern), and several other period homes as well as blacksmithing and woodworking demonstrations. It makes for a fascinating morning.

LUNCH: Nearby, follow your nose to the pleasant **Spanish Bakery** (42½ St. George Street; no phone; inexpensive), which sells wonderful baked products and features a daily lunch special of soup, bread, and beverage.

Afternoon

St. Augustine is steeped in history, but there is also a (slightly) more modern attraction that has made history of its own. This very popular "theme park" is a throwback to an earlier Florida, when Walt Disney World didn't exist. **St. Augustine Alligator Farm** (999 Anastasia Boulevard; 904–824–3337; entrance fee) opened in 1893 and still features a wide range of alligators, crocodiles, and other similar species as well as specific shows, exhibits, and other animals. In many ways, it's the original Florida theme park.

Get back on I–95 south and take it to I–4 west toward Orlando.

THERE'S MORE

Other sightseeing attractions: St. Augustine rivals the Orlando area in the number and quality of sightseeing possibilities. Some of the numerous additional options include the huge **Ripley's Believe It or Not! Museum** (19 San Marco Avenue; 904–824–1606; entrance fee); more than 150 historical wax figures at **Potter's Wax Museum** (17 King Street; 904–829–9056; entrance fee); the reconstructed sixteenth-century **Government House Museum** (48 King Street; 904–825–5033; entrance fee); a reconstructed **Spanish Military Hospital** (3 Aviles Street; 904–825–6808; no entrance fee); and the worldwide historical **Lightner Museum** (75 King Street; 904–824–2874; entrance fee), which was originally the Alcazar Hotel.

Organized tours: Tourist-oriented St. Augustine has many excellent organized tour opportunities, including open-air trolley tours with **St. Augustine Historical Tours** (167 San Marco Avenue; 904–829–3800 or 800–397–4071) and **St. Augustine Sightseeing Train** (170 San Marco Avenue; 904–829–6545 or 800–226–6545); fascinating city tours with **St. Augustine Transfer** (115 La Quinta; 904–829–2391); and well-run Matanzas Bay tours with **St. Augustine Scenic Cruises** (Municipal Marina; 904–824–1806 or 800–542–8316).

SPECIAL EVENTS

January. Royal Family Transfer of Office re-creation, St. Augustine. Natives portray the Spanish Royal Family; (904) 829–2992.

March. St. Johns County Fair. Regional exhibits and events; (904) 829–5681.

Easter Weekend Seafood Festival, Sunday Promenade, Easter Parade, Blessing of the Fleet, and other events; (904) 829–1711 or (800) OLD–CITY.

September. Founders Day, Menendez Landing. Reenactment of the first Catholic Mass in America; honors the arrival of city founder Don Pedro Menendez de Aviles; (904) 829–1711 or (800) OLD–CITY.

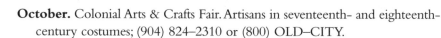
October. Colonial Arts & Crafts Fair. Artisans in seventeenth- and eighteenth-century costumes; (904) 824–2310 or (800) OLD–CITY.

November. Nights of Lights Festival. Millions of tiny white lights outline the historic city, historic reenactments, B&B tours, caroling, a lighted boat parade, and more. Through the end of January; (904) 829–1711 or (800) OLD–CITY.

OTHER RECOMMENDED RESTAURANTS AND LODGINGS

Though St. Augustine lodging establishments seem to specialize in B&Bs, there are also some excellent traditional hotel possibilities. The family-run **Quality Inn Alhambra** (2700 Ponce de Leon Boulevard; 904–824–2883 or 800–223–4153; inexpensive) is one of the best choices, with an architectural style similar to many buildings in the area and a friendly and helpful atmosphere situated away from the downtown hustle and bustle. Other hotel or resort options include the **Radisson Ponce de Leon Golf & Conference Resort** (4000 US 1 North; 904–824–2821 or 800–228–2821; inexpensive to moderate); the **Casa Monica Hotel** (95 Cordova Street; 904–827–1888 or 800–648–1888; moderate to expensive), a magnificent restoration of a luxurious 1888 hotel; and the **Marriott at Sawgrass Resort** (1000 TPC Boulevard, Ponte Vedra; 904–285–7777 or 800–457–GOLF; moderate to expensive) or the **Ponte Vedra Inn & Club** (200 Ponte Vedra Boulevard, Ponte Vedra; 904–285–1111 or 800–234–7842; moderate to expensive), both up in the golf and beach town of Ponte Vedra.

Other dining options in the St. Augustine area include **Salt Water Cowboy's** (299 Dondanville Road; 904–471–2332; inexpensive to moderate); **Creekside Dinery** (160 Nix Boat Yard Road; 904–829–6113; inexpensive to moderate); and **A1A Ale Works** (1 King Street; 904–829–2977; inexpensive to moderate).

FOR MORE INFORMATION

St. Augustine, Ponte Vedra & The Beaches Visitors & Convention Bureau, 88 Riberia Street, Suite 400, St. Augustine, FL 32084. (904) 829–1711 or (800) OLD–CITY.

St. Augustine Visitor Information Center, 10 Castillo Drive, St. Augustine, FL 32084. (904) 825–1000.

Amelia Island

NORTHEAST FLORIDA AT ITS FINEST

2 NIGHTS

B&Bs • History • Beach • Golf

In many ways, northeast Florida's Amelia Island is more like a Georgia barrier island than a typical Florida beach destination. From the Spanish moss in the trees to the Victorian-style town of Fernandina Beach, Amelia Island is a far cry from the rest of what most people think of as the Sunshine State.

An escape to Amelia Island provides plenty of options for varying styles of weekends. With so many beach possibilities throughout the state, you might enjoy staying away from the beach in a historic Fernandina Beach B&B, while still exploring the beach and the rest of the 13-mile-long island. Of course, you can also stay right on the beach at one of many accommodations.

Amelia Island activities include going to the beach, exploring the charm of Fernandina's Centre Street and further afield, renowned golf, tennis, horseback riding, visiting Civil War–era Fort Clinch State Park, or heading into Jacksonville for some big-city life.

DAY 1

Afternoon

From Orlando, take I–4 east over to I–95 north. Drive through Jacksonville on I–95 and take US A1A/200 east over to Amelia Island. The drive takes about three hours, so you may want to stop in Daytona Beach (Orlando Escape Five) or historic St. Augustine (Orlando Escape Thirteen) along the way.

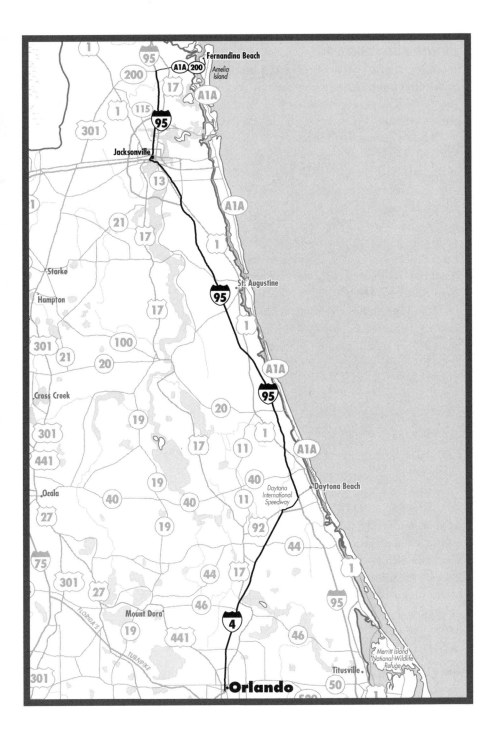

ESCAPE FOURTEEN

ORLANDO

DINNER AND LODGING: As can be expected, there are many excellent lodging choices on Amelia Island. From historic B&Bs to beachfront inns, hotels, and condominiums, you can sleep in almost any style you desire. However, since beach accommodations are so plentiful in Florida, perhaps a B&B in historic Fernandina provides a unique choice.

The Fairbanks House (227 South 7th Street; 904–277–0500 or 800–261–4838; moderate to expensive) is typical of many excellent B&B inns in Fernandina Beach. This 1885 Italianate villa and its owner/operators Theresa and Bill Hamilton greet visitors with polished hardwood floors, 12-foot ceilings, ten stately fireplaces, and twelve varied accommodations.

From wonderfully renovated guest rooms to your own private suite or cottage, this is not your average B&B. Every room offers a private bathroom, cable television, and a telephone. Additional amenities include a gourmet breakfast, enchanting gardens, a courtyard pool, and the hospitality and local help of Theresa and Bill.

The Hamiltons have collected a notebook full of local restaurant menus, and they highly recommend **The Beech Street Grill** (801 Beech Street; 904–277–3662; moderate to expensive), which is just around the corner from The Fairbanks House in a huge old home. Quite simply, Rick Erickson and Liz Smiddy have fashioned one of the most creative restaurants in the state. Rick ensures the best the globe has to offer in cuisine components—from Midwestern grain-fed lamb and Newfoundland mussels to the freshest regional produce and seafood. Liz has built a wine lover's haven, with an award-winning list that includes many excellent choices by the glass. The service is impeccable.

Evening

Before or after dinner, you may want to walk up to Centre Street for a drink at the **Palace Saloon** (117 Centre Street; 904–261–6320). This huge watering hole claims to be Florida's oldest and features a mahogany bar and live entertainment.

DAY 2

Morning

BREAKFAST: The Fairbanks House. Served in the dining room on the porch, the breakfast is typically creative and filling.

The morning offers a perfect time to walk around historic Fernandina Beach, concentrating on Centre Street and the surrounding side streets. After the Civil War, Fernandina grew as a commercial port and vacation destination. Many large homes and commercial buildings were built then and still exist.

Centre Street lies at the heart of the 52-square-block area designated as a National Historic District. Stop by the **Fernandina Beach Chamber of Commerce** (102 Centre Street; 904–261–3248 or 800–2–AMELIA) at the Old Fernandina Depot for more information. Some of the highlights include the **Nassau County Courthouse** (Centre and 5th Streets); the **Tabby House** (Ash and 7th Streets); and **Villa las Palmas** (315 Alachua Street). Of course, all of the late nineteenth- and early twentieth-century homes (many of which are now B&Bs) are eyecatchers during your strolls along the streets.

If you're really into the history of the area, be sure to visit the **Amelia Island Museum of History** (233 3rd Street; 904–261–7378; entrance fee). Located in the old Nassau County Jail building, this unusual oral history museum features docents who provide tours of the museum's many displays, ranging from Native Americans to the area's early twentieth-century growth. The museum also offers interesting walking tours of the town.

Fernandina features an eclectic array of shopping options on or just off Centre Street. Some unusual options include the **Eight Flags Antique Market** (602 Centre Street; 904–277–8550); travel accessories at **Last Flight Out** (114 Centre Street; 904–321–0510); gifts at **Southern Touch** (301 Centre Street; 904–261–5377); a wide variety of art at the **Island Art Association Co-op Gallery** (205 Centre Street; 904–261–7020); and a huge selection of new and used books at **Books Plus** (215 Centre Street; 904–261–0303) or **The Sailor's Wife Book Exchange** (310 Ash Street; 904–261–5845).

LUNCH: The Centre Street area offers many casual lunch spots. For something in keeping with the town's history, head to the **Florida House Inn** (22 South 3rd Street; 914–261–3300; moderate), where you'll dine in Florida's oldest hotel and Fernandina Beach's oldest dining room (dating from 1865). Homestyle cooking is served boarding-house style from heaping plates and bowls. It's all-you-can-eat for lunch or dinner.

Afternoon

If you're finished touring Fernandina Beach in time, the afternoon provides a perfect opportunity to drive around the island or down into Jacksonville for a quick look at this thriving city on the St. Johns River.

Whether you're just touring the island or driving into Jacksonville, take Centre Street east, which turns into Atlantic Avenue/A1A. You'll pass Fort Clinch State Park on the left (see Day 3). Continue on Atlantic to the ocean, turning right to follow A1A, which is now South Fletcher Avenue.

South Fletcher Avenue follows along the beach, providing glimpses of old beach houses and stunning new homes. Continue along A1A, which turns inland and runs through Amelia Island Plantation (see Day 3), a highly successful resort with condominiums and homes that is an ideal beach base for families. Several excellent shops also line A1A in this area.

If you're continuing on to downtown Jacksonville, you'll follow A1A to 9A north, which intersects with both US 17 and I–95 for the short drive into the downtown area. **Jacksonville Landing** (2 Independence Drive; 904–353–1188) is the focal point of downtown Jacksonville. Opened in 1987, this riverfront "festival marketplace" features a wide variety of shops and restaurants. On the opposite side of the St. Johns River, **The Riverwalk** (904–396–4900) is the site of even more restaurants, the world's largest self-contained fountain, small maritime museum, and the city's science and history museums.

Other options either downtown or nearby include the **Cummer Museum of Art & Gardens** (829 Riverside Avenue; 904–356–6857; entrance fee); the **Anheuser-Busch Brewery** (111 Busch Drive; 904–751–8118; no entrance fee); **Jacksonville Zoological Gardens** (8605 Zoo Road; 904–757–4462; entrance fee); the **Jacksonville Museum of Modern Art** (333 North Laura Street, Hemming Plaza; 904–366–6911; entrance fee); and the nineteenth-century **Zephaniah Kingsley Plantation** (11676 Palmetto Avenue; 904–251–3537; entrance fee). It's located on State Route A1A between Amelia Island and Jacksonville.

DINNER: Besides the Beech Street Grill recommended for Day 1, Fernandina Beach features many other creative restaurants. If you didn't try the Florida House Inn (see above) for lunch, they also serve similar family-style suppers. Otherwise, head to the corner of Eighth and Ash Streets for some innovative island cuisine at **Horizons** (802 Ash Street; 904–321–2430; moderate).

LODGING: The Fairbanks House will become your home-away-from-home by the second night. However, the large number of B&Bs in Fernandina Beach also makes it easy to try another one. Better yet, stay put and visit some other B&Bs as research for your next Amelia Island escape.

DAY 3

Morning

BREAKFAST: The Fairbanks House (eat lightly if you plan to go to the Sunday Brunch at Amelia Island Plantation, see below).

If you're visiting on the weekend, Sunday morning is a perfect time to check out **Fort Clinch State Park** (2601 Atlantic Avenue; 904–277–7274; entrance fee). This perfectly preserved nineteenth-century fort was completed during the Civil War. Along with tours of the fort's garrison, barracks, and other buildings, the park also has a fine beach, hiking, biking, and camping.

LUNCH: Sunday brunch at Amelia Island Plantation's oceanfront **Amelia Inn Restaurant & Lounge** (3000 First Coast Highway; 904–321–5050; expensive) is worth the drive to Amelia Island from anywhere in the Southeast. The huge buffet, featuring Southern cooking and a variety of fresh seafood, is matched by one of the finest ocean views available and accompanied by live piano. Save room for the award-winning desserts.

Afternoon

The afternoon can be spent exploring a bit more of Amelia Island Plantation, playing a round of golf (see below), lounging at the beach, or getting an early start on the drive back south. Take US A1A/200 back to I–95, heading south, before joining I–4 west to Orlando.

THERE'S MORE

Golf: Golf is a duffer's delight on Amelia Island. The options include **Fernandina Beach Golf Club** (2800 Bill Melton Road; 904–277–7370), which is open to the public; **The Golf Club of Amelia Island** (904–277–8015), which is open to members and resort guests; **Royal Amelia Links** (904–491–8500), which is open to members and resort guests; and Ocean Links and Long Point at **Amelia Island Plantation** (904–261–6161 or 800–874–6878), which are also open to members and resort guests.

SPECIAL EVENTS

April. Annual Bausch & Lomb Tennis Tournament, Amelia Island Plantation; (800) 874–6878.

May. Fernandina Beach Shrimp Festival, Fernandina Beach. A huge event, with lots of food and fun events; (904) 261–0203.

July. Fernandina Beach has its own July 4th celebration; (904) 277–8617 or (800) 2–AMELIA.

Kingfish Tournament, Fernandina Beach anglers' delight; (904) 277–8617 or (800) 2–AMELIA.

September. Festival of Wine & New World Cuisine, The Ritz-Carlton; (904) 277–1100.

December. Holiday Tour of Historic Treasures. A great way to see the island's varied accommodations; (904) 277–0717 or (800) 2–AMELIA.

OTHER RECOMMENDED RESTAURANTS AND LODGINGS

In addition to The Fairbanks House, Amelia Island features a number of accommodations, ranging from other B&Bs to inns to condos to three major resorts, including a Ritz-Carlton. If The Fairbanks House is full or you want to try something different in Fernandina Beach, contact **Addison House** (614 Ash Street; 904–277–1604 or 800–943–1604; moderate); **Bailey House** (28 South 7th Street; 904–262–5390 or 800–251–5390; moderate); **Hoyt House Bed & Breakfast** (804 Atlantic Avenue; 904–277–4300; moderate); **Florida House Inn** (22 South 3rd Street; 904–262–3300 or 800–258–3301; moderate); **Amelia House Bed, Breakfast & Sail** (222 North 5th Street; 904–321–1717 or 800–980–3629; moderate); **1735 House B&B** (584 South Fletcher Avenue; 904–261–4148 or 800–872–8531; moderate); **Walnford Inn** (102 7th Street; 904–277–6660 or 800–277–6660; moderate); or **Amelia Island Williams House** (103 South 9th Street; 904–277–2328; moderate). The **Harborfront Hotel** (19 South Second Street; 904–491–4911; moderate) is a modern hotel overlooking the harbor.

Perhaps your idea of an island escape is a beachfront inn. If so, contact **Elizabeth Pointe Lodge** (98 South Fletcher Avenue; 904–277–4851 or 800–772–3359; moderate to expensive). This shingle-style inn offers twenty modern "Main House" rooms, four larger deluxe sitting rooms in the "Harris Lodge," and the two-bedroom "Miller Cottage." In addition to representing Elizabeth Pointe Lodge, **Lodging Resources** (98 South Fletcher Avenue; 904–277–4851; inexpensive to expensive) also arranges accommodations in a lighthouse replica, oceanfront villas, and private homes.

For all of the amenities of home or if you're traveling as a family, **Amelia Island Plantation** (3000 First Coast Highway; 904–261–6161 or 800–874–6878; moderate to expensive) is a perfect pick. This huge property occupies more than 1,250 acres, with one-, two-, and three-bedroom villas all along the ocean and among the trees. Amenities include top golf and tennis, a full-service fitness center and spa, twenty-one pools, beachside activities, nature programs, children's programs, dining, shopping, and much more.

For an Amelia Island splurge, it doesn't get any better than **The Ritz-Carlton Amelia Island** (4750 Amelia Island Parkway; 904–277–1100 or 800–241–3333; moderate to expensive). This large oceanfront resort has all of the typical Ritz-Carlton amenities, with superb dining and excellent children's programs among its many features.

The dining scene is just as varied as the lodging outlook. In Fernandina Beach, in addition to those mentioned above, the possibilities include great sunsets and seafood at **Brett's Waterway Cafe** (Fernandina Harbor Marina at the foot of Centre Street; 904–261–2660; moderate); creative seafood at **The Golden Grouper Cafe** (201 Alachua Street; 904–261–0013; moderate); or Irish food, drink, and entertainment at **O'Kane's Irish Pub & Eatery** (318 Centre Street; 904–261–1000; inexpensive to moderate).

Elsewhere on the island, try the serious barbecue at **Sonny's Real Pit Bar-B-Q** (642 East SR 200; 904–261–6632; inexpensive); seafood, steaks, and chicken with a flair at **The Southern Tip** (Palmetto Walk, Amelia Island Parkway; 904–261–6184; moderate to expensive); or fresh seafood at **Down Under** (under the A1A bridge heading off the island; 904–261–1001; moderate).

FOR MORE INFORMATION

Amelia Island Tourist Development Council, 102 Centre Street, Fernandina Beach, FL 32034. (904) 277–0717 or (800) 2–AMELIA.

Jacksonville and the Beaches Convention and Visitors Bureau, 3 Independent Drive, Jacksonville, FL 32202. (904) 798–9148.

INDEX

ABOUT THE AUTHOR

Lynn Seldon, the author of ten travel books, also writes for many national publications, including *USA Today, The L. A. Times, The New York Post, Rodale's Scuba Diving, GOLF Magazine, SKI Magazine, Backpacker, Caribbean Travel & Life, American Heritage, Smithsonian, Arthur Frommer's Budget Travel, Travel America,* and many more.